Anxiety Disorders

Anxiety Disorders
A PRACTITIONER'S GUIDE

PAUL M.G. EMMELKAMP
THEO K. BOUMAN
AGNES SCHOLING
University of Groningen, The Netherlands

JOHN WILEY & SONS
Chichester · New York · Brisbane · Toronto · Singapore

Original Dutch edition published under the title of *Angst, fobieën en dwang: diagnostiek en behandeling.*
Copyright © 1989 by P. Emmelkamp, T. Bouman and A. Scholing

English language edition copyright © 1992 by   John Wiley & Sons Ltd,
Baffins Lane, Chichester,
West Sussex PO19 1UD, England

Other Wiley Editorial Offices

John Wiley & Sons, Inc., 605 Third Avenue,
New York, NY 10158-0012, USA

Jacaranda Wiley Ltd, G.P.O. Box 859, Brisbane,
Queensland 4001, Australia

John Wiley & Sons (Canada) Ltd, 22 Worcester Road,
Rexdale, Ontario M9W 1L1, Canada

John Wiley & Sons (SEA) Pte Ltd, 37 Jalan Pemimpin #05-04,
Block B, Union Industrial Building, Singapore 2057

Library of Congress Cataloging-in-Publication Data

Emmelkamp, Paul M. G., 1949–
    [Angst, fobieën, en dwang. English]
    Anxiety disorders : a practitioner's guide / Paul M. G. Emmelkamp,
Theo K. Bouman, Agnes Scholing.
        p.   cm.
    Translation of: Angst, fobieën, en dwang.
    Includes bibliographical references and index.
    ISBN 0-471-93112-8 (ppc)
    1. Anxiety. 2. Phobias. 3. Obsessive-compulsive disorder.
I. Bouman, Theo K. II. Scholing, Agnes. III. Title.
    [DNLM: 1. Anxiety Disorders. WM 172 E54a]
    RC531.E4413   1992
    616.85'22—dc20
    DNLM/DLC   92–18107
    for Library of Congress   CIP

British Library Cataloguing in Publication Data

A catalogue record for this book is available from the British Library

ISBN 0-471-93112-8

Typeset in 10/12pt Times from author's disks by Text Processing Department,
John Wiley & Sons Ltd, Chichester
Printed and bound in Great Britain by Biddles Ltd, Guildford and King's Lynn

Contents

Preface

The purpose of this book is to give an overview of recent developments in the assessment and treatment of anxiety disorders. For an audience the book aims at interested professionals, such as psychologists and psychiatrists, general practitioners and social workers, and trainees in these fields. The overwhelming amount of literature on the subject makes it impossible to summarize here all the studies into anxiety disorders that have appeared in the past few years. Therefore, our scope is restricted to the main issues.

In nearly all chapters of the book, case descriptions and examples are included to alert workers in (mental) health care to the various manifestations of anxiety disorders. The clinical description of the disorders is based upon the classification principles according to the third revised version of the *Diagnostic and Statistical Manual of Mental Disorders* (DSM-III-R) from the American Psychiatric Association (APA, 1987). Thus the book can be regarded as an annotated version of these widely used diagnostic criteria pertaining to anxiety disorders. In this sense the information is also of relevance for those interested in diagnostic issues, and for those wanting to gain insight into possibilities for referral.

A major part of the text is devoted to treatment guidelines. However, it should be emphasized that this book cannot be considered a treatment manual. The latter implies an extensive knowledge about and training in general psychopathology, in which professional activities carried out under supervision are an important ingredient. The chapters on treatment depart from a (cognitive) behavioural point of view, because of the important results in the treatment of anxiety disorders. It should be pointed out that, although the description of the procedures is restricted to the treatment of outpatients, most techniques can easily be adapted to inpatient settings.

Details of case descriptions have, of course, been changed in such a way as to guard the patients' privacy. Furthermore, we choose to use the word 'patient' instead of 'client'. This choice, however, does not imply we adhere to a medical model of psychopathology; it merely reflects the current use in general textbooks.

We wish to conclude by expressing our hopes that this book will be of value in the training and practice of mental health care.

Paul Emmelkamp
Theo Bouman
Agnes Scholing
Groningen, The Netherlands, February 1992

1 Phenomenology

WHAT ARE ANXIETY DISORDERS?

Anna is sitting pale and nervous at her doctor's desk. It has taken her weeks to get this far and now she can hardly find the words to explain. Will he think she is mad? Will she have to be admitted to a mental hospital? How will she get out of this mess? These and many more thoughts beat through her head and make her more nervous than when she left home. The doctor looks at her understandingly and asks: "What exactly are you afraid of?" Yes, exactly what? It looks as if for the last six months she has not been able to do anything without fear. When she is at home, her heart beats in her throat and every now and then she is very, very frightened. She dare not go in the street at all; imagine she should panic there, what would the neighbours think? Anyway, Anna does not feel very much at ease with other people. Their presence makes her insecure. It makes her watch herself all the time and she never knows if she is doing things right. To make matters worse, her husband Jim seems to understand only very little of it. He often says that she should not exaggerate and that nothing can happen. The fear, the domestic troubles, the hopelessness have made her feel rather depressed lately. If Jim is not at home, she is often crying and cannot get started with her chores. At her previous visit to her doctor he prescribed some tranquillizers, but she does not believe that these are doing any good. Now that she is there again, he will probably think she is an enormous bore. But the doctor is very nice and he wants to know everything about her fears and worries. That is quite a relief and, gradually, Anna gets the idea that at least somebody understands what is bothering her. Finally, the doctor says: "It seems a sensible thing to refer you to a specialized unit. The people there know a lot about these kinds of problems and their treatment. I'll write a letter of referral if you like." There is not much choice, Anna thinks, something should happen.

People with problems similar to Anna's often turn to institutions of mental health care. Some of them are able to pinpoint exactly what they are afraid of, others experience their whole daily life as an enormous burden. When we summarize Anna's problems a number of different manifestations of anxiety emerge. She is afraid to be at home alone, she is afraid to be on her own outside the house, and she gets tense when she is interacting with other people. The anxiety can be held responsible for the marital rows, for the difficulty in maintaining her house, and for her gradually developing depression. When we want to help people in this situation, the first thing to do is to analyse their problems. What exactly are the complaints? What exactly is the person afraid of? What does the person think and experience when anxious? The delineation of anxiety disorders is the subject of this first chapter. In the course of time, various attempts have been made to order the often very imprecise and unclear labels of these phenomena. This has resulted in the formulation of diagnostic criteria. At present the *Diagnostic and Statistical Manual of Mental Disorders* (Third Edition, Revised, DSM-III-R) of the American Psychiatric Association (APA, 1987) is the most widely used manual. The authors point out that it is an atheoretical approach in which manifest symptoms are taken up as criteria. The system departs from a multi-axial approach in which "... every case be assessed on several 'axes', each of which refers to a different class of information" (APA, 1987, p. 15). The five axes refer to:

1. Axis I: Clinical syndromes.
2. Axis II: Developmental and personality disorders.
3. Axis III: Organic disorders.
4. Axis IV: The severity of social stressors.
5. Axis V: The highest level of adaptive functioning during the past year.

It should be pointed out that this classification system aims at the classification of disorders, instead of the classification of persons. One of the consequences is that the system allows for diagnosing more than one anxiety disorder on Axis I. In the same way, different clinical syndromes, for example depression, hypochondriasis and an anxiety disorder can be present in one person. Such a categorical classification system could create the impression that anxiety is a phenomenon clearly delineated from other psychic states. This is obviously not true, since anxiety can be part of many other psychopathological pictures. An extensive overview of the backgrounds of DSM-III-R and of the operational criteria of various diagnostic categories can be found in the original text. Finally, one should realize that DSM-III-R is based on the consensus among a number of clinicians regarding psychopathology. The system is no direct reflection of reality and thus is open to criticism and reformulation. Anxiety disorders are assigned to Axis I (Clinical syndromes) and are in turn subdivided as indicated in Table 1.1. The authors of DSM-III-R designed a decision tree for the diagnosis of anxiety disorders, in which two observations are determinant for the question whether a further exploration of anxiety complaints is necessary. First, there should be phenomena of irrational and excessive anxiety or of worrying, avoidance behaviour or increased arousability which cannot be ascribed to a psychotic disorder. Second, there should not be any organic factor causing or maintaining the disorder. Only if both conditions are fulfilled, can one speak of the presence of one or more anxiety disorders. In the next sections of this chapter each anxiety disorder is presented with an overview of the diagnostic criteria according to the DSM-III-R classification. Apart from that, the clinical picture is discussed and illustrated with case histories. The category "anxiety disorders not otherwise specified" will not be discussed. This category implies anxiety disorders not fulfilling DSM-III-R criteria, a diagnosis which is made only after exclusion of the other anxiety disorders.

Table 1.1. DSM-III-R categories of anxiety disorders

Panic disorder with agoraphobia
Panic disorder without agoraphobia
Agoraphobia without history of panic disorder
Social phobia
Simple phobia
Obsessive-compulsive disorder
Post-traumatic stress disorder
Generalized anxiety disorder
Anxiety disorder not otherwise specified

PANIC DISORDER

"I thought I was going to die", replies Charles (34) as the psychologist asks him how he had felt on that particular evening. He made an appointment for an admission interview on the advice of his general practitioner and is now telling what frightened him so. On an ordinary night, 8 months before, he felt terrible. He was sitting on the couch, watching football on television just like every other Sunday night. His wife had put the children to bed and they had just had a few cups of coffee. Suddenly (and he still does not know how it happened) his heart started beating like mad. He felt dizzy, lightheaded, was sweating, and became terribly frightened. The anxiety increased when he also felt a sharp pain in his chest that radiated to his left arm. "Call the doctor", he cried to his wife. He lay down on the couch and hardly dared to move. Over and over again he thought that his last hour had come. It seemed like hours before a colleague of his general practitioner arrived. The doctor examined him briefly, listened to his heart, felt his wrist, and said: "Just go to bed and relax. These are all just tensions. There is nothing wrong with your heart, it's just psychic." Hardly reassured, Charles spent half the night awake while checking his heart-beat. The next day his own general practitioner told him the same story and added the advice that he should take things a bit easier. It was true, he had been very busy lately, he had helped his parents-in-law with redecorating their house, he had done his regular job during the day, on Saturday he was playing football, on Sunday he was entertaining his children, and he went to the snooker club for three nights in a week. Charles took his GP's advice seriously, but after a few months of taking life more calmly, it did not seem to help. He was still afraid of having a new attack and he actually did have more attacks. He just could not tell, it simply happened. Now he is finally sitting in the psychologist's office. The therapist asks him whether he has started avoiding certain situations. But Charles denies that he has. He dares to do everything he did before. The only remarkable thing is that he feels more safe when he has his car at hand. If anything happens he can be home really fast. For fear of another attack, he has just stopped taking part in active sport.

DSM-III-R criteria

Crucial to the panic disorder is the panic attack, that is a discrete period of intense fear or discomfort, often occurring unexpectedly. In the DSM-III-R chapter on anxiety disorders panic attacks play an important role. The diagnosis of some disorders, particularly panic disorder with or without agoraphobia, depends upon the presence of panic attacks, whereas the diagnosis of other anxiety disorders can only be made when it is demonstrated that panic is not the central theme, for example, in social phobia or generalized anxiety disorder. First, panic disorder will be discussed. Next, we will highlight its relationship with agoraphobia. According to DSM-III-R, the central feature of panic disorder is a number of panic attacks during a predetermined amount of time. Those attacks have to be unexpected (at least at the start); that is they do not occur immediately before or after exposure to a situation that nearly always causes anxiety. Neither are the attacks the result of situations in which the person is the focus of others' attention. Within a period of 4 weeks either four of those attacks should occur, or one or more attacks should be followed by a period of at least one month during which a persistent fear of having another panic attack exists. During at least one of the attacks four of the following symptoms occur within 10 minutes of the beginning of the first symptom with which the attack commences. If there are less than four symptoms, DSM-III-R speaks of a limited symptom attack.

1. Shortness of breath (dyspnea) or smothering sensations.
2. Dizziness, unsteady feelings, or faintness.
3. Palpitations or accelerated heart rate (tachycardia).
4. Trembling or shaking.
5. Sweating.
6. Choking.
7. Nausea or abdominal distress.
8. Depersonalization or derealization.
9. Numbness or tingling sensations (paresthesias).
10. (Hot) flushes or chills.
11. Chest pain or discomfort.
12. Fear of dying.
13. Fear of going crazy or of doing something uncontrolled.

Exclusion criteria concern the existence of organic factors, such as amphetamine or caffeine intoxication or hyperthyroidism, as a causative or a maintaining factor. Regarding the severity of the panic attacks, DSM-III-R discerns a mild, moderate or severe intensity. In mild panic disorder there has been at most one attack during the previous month or all attacks were in fact limited symptom attacks. A severe panic disorder indicates at least eight panic attacks over the past month. The moderate panic disorder is in between mild and severe.

Clinical picture

An important diagnostic criterion is the unexpected nature of the panic attack. Some speak of a "spontaneous" attack, indicating that the phenomena apparently come out of the blue. In an early phase of the treatment, the actual reason for an attack is indeed mostly unclear. In the course of psychological treatment insight will be gained into the nature of the direct precursor of an attack (see Chapter 6). Physical symptoms of panic such as sweating, trembling, chest pain, fear of fainting, and sudden changes in temperature show great similarities with the bodily symptoms of hyperventilation (Ley, 1985). DSM-III-R, however, does not mention such a relationship. The phenomenon of hyperventilation refers to a breathing pattern which is too fast or too deep at a time when the body does not need it. During physical exercise breathing also increases because more oxygen is used and more carbon dioxide is produced. In these moments the breathing pattern adapts to the needs of the body. When a person is hyperventilating, his breathing is stronger than necessary to provide those needs. This results in a stronger exhalation of carbon dioxide than is usually the case. The consequence is a decrease of the carbon dioxide level in the blood and a decrease of the acid level. This phenomenon is called "respiratory alkalosis". As a result of the accelerated and deepened exhalation a number of bodily complaints may occur which are called the "hyperventilation syndrome". These complaints vary considerably over persons, and can be summarized in the following categories:

1. Respiratory complaints (such as tightness around the chest, a sensation of being unable to breathe).
2. Paresthesias (tingling or numbness of the limbs, especially hands and feet, sometimes also around the mouth).
3. Neuromuscular complaints (stiffness, tremor or tetanic sensations in the limbs).
4. Cerebrovascular complaints (such as dizziness, blurred vision, feeling of fainting).
5. Cardiac complaints (such as a strong increase in heartbeat frequency, irregular heartbeat, pain in the cardiac area).
6. Temperature sensation.
7. Gastro-intestinal complaints (such as nausea, aerophagia).
8. Psychic complaints (such as anxiety, feelings of unrest and tension).
9. General complaints (such as fatigue and weakness).

Hyperventilation can in many cases be regarded as the somatic component of the panic attack. It can be assumed that in hyperventilant patients the breathing system is in a state of specific overresponsiveness, which can be determined by genetic factors or by learning processes. Some authors (Ley, 1985) regard hyperventilation as a response to a threatening situation: some people tend to respond more quickly with hyperventilation to an anxiety-inducing situation than other people. The acute and intense experience of anxiety can be considered the psychological component of panic and is held responsible for the tendency to escape which is characteristic of the panic attack ("I've got to get out of here as soon as possible"). Escaping behaviour aims at stopping the attack, but is sometimes effective only after a certain period of time. When a situation does not allow for an escape, for example when the person is at home, some patients start walking about restlessly or talking incessantly. Hibbert (1984a) investigated the cognitions of people with panic attacks and found their thinking to be concentrated around the theme of "personal danger". This became most clear with regard to bodily symptoms in which patients suffering from panic attacks "systematically misconstrue their somatic experiences as dangerous ..." (p. 622). Patients without panic attacks had significantly less anxious cognitions and also less severe bodily symptoms. Very often cognitions are characterized by anticipation of the feared situation ("anticipatory anxiety"). This causes an increase in arousal even before the patient actually enters such a situation. One of our patients once said: "Last time I felt very dizzy so I'll be unwell the next time. Maybe I'll really faint this time." Quite remarkable in patients with panic attacks is the experience of (fear of) losing control of part of their functioning. In such cases the anticipatory anxiety which occurs in between the panic attacks is strongly coloured by the threat of such a loss of control. We may roughly discern four themes of loss of control: fear of somatic, psychic, behavioural and social loss of control.

1. First, there are people whose pattern of complaints is dominated by a fear of somatic loss of control. They fear a heart attack, a stroke or fainting, or, more generally speaking, a severe dysfunction of their body. This fear induces patients to make a strong appeal to medical services, such as medical specialists, cardiologists and neurologists. The latter are unable to diagnose any organic disorders, leaving the patient feeling increasingly insecure and anxious.

2. In the case of fear of psychic loss of control, the person's attention is particularly focused on losing control over situations. The anxiety centres around patients' belief that they are possibly going mad: "Unusual things are happening which are beyond my comprehension." This fear may induce the fear of mad people, of abnormal behaviour, and may in time lead to specific avoidance behaviour. One of our patients for example dared not watch television for fear of seeing programmes about people who had left home in stressed circumstances. She feared she would do the same. When patients realize they can no longer think properly, the realization itself can trigger a panic attack. It is our impression that it is especially people who are used to getting things organized and who tend to rationalize, who are very anxious when experiencing this type of panic attack.

John, a 28-year-old man, gives a tense and depressed impression at the admission interview. He has gradually begun to doubt every aspect of his own person. He used to have things organized, knew what he wanted, and achieved much. Now he is sitting there, a miserable human being, wanting help and losing control over his life. His friends always believed him to be a strong and self-confident person. After a sudden panic attack, his view of himself has changed totally. He had never before experienced such an event. One day he was walking with his dog when all of a sudden he felt a surge of fear. Not just fear, but a kind of deadly fear, which made him stop thinking. His heart palpitated as if it would jump out of his chest. He started sweating and ran home. But what frightened him most was that he could not organize his thoughts. Whatever he said to himself, nothing helped. He was at a complete loss and lost his orientation in the street. How could this happen to him, he who was always so cool and rational? He ran home as fast as he could and since that day he has hardly gone out.

3. To another group of patients, losing control over their own behaviour is the most frightening idea. They fear total dysinhibition, throwing things, hurting themselves, screaming or yelling. One of our patients, for example, feared that he would jump into a canal while having a panic attack. It is important to discern between this kind of panic attack and a so-called harming obsession. The latter phenomenon is not restricted to an attack of fear.

4. People who fear loss of control in a social respect often feel shame about the alleged signs of increased arousal. Some of them are ashamed of sensations which actually occur, such as nervousness, trembling, wanting to leave. They have thoughts like: "People will find it strange when I leave the meeting unexpectedly", or "People will think I'm mad". Other patients visualize what would happen if they really lost control, although this has never happened. They think: "Just imagine that I'm lying on the ground and everybody is looking at me; I would die."

At the admission interview it is very relevant to obtain a clear picture of the way in which the patient experiences his loss of control, because this information gives important points of impact for treatment. Many panic patients tend to avoid situations or activities which are supposed to trigger panic attacks, sometimes starting immediately after their first panic attack. Extensive avoidance behaviour may prevent a person from having a panic attack, but at the same time it will prevent him or her from leaving the house. A diagnosis of panic disorder with agoraphobia is made when the complaints meet the criteria of panic disorder and those of agoraphobia as well (see below). A study by Garssen, Veenendaal and Bloemink (1983) showed that 60% of agoraphobics complain of hyperventilation symptoms and that 60% of patients with hyperventilation show agoraphobic behaviour. In many cases these attacks are relatively infrequent; sometimes it is even years or months since the most recent panic attack happened. Williams (1985), Thyer, Parrish, Curtis, Nesse and Cameron (1985) and Turner, Williams, Beidel and Mezzich (1986c) remarked that people suffering from a panic disorder are in general also suffering from agoraphobic fears. Research shows that panic patients, compared with agoraphobics, show the same type of bodily symptoms, but to a lesser extent. It is quite remarkable that groups without psychiatric problems also seem to be troubled by panic attacks: 24% of a group of students, 21% of their partners, and 5% of senior citizens reported having had at least one attack in the previous week (Craske, Sanderson and Barlow, 1987). Turner et al. (1986c) suggested a temporal relationship between panic disorder and agoraphobia: agoraphobic symptoms develop later and as a function of a panic attack. Thus panic is regarded as a precursor of agoraphobia. Thyer and Himle (1985) and Garvey and Tuason (1984) suggested a similar relationship: agoraphobia as a secondary manifestation of panic. According to Williams (1985), however, the fact that agoraphobic behaviour is maintained for a longer period without panic attacks could be an argument against panic being the primary cause of agoraphobic avoidance: "Rather it appears that any relationship existing between panic attack and avoidance must be mediated primarily by cognitive factors" (p. 115). In an influential article by Goldstein and Chambless (1978) the concept of "fear of fear" was introduced as the core element of agoraphobia. People with a history of panic attacks tend to be hyperalert regarding their bodily sensations and interpret these sensations as precursors of an imminent catastrophe. Last (1984) discussed the role of cognitions in a cognitive behavioural framework in which "maladaptive cognitions are conceptualized as primarily responsible for the maintenance of fear and avoidance patterns characteristic of phobic disorders" (p. 66). This author stated that these cognitions trigger anxiety preceding and during the contact with phobic stimuli and would increase physiological arousal, which in turn enhances anxiety and finally results in avoidance behaviour.

Differential diagnosis

Although panic disorder consists of a number of discrete episodes of fear, it can easily be mistaken for other disorders. Among other things, panic should be distinguished from a number of disorders, such as hypochondriasis and generalized anxiety disorder. Hypochondriasis is the persistent conviction of having a disease, attendant with fear and with a tendency to seek reassurance. In panic disorder the disease conviction is predominantly restricted to the period of the attacks themselves, in between the patient is capable of feeling less concerned. Furthermore, in panic disorder somatic preoccupations relate to phenomena occurring during the attack, such as headache, palpitations or dizziness. Generalized anxiety disorder is characterized by a substantial increase in arousal encompassing a variety of situations. In some cases panic disorder resembles generalized anxiety disorder, for example with respect to the intensified fear or tension in between the attacks. The fear is mostly caused by anticipation anxiety or anxious expectations concerning a new attack. The difference between panic disorder and social phobia will be highlighted in the section on "Social phobia". Organic causes of increase in arousal, such as hyperthyroidism, should be excluded. Excessive use or abuse of certain substances (such as coffee, caffeine-containing products; DSM-III-R, p. 139) may lead to a number of panic-related symptoms such as restlessness, nervousness, increase in heart-beat, and even withdrawal symptoms or a hangover caused by, for example, alcohol (with phenomena such as anxiety, or autonomic hyperactivity, such as palpitations, sweating and hypertension; DSM-III-R, p. 130). Finally, the rebound effect of tranquillizers should be mentioned.

AGORAPHOBIA

Rita, a 35-year-old housewife, is referred by her general practitioner because of her "fears". For the last few weeks she has found it more and more difficult to leave home. She is no longer able to take her six-year-old son to school. Being in the street alone among people makes her lose all her self-confidence. When she is walking there, she feels dizzy and lightheaded. It feels just as if she is walking up a slope. Her knees feel wobbly, which causes her to be afraid of fainting. Because she does not feel safe outdoors, she tends to stay at home more and more, because she thinks nothing can happen to her there. Her husband does the shopping, and has to leave his work about 45 minutes earlier. When the therapist asks his opinion, her husband says he does not mind, because he likes to do something for his wife, now that she is in trouble. The only thing is he has to hurry every now and then if his work takes a little longer. Over the past three years (the problems have existed this long) there could hardly be a mention of holidays and this is the most important thing the family has to miss. When they planned to go abroad, some years ago, they had to return home after a few miles because Rita got into serious trouble. She could not be prompted to do anything, which made them spend their holiday at home. Currently, Rita just goes into town accompanied by her mother, who luckily lives only a few blocks away. This is only the case on "her good days". She can never tell beforehand when she is going to feel good. Therefore it is very hard for her to make any appointments and she has to cancel a lot of them. Everybody is very concerned about her and tries to help as much as possible.

DSM-III-R criteria

DSM-III-R discerns two kinds of agoraphobia, that is agoraphobia in connection with panic disorder and agoraphobia without a history of panic attacks. This distinction predominantly relates to the motives urging a person to avoid situations. Agoraphobia as connected with panic disorder is described as a fear of being in places or situations from which it is difficult to escape, or in which there is no help at hand in case of a panic attack. In agoraphobia without panic disorder there is a fear of suddenly emerging symptoms which may cause embarrassment to the person or make him or her in need of help. Often the theme of the fear is to lose control over the bladder or bowels, to have to vomit, depersonalization or derealization, and dizziness. This fear causes a restriction in travelling or dictates the need for leaving the house only in company. In some cases the person enters the feared situation although the anxiety is substantial. According to DSM-III-R several gradations of intensity of these complaints can be distinguished: mild, moderate and severe. Mild agoraphobia implies the existence of some avoidance, but on the whole the person concerned leads a relatively normal life. This may be the case when a person is able to leave the house when necessary, but abstains from further travelling alone. Moderate agoraphobia, according to DSM-III-R, is characterized by a restricted life style in a sense that the person dares to leave home, but dare not be more than a few kilometres away from home without company. When a person is totally housebound and hardly dares to leave home, this is called a severe agoraphobia.

Clinical picture

From the paragraphs above it becomes clear that avoidance behaviour is one of the most characteristic features of agoraphobia. The number of situations agoraphobics would call anxiety-provoking is quite large. The popular notion that agoraphobia is equal to fear of streets or markets or open spaces in fact bears no relation to the diversity of situations which are indicated as difficult by the patients themselves. In reality, the central theme is "not being able to leave" or "being stuck", and this theme is more important than the open space itself. Sometimes it is not the open spaces but the restricted situation in which a person feels imprisoned. Some examples of such situations are:

- standing in a queue;
- being in a large shop or shopping centre;
- travelling by public transport (bus, train or aeroplane);
- crowds, busy streets, large gatherings;
- driving a car on a motorway (the impossibility of turning on the road);
- being in a traffic jam;
- crossing a bridge or being on a bridge;
- sitting at the barber's;
- being in conversation with some person on the street.

The desire to be able to leave as quickly as possible prompts some people to take their own precautions. As an example, they never leave home without a bicycle or car, so that if something should happen they will be able to get home as soon as possible. These and other forms of avoidance behaviour should be assessed by the therapist as accurately as possible, because sometimes they are very subtle in nature.

Mr Rose, 40 years old, has been troubled by agoraphobic problems since his divorce from his wife. In the course of time it has become more and more difficult for him to leave home on his own. He lives in the east part of the country and likes to visit his family in the west. Driving his car is something he has given up: "If something happens to me while driving a car, I can be in big trouble and may cause a fatal accident." It all started when he realized that one cannot turn a car and drive back on the motorway, but has to drive all the way to the next exit instead. If he felt very anxious such a distance would be just too much. When he noticed he could not concentrate while driving a car, he grew more and more fearful and decided to use his car only for short drives near where he lives. He seemed to be able to cope with it until after some time he found that it was impossible to get on the train. The idea of not being able to leave the very instant he felt fearful started to worry him more and more, which made him more and more nervous while on the train. In summary, in the course of time, his reach has been considerably restricted. At the moment he is able to move without fear only within his own village and has therefore applied for treatment.

Some authors, including Goldstein and Chambless (1978), have argued that in the first place agoraphobia is a fear of fear and not so much a fear of certain places. Chambless (1982) holds the opinion that agoraphobia cannot be defined as a fear of public places. She thinks that fear of leaving the house and the familiar environment (places and people that warrant psychological reassurance) should be mentioned as well. Most agoraphobics, 35% according to Marks (1969), are therefore much more fearful when alone. They often avoid being alone and feel less anxious when accompanied by a trusted person, for example a partner or a person who is aware of their problems. Consequently, an agoraphobic may be able to cope with several kinds of situations as long as he is not alone.

At the admission interview, Mrs Finchley is asked what she usually does. This seems to be quite a lot. When the therapist asks what she does on her own, she has to admit that there are only a few things left. In fact, she hardly dares to do her shopping at the butcher's at the corner. When, on the other hand, she is accompanied by someone she dares to go nearly everywhere. The therapist asks whether she means that all company is equally suitable for that purpose, or whether there is a difference between people with whom she feels safe and those with whom she does not. Mrs Finchley's answer indicates that she is most at ease with her sister-in-law. The latter knows of her fears and would understand if she were attacked by fear when outside the house. She does not feel at ease with her husband when she is outside. He provokes her every now and then and leaves her standing somewhere on her own: "just for practice", he then says. Her husband's unpleasant surprises make Mrs Finchley even more nervous, so that she goes out with him less and less. When the therapist asks what her sister-in-law could do if she should have an attack, the patient answers: "Well, nothing really, just being there". In fact she realizes that it is not rational to expect help in this way but, one way or another, it works.

The anxiety-reducing role of company appears to be one of the most important maintaining factors of agoraphobia. As in Mrs Finchley's case, it does matter who this company is; preferably a person who knows or understands what it means to be fearful and not to dare to do very much. However, not all agoraphobics feel comfortable in company. A number of them report quite the contrary. When they are accompanied by a person while outside, they are more nervous and anxious than when they are alone. If you want to escape, you will be stuck with this company and you will have to excuse yourself. The distinction between somatic loss of control (fear of becoming sick and needing support) and social loss of control can be made here. In the latter case, panicking in the company of other people is more embarrassing than having a panic attack when alone. For some agoraphobics the presence of young children appears to be an additional source of worry instead of being a comfort, especially in cases in which the patient feels responsible for the children. The existing tension only increases, which makes it more difficult to leave the house with than without the children. Regarding catastrophic thoughts, Last and Blanchard (1982) found a significantly greater amount of catastrophic thoughts in agoraphobics than in patients with panic attacks without avoidance of situations. Moreover, in the agoraphobic group more persons with catastrophic thoughts were found than in the group of panic patients. Reiss, Peterson, Gursky and McNally (1986) also indicated that anxiety sensitivity (the thought that experiencing anxiety can have negative implications) is more strongly associated with agoraphobia than with other anxiety disorders.

Differential diagnosis

Situational avoidance is not found only in agoraphobia with or without panic attacks, as mentioned above, but can also be related to other psychopathology. In depressed patients one often observes a lack of interest and initiative, leading to avoidance of outdoor activities. Because of the fact that depression also involves a certain extent of fear, such avoidance behaviour can easily be mistaken for agoraphobia. The motive for this behaviour, however, is not fear of a possible catastrophe, as may be learned from the patient. Another source of avoidance is social phobia. Many social phobics fear travelling on their own or being in public, because of the fear they experience in being among other people. At first sight one would consider the diagnosis "agoraphobia", but here is another example where the motive to avoid is crucial. Going out on your own implies being in contact with strangers, which can be prevented by an accompanying partner. In the section on differential diagnosis of social phobia this will be highlighted further.

SOCIAL PHOBIA

Alex, a 21-year-old young man, is referred to us through his family doctor. His major problem is that he feels quite uncomfortable and anxious in almost every social situation. His anxiety is strongest within a group but is also present when he is talking to a single person. Alex has a brother and a sister and lives at his parents' home. The idea of moving to lodgings occasionally runs through his mind; however, his fear of becoming totally isolated keeps him from taking concrete steps. Since he got a Lower Secondary Education degree at 16 he has made hardly any contact with others, except for his own family. When he was at Secondary School he still had some friends he knew from Primary School, but after his final exam these contacts faded away rapidly. Alex blames himself for it because he did not take any steps at all to maintain them. After he left Secondary Education he began to apply for jobs. At 17 he got an invitation for an interview for a job at a neighbouring supermarket. He came out of it rather depressed because he had completely clammed up within five minutes. After that he had to run away. Since then he has kept away from that particular supermarket and from job interviews in general. In the years afterwards he worked in his uncle's shop at regular intervals as he actually wanted to do something. At the age of 20 he decided not to carry on like this and enrolled for a two-year clerical training course. At the moment the training itself gives no problems whatever, but here again his social anxiety makes itself felt. This time it has become the direct reason for calling for help. True, he had been treated by a psychiatrist once before but had stopped treatment after a few months without having experienced any change for the better. Alex himself has the idea that he has always been silent and shy. It only became a real problem for him when he was at college. Checking a list of social situations during the initial interview shows that the fear has been generalizing considerably and it is obvious that Alex is avoiding many situations. For example, he finds it very hard to make telephone calls. He calls only if it is absolutely necessary and only after he has put it off for some days. Before calling he makes sure that there is nobody around and that everything he wants to say is written down beforehand. He goes to birthday parties only if relatives are involved (meanwhile, other people do not invite him any longer) and keeps a low profile all evening. In the doctor's waiting-room or other public instances he rehearses over and over again what he is going to say, meanwhile having frightening images about clamming up once more. He can hardly get himself to start a little chat, usually leaving the initiative with others. To get into conversation with girls is even more difficult than with boys. At first, Alex performed reasonably well in his present class. He was indeed silent but determined not to stand out from the rest of the students. As the school year progresses Alex gets more in to trouble. He knows for certain that little by little other people will have found out how shy he really is.

DSM-III-R criteria

In DSM-III-R "social phobia" is described as a persistent fear of one or more situations in which the person is exposed to possible scrutiny by others, and fears to behave in a way that will be embarrassing. The fear must be unrelated to other Axis I disorders (such as panic disorder) or Axis III disorders. As an example, fear of trembling that results from Parkinson's Disease does not justify a diagnosis of social phobia. Confrontation with the feared situation usually elicits an anxiety response, and those situations will generally be avoided or endured only with intense anxiety, if avoidance is impossible. The avoidance behaviour interferes with occupational or social functioning. Moreover, the person recognizes that the fear is excessive and disproportional to the factual risk that is present. If the person is under 18, the diagnosis 'Avoidant disorder of childhood or adolescence' should be excluded (DSM-III-R, pp. 61–63).

Clinical picture

For most people, temporary feelings of distress in specific social situations are a familiar phenomenon. It is not exceptional that applicants avoid touching the cup of coffee offered them during an interview with their possible employer, as they are afraid that they cannot drink it without spilling. Likewise, many people get nervous when they are invited to make a speech in public. This situation has often been associated with distress, displaying itself by physical symptoms, such as sweating hands, blushing, a trembling voice and palpitations. These symptoms are frequently elicited by a common element: the fear of being in the centre of others' attention and in particular the fear of being judged. For most people this arousal is not a motive to avoid such situations. On the contrary, the attendant alertness is frequently considered as conducive to one's performance. These examples show the complications that arise when a line has to be drawn between "normal" feelings of discomfort in social situations and clinically relevant social anxiety. Alex's case clearly shows that some people can feel so inhibited by their anxiety in (specific) social situations that help becomes necessary. In view of the serious character of the problems in those cases the diagnosis "social phobia" must be given. The diagnosis "social phobia" has found general acceptance only recently; to be exact, since the introduction of DSM-III (1980), classifying it among the anxiety disorders. In this edition social phobia was described as a persistent fear of one specific social situation, the wish to avoid this situation and the individual's recognition that the anxiety is basically irrational. According to DSM-III, fears for more than one situation could not be classified as social phobia, but as "avoidant personality disorder". In contrast, DSM-III-R categorizes patients with fear of several social situations as "social phobia", with the addition "generalized type". The phenomenon "social phobia" as such has been described long before. The term was introduced by Marks and Gelder in 1966 and defined as a "fear of eating, drinking, and writing in the presence of other people; specifically a fear of blushing, of trembling or vomiting". They stated that the essential characteristic of social phobics was the fear of making a fool of themselves in the eyes of other people. Since then several studies on similar phenomena have been published. However, the problem was the lack of conformity regarding the terminology to be used and also about the respective shades of meaning. Terms such as shy, unassertive, fear of company, socially inhibited, fear of speaking, social anxiety and interpersonal anxiety were used, often without supplementary exact description. This made comparison of the results of studies rather difficult. Additionally, the group under study often consisted of psychiatric patients with various disorders, the social anxiety often constituting a point of minor importance. The same goes for groups of students or "normals" with a light form of social anxiety. In a way the description as stated in DSM-III was indeed an important step forward. In the early 1980s, however, this definition proved unsatisfactory on many counts. The main point of criticism was the DSM-III notion that the patient is afraid of only one social situation. A "specific" social phobia of that kind, such as a fear of writing or eating in the presence of others, or of looking in the hairdresser's mirror, seems to be a comparatively rare phenomenon. Research by Turner, Beidel, Dancu and Keys (1986a) demonstrated that out of a group of 21 social phobics almost everyone had difficulty with at least two different situations and nearly 50% revealed that they felt anxious in three or more situations. Our personal experiences with patients suffering from social anxiety underline the fact that most patients fear more than one situation. Observable behaviour, relevant in social phobia, can be divided into two components: social skills and avoidance behaviour. Results from research concerning the first aspect are somewhat ambiguous. Some researchers found that independent raters classified socially anxious persons as having less adequate social skills than non-anxious persons (Twentyman & McFall, 1975; Arkowitz, Lichtenstein, McGovern & Hines, 1975). However, when comparing specific social skills (such as keeping prolonged eye-contact and the overall length of speaking time) these differences could not be established (Monti, Boice, Fingeret, Zwick, Kolko, Munroe & Grunberger, 1984). Observational research data about avoidance behaviour of social phobics compared to normals have not yet been published, but self-report data indicate that social phobics avoid many situations. Often, they do not avoid the situation as a whole but show more subtle avoidance while actually in the situation, trying to behave as unobtrusively as possible. For assessing the seriousness of the problems and during treatment it would be wise, of course, to chart this avoidance behaviour, which will be discussed in detail under the description of the treatment of social phobia (Chapter 7). The cognitive component of social phobia is often understood to mean the way in which a social phobic judges and appreciates his own behaviour and that of others. In a review Arkowitz (1977) gives the following five cognitive mechanisms and modes of thought:

1. To begin with, roughly speaking, social phobics display considerably more negative self-statements in social contacts than non-anxious persons. To give some examples, these are thoughts like: "Just look how I'm messing up things" and "It'll come to nothing again, I tell you".
2. Also, social phobics tend to evaluate their own (social) behaviour in an excessively negative way.
3. Related to the above, social phobics appear to make exorbitant demands on their own behaviour, in general much more demanding than on the behaviour of others ("applying double standards").

4. They are rather selective in their recollections: pleasant or positive situations or events are forgotten or brushed aside as being unimportant, whereas dissatisfying events are remembered and emphasized over a long time.
5. Finally, they are often inclined to seek the reason for social contacts passing off smoothly outside themselves ("external attribution"), whereas in disappointing situations they rather seek the cause within themselves.

In research on social phobia, several attempts have been made to name subtypes within the scope of this disorder. One of the reasons for this is the fact that treatment effects have been rather diverse until now. Various types of treatment produced positive results when large groups were compared. However, in some individual cases the same treatments seemed to produce a minimal effect. This may relate to the wide disparity existing within the group of social phobics. DSM-III-R does not explicitly discriminate between subtypes. The only suggestion pointing in this direction is that persons suffering from fears in a wide variety of social situations must be categorized as "generalized type". This addition, however, is too restricted. For example, during the treatments we implemented over the years, it became clear that patients who are afraid of blushing (erytrophobia), of trembling (tremophobia) or of sweating (hydrosophobia) when in company, often find little benefit in the usual kinds of treatment, such as social skills training or cognitive therapy. Although, according to DSM-III-R, similar problems can be regarded as a specific social phobia, one may argue that they seem to be of a slightly different nature from, for example, the fear of making telephone calls. Up to this moment the literature on social phobia has shown a lack of interest in these kinds of problems. In a review of the literature on fear of blushing (Vandereycken & Pollentier, 1986) it is taken as self-evident that fear of blushing has to be clearly distinguished from blushing itself. Little concrete information is available on the question as to whether specific persons are quicker in blushing than others, owing to their physical constitution (e.g. a thin skin or vasomotoric instability). Anyhow, the answer to this question seems irrelevant. Several erytrophobic patients walk around nearly all day with a continuous fear of blushing, whereas this phenomenon actually hardly occurs at all. On the other hand a great many people can blush without being distressed about it.

Rob is a 26-year-old bachelor who was referred to us through his family doctor. During the first interview the following points attracted attention. He has a beard which covers the greater part of his cheeks; he wears spectacles with dark glasses that make his eyes almost invisible. His handshake is clammy. He tells us that for the last 10 years he has been afraid of blushing and sweating in company. He can clearly remember what triggered off this fear. During his first term in college his classmates were kidding him when one of the most popular girls in class sat down next to him. This made him blush, which in turn stirred up new comments. Suddenly he was seized by panic. He got the sensation of blushing to the roots of his hair and felt cold sweat coming all over his body. This was the moment that he ran away from class. Ever since that shocking experience he has been living in constant fear of recurrence. He has avoided the company of girls, especially in school. He has tried to dodge school parties with lame excuses. Before the "traumatic event" he did reasonably well in class, though he was no "whizz kid". Soon his school performances started to change for the worse. He had to stay down at the end of the year and decided to go to a Polytechnic. Looking back, he regrets his choice. He feels sure that he could have finished his studies at college if he had not been hindered by his fear of getting another attack in class. His choice in favour of a Polytechnic was not so much based on his wish to become a professional engineer as on his special wish not to sit in class with girls. Anyhow, he did well at Polytechnic and went to Technical College afterwards. Here he got into trouble again as stiffer demands were put on oral presentation. He had to make speeches in class at regular intervals, a situation he could cope with only by pumping the text into his head word for word. When questions were asked unexpectedly he got rattled and started to blush again. He shuddered to think of the final oral exam, yet it passed off smoothly. In the mean time he had reached his early twenties and although he had some close friends it was not easy for him to come into contact with women. He sometimes tried to but soon discovered that in no time he started to blush and to sweat. His sweating in particular was an important reason for him to avoid any form of physical contact. When a woman touched him fleetingly—casually or not—he would break out in a sweat. He has a good job now as a technical engineer and holding his own is no problem. Nevertheless, he is still having problems outside his work, that is to say in the informal sphere. Social evenings and parties are hard to get through, especially when the guests are expected to dance. Some months ago he began an intimate relationship with a woman for the first time in his life, or rather, he joined in her initiatives. In these matters too his anxiety about physical contact was playing tricks on him. He shrank back from touching her and as he was deeply ashamed of his sweating he had great difficulty in making love. This and other problems made a complete failure of the relationship. This time it is the immediate reason for Rob's going to do something about it. After drawing an outline of his avoidance behaviour, it is all too evident to what extent his life is dominated by problems. He avoids situations that might provoke blushing or sweating as much as possible. It means that he avoids not only direct contact with women but also situations in which allusions to relationships between men and women or sexuality can be made. To give an example of what situations can elicit feelings of stress, he tells us that once he began to blush when he heard a woman say in a doctor's waiting room that she was pregnant.

Tremophobia (fear of trembling) is a similar problem, although situations in which the fear is felt can usually be more easily avoided. Examples are eating or drinking in public (soup, coffee and tea) or signing a paper. Paying cash can raise problems as well, especially when paying in small change. One of our patients said that she never wrote out cheques, adding that she always paid in "big notes". She did not check how much she got back as she was afraid to draw attention to her trembling hands. Sometimes these situations can hardly be avoided, which makes a call for help increasingly urgent. A nurse explained to us that she could not do her work properly any more, because at times she started to tremble terribly when giving injections, especially when a doctor was around. Characteristic for the groups with fear of the physical symptoms mentioned above is the existence of the vicious circle which is also found in patients with panic disorder. The anticipatory anxiety is responsible for calling up the very symptoms the patient is afraid of (i.e. blushing or a fit of panic). For that reason people with a fear of blushing, trembling or sweating can be considered a separate group that needs a treatment more attuned to the problems as such. Experiences with this group of patients show that to some extent they seem different from other social phobics. First of all, relatively young, well-educated people are involved, people who seem to have adequate social skills. A significant part of this group seems to be focused on a number of characteristic cognitions, such as "I must keep everything under control, and cannot allow myself to show weak spots", "I cannot allow myself to make mistakes". Apart from this group other subtypes may be distinguished, emphasizing the following dimensions:

- social ability versus social inability;
- rational versus irrational way of thinking;
- secondary versus dominating avoidance pattern;
- difficulties emerging from situations with familiar people versus unknown persons;
- difficulties in a group versus situations with one or two other persons.

In many of the situations mentioned above these patients try to maintain themselves by using anxiety-reducing strategies, such as distraction. Many social phobics use alcohol to reduce the distress. No studies have been conducted so far on the differences between "normals" and social phobics as to their respective alcohol consumption. Yet research has revealed that social phobics in particular take alcohol before meeting people, as they do not dare to leave home without it ("anticipatory drinking"). This can sometimes assume extreme dimensions, adding to the social phobia an alcohol addiction as well.

To serve as an example there is the story of a man (29), who for years has been used to knocking down at least six glasses of liquor before meeting people. When he is on his own he hardly drinks any alcohol. Although he knows very well why he drinks, he cannot get himself to stop it. His fear of an alcohol addiction is the immediate cause of his looking for help for his social anxiety.

Alcohol consumption in turn often escalates social anxiety. As people are ashamed of drinking, all sorts of excuses have to be invented. The study by Amies, Gelder and Shaw (1983) pointed out that 20% of a group of social phobics showed excessive alcohol consumption compared to 7% of a group of agoraphobics. More recently, van Ameringen, Mancini, Styan and Donison (1991) found that among social phobics 28.1% suffered from alcohol dependence and 15.8% from substance abuse once in their life. The opposite, that is the occurrence of social phobic complaints among alcoholics, has also become the object of some studies. The results are not identical on all points. A study by Mullaney and Trippett (1979) found that 23% of all alcoholics were also suffering from social anxiety, while in another study only 2 in 84 persons were involved (Weiss & Rosenberg, 1985). True enough, it was evident that the phobic complaints became apparent at an earlier stage than the alcohol problems. Finally, Kushner, Sher and Beitman (1990) reported that in agoraphobia and social phobia alcohol problems often seemed to be a consequence of attempts at self-medication of anxiety symptoms, while panic disorder and generalized anxiety disorder were more likely to follow from alcohol abuse.

Differential diagnosis

The improved criteria according to DSM-III-R certainly do not solve the problems about assessment of social phobia. For the moment it is in fact hardly possible to discriminate between social phobia, generalized type, and avoidant personality disorder, since six out of the seven criteria given for this type of personality disorder overlap the phenomena of generalized social phobia (cf. DSM-III-R, pp. 241–243 and 351–353). In addition, there is no clear-cut demarcation line between anxiety disorders. Partly, this is due to the fact that DSM-III-R was set up as an atheoretical, purely descriptive system, based on a dichotomic (somatic medical) model. This means that similar phenomena should be classified under the same diagnosis, irrespective of causes, and also that a disorder is either present or not present. However, for correct classification, and especially for treatment, it is very important for clinicians to ask for the reasons why a person fears and avoids specific situations. The following case study may illustrate the importance of this point, already mentioned earlier, in the differential diagnosis of agoraphobia.

Social services have referred Bert, a 19-year-old young man, to our department because of agoraphobic complaints. At the first interview he is in his mother's company. She takes for granted that there can be no admission interview without her being present, because "... he never knows what to say...". The therapist prefers to have a session with Bert alone first, and proposes that the mother should join them after he has finished the first part of the interview. The session with Bert is dragging on. He has evidently got used to his mother doing the talking for him on any occasion and therefore he can carry on a conversation only with great effort. However, he actually manages to give the reason for his coming. After staying at home for some years out of work, he now can get a job in a warehouse of a department store in the centre of the city. His problem is that he has not ventured out of doors alone, that is to say without his mother, for years, because he has not got the nerve for it. Just as big a problem is travelling alone by city buses. He dare not enter busy shops and shopping centres without his mother being with him. At first glance this is a serious form of agoraphobia. As yet he has never been seized by panic in such situations. At first he is unable to answer the question as to what exactly makes him anxious. Only after a while does he speak about his great difficulty in meeting people in the street, above all his neighbours, because he is afraid that they will notice that he is insecure and has nothing to say to them. When he is with his mother no problems arise, as on such occasions he can keep silent. In view of the above the diagnosis "social phobia" appears to be more applicable.

This example shows the importance of making thorough enquiries about the fears of the patient when phobic disorders are concerned. An essential aspect of social phobia is the experience of anxiety in contacts with other people, in particular the fear of (adverse) judgements. On the other hand, when panic disorder and agoraphobia are involved, it is the fear of falling victim to panic, of losing one's self-control or becoming helplessly alone that predominates. Social phobics, for example, may say that they dare not leave home and certainly dare not go to shops in their home town, whereas the same person does not mind travelling to an unknown city to do the shopping there all alone. The difference is that they are afraid of running into acquaintances in their home town, which is not likely to happen elsewhere. Likewise, some social phobics manage to go on holiday alone reasonably well, engage in several sorts of social contacts with strangers and mix relatively easily in groups. One of our patients told us by way of illustration that he found it easy to get off with a girl when he was on holiday and that he already had several holiday affairs behind him. However, the mere thought of having to talk to a girl he liked in his daily environment made him break out in a cold sweat. Agoraphobics, on the other hand, become increasingly anxious when they are alone a long way from home. In a few studies, differences have been established between somatic phenomena as experienced by social phobics and "normals" or agoraphobics. A study by Turner, Beidel and Larkin (1986b) showed that persons with social phobia had a raised pulse rate and blood pressure, both significantly higher than for "normals", during a behaviour rating, including a conversation with a member of the opposite sex. Another study made it clear that in comparison with agoraphobics, social phobics differ chiefly in the nature of their physical symptoms: the latter group complained about blushing and twitching of muscles in particular, while agoraphobics made special mention of breathing difficulties, weakness in limbs, and dizziness as their greatest problems. As to palpitations, a dry throat, trembling and sweating, no significant differences between the two groups were found (Amies, Gelder & Shaw, 1983). It is often hard to discriminate between panic disorder patients and social phobics. Many phobics report that they feel ill at ease in company, because on such occasions all sorts of physical symptoms become apparent, which make them anxious. The diagnoses are not mutually exclusive, although in these cases establishing the primary diagnosis may be difficult. With regard to social phobics, these experiences and physical symptoms are (almost) exclusively elicited in social situations, and their fear is not in the first place for the symptoms as such, but for their possible observation by other people. The primary diagnosis "panic disorder" is adequate when feelings of discomfort are induced by (anticipatory) fear to a panic attack. This fear can also occur in non-social situations, for example when the person is alone at home. If it occurs in social situations the patient is primarily afraid of having a fit of panic or even a heart attack rather than of his own social (dis)functioning. Dysmorphophobia or body dysmorphic disorder is a complaint that may show some similarities with social phobia. According to DSM-III-R this disorder is not classified among the anxiety disorders but among the somatoform disorders. The diagnosis is made on people who are preoccupied with certain parts of their body. They think that something is wrong with them while, from an objective point of view, there is no reason for it. If a slight physical "anomaly" is really evident, the diagnosis is given only when the preoccupation or fear on that point is exaggerated. Some examples of the disorder are:

- to be convinced of having all kinds of unsightly hairs on one's face or all over one's body, and to think that other people are constantly looking at it and making jokes about it;
- to be convinced one is spreading a nasty, pungent smell;
- to be convinced that something is wrong with the shape or size of one's genitals or other parts of the body, such as ears or nose.

Given the obsessional character of the disorder, one may ask whether this disorder is related to the obsessive-compulsive disorder. Hardy and Cotterill (1982) compared dysmorphophobics with obsessive-compulsives on the one hand, and psoriasis patients on the other, on several variables. Dysmorphophobics appeared to score higher on depression than psoriasis patients. In both groups obsessional symptoms were more outspoken than in a control group of "normals". This study did not, however, endorse the hypothesis that dysmorphophobia should be rated among obsessive-compulsive disorders. The fact that the majority of dysmorphophobics feel especially uncomfortable in social contacts and frequently try to avoid these situations, sometimes makes it hard to distinguish them from social phobics. A study by Marks and Mishan (1988) on the effects of the treatment of this disorder brought to light that four out of five dysmorphophobics had to cope with social anxiety and avoidance behaviour as a result of the disorder. By the time the dysmorphophobia had declined the anxiety had disappeared.

SIMPLE PHOBIA

Peter, a man aged 43, applies to us because of growing phobic complaints and depression. He has been married for 23 years and has three children. During the first interview a serious form of claustrophobia became apparent which, true enough, does not hamper him very much in daily life, but occasionally rouses fierce outbreaks of anxiety. Problems have been increasing over the last few months. It has recently become impossible for him to use the cubicles in a swimming pool which he visits three times a week. Moreover, he finds it increasingly difficult to sit in a car on his own. It has also been a long time since he got in the back of a car with childproof locks or into a two-door car. Illustrative of the seriousness of his anxiety about being locked up is that he is resolved that, if he should get cancer, he will refuse to submit to radiation treatments, even if it should result in dissemination of the disease. And, furthermore, he has made his family promise to take care that in the event of an accident he will not be put in a plaster cast and connected to all sorts of terrifying equipment. He declares that he would rather die than be locked up like that. Peter cannot remember exactly when the first problems manifested themselves. One event is indelibly stamped on his mind: he was 10 years old and got locked up in a lavatory in a swimming pool for half an hour. He can still remember being scared to death, especially because it was Saturday afternoon and nearly closing time, so that he expected to have to stay there all over the weekend. To his great relief he was set free. Although he took great care not to lock himself in again for at least a few months after the incident, he is sure that this anxiety has not troubled him for years.

DSM-III-R criteria

Characteristic of simple or specific phobias, according to the DSM-III-R definition, is a persistent and irrational fear of a specific object or a specific situation. A compelling desire to avoid the object or the situations in question is evident and may cause considerable inconvenience. When the person involved is exposed to the feared stimulus, a reaction of fear will follow almost immediately. The fear is not of having a panic attack (as in panic disorder), of humiliation and of loss of face (as with social phobia) or of contamination (as with obsessive-compulsive disorder). Finally, the person in question realizes that the fear is disproportional and irrational.

Clinical picture

The picture of simple phobia arises from the diagnostic criteria as a residual category. Although the "phobic stimulus" can differ, the various forms of this anxiety disorder agree essentially. Simple phobia is like social phobia in at least one respect. Both phobias are widespread (in a mild form) among the "normal" population and the difference between normal anxiety and its phobic variant develops smoothly. Moreover, where simple phobias are concerned, the phobic stimulus can be quite easily avoided, which seems also to be the reason why only a few phobics choose to be treated. Bringing together the various types of fears known as simple phobias, fears concerning height, enclosure, animals, blood, and so on can be distinguished. Sometimes their Greek names are used, and incidentally the use of pseudo-Greek terminology has led to notable extravagances, as emerges from a summary in a handbook which enumerates up to 275 possible "phobias". Some examples are: fear of books (bibliophobia), fear of new things (cainophobia), fear of joy (cherophobia), fear of money (chrematophobia), fear of stealing (kleptophobia), fear of nosebleed (epistaxiophobia), fear of marriage (gamophobia), fear of sermons (homilo- phobia), and fear of the unlucky number 13 (triskaidekaphobia). The term hellenogophobia covers the notion of fear of complicated, pseudo-scientific linguistic usage. To conclude with, to round things off: fear of phobias is quoted as phobophobia. Ranking foremost in clinical practice are phobias of certain kinds of animals, of small locked-up rooms, of height, of blood and medical surgery (injections, dentists, etc.), of thunderstorms and of eating (specific kinds of) food. Blood and swallow phobias are in separate classes by themselves; they will be discussed later. With animal phobias in many cases no other (anxiety) disorders are present, and if they do occur together, there seems to be no connection with the animal phobia. Characteristic of an animal phobia is a lasting, persistent fear of a specific animal which is not connected to the fear of getting contaminated. This latter fear should rather be classified among the diagnostic category of obsessive-compulsive disorders. All animal species can feature as possible phobic objects, but generally speaking one particular person usually has fear of one single species. The fears that occur most frequently are those of spiders, mice, cats, dogs and horses. Movements of the feared animals in particular will bring about feelings of anxiety, sometimes leading to strong avoidance responses, disproportionate to the actual danger. Marks (1987) gave an example of a woman who was so afraid of spiders that—while in the middle of a lake—she jumped out of a rowing-boat without a moment's thought, although she could not swim. A big spider had prompted her to do so. An animal phobia is hardly ever the only reason for calling for help. But if this does occur nevertheless, it often appears that a person's actual living conditions have changed in such a way that confrontation with the awe-inspiring animal has become much more frequent. This will happen, for instance, after moving from an urban upstairs flat to a house in the country where spiders and mice are more frequent.

A 19-year-old woman asked for treatment because of her deep fear of spiders. Though she had always felt a little anxious, she had never before felt inhibited by it. Only recently, however, she had begun to live with her friend. The house was at ground level; it had a garden and a shed. After she had occasionally come across a spider in the shed, her fear had increased quickly. The situation turned into a real problem, however, when she chanced upon a spider in her house. Since then she had not dared to stay at home alone and kept the windows and doors at the back of the house hermetically sealed, as well as all the cupboards in every room. Her fear made her sleep badly, which in turn had negative effects on her work as a secretary. The effects of increasing tiredness and irritability ended in a growing number of conflicts with her colleagues, as well as with her friend.

One reason for women to call in help is sometimes the worry of transferring their own problems to their children. Another type of simple phobia is claustrophobia, that is the fear of being locked up in enclosed places. A variety of situations can cause difficulties, such as lifts, lavatories or shower rooms (especially unknown ones with locked doors), bathing cubicles in swimming pools, cellars and sitting in the back seat of two-door cars. Men who have been in the army quite often mention foxholes. If the phobia leads to serious problems at work or in daily life in particular, help will be needed. Illustrative is the story of a window-cleaner who functioned well for years until the day he got involved in an accident, 8 months earlier. The experience made him develop a fear of heights and he has been unable to climb even small ladders since. Apart from the above situational phobias, some patients report specific object phobias. Food and swallow phobias are basically two entirely different problems, although, as a matter of fact, only the latter is relevant to clinical practice. Strictly speaking, food phobia, as it is sometimes called, should not be defined as a phobia but as an aversion to certain kinds of food. Consumption of this food does not usually result in anxiety, but primarily in nausea and in (a tendency to) being sick. Such aversions can develop in childhood (the well-known aversion to sprouts, onions or chicory) or at a more advanced age. In the latter case aversive experiences associated with the food in question play an important role. As it is nearly always possible to keep away from unwanted food, treatment will hardly ever be necessary. This is entirely different from swallowing phobias which generally are not linked to the taste of certain kinds of food. The main characteristic of a swallowing phobia is the fear of being choked by the food. That is why fears of food generally are stronger for solid than for liquid food. This phobia can grow to such an alarming extent that in some cases considerable loss of weight can be the result. Such phobias usually have additional far-reaching consequences for one's social life, as in serious cases eating or drinking in company is not at all or barely possible.

Blood and injury phobias

The mere sight of blood or physical injury can arouse in many people a feeling of uneasiness, not to mention nausea. Many nurses and medical students who, as trainees, are first confronted with situations involving blood, find it exceptionally hard to get their physical reactions and their urge to escape under control. According to research carried out by Lapouse and Monk (1959) a minor fear of blood is prevalent among 44% of 6- to 8-year olds, and among 27% of 9- to 12-year olds. Blood phobias as such can be found in about 2–3% of the "normal" population, and undeniably feature as one of the most prominent phobias in adults (Agras, Sylvester & Oliveau, 1969; Miller, Barrett & Hampe, 1974). In some respects blood phobias differ remarkably from other simple phobias. Notable aspects are the physical symptoms, the attendant feelings and the fact that blood phobias seem to be partly familially determined. These items will be discussed briefly in consecutive order. It is a well-known fact that, speaking of animal phobias, situational phobias (height and claustrophobias) and of other object phobias, the fear reveals itself in elevated physical arousal such as accelerated heart-rate. Apart from that, the persons involved report feelings of near fainting ("weak feeling in the legs, dizziness") when confronted with the phobic stimulus. However, these problems hardly ever lead to actual fainting. On the other hand, blood phobias can bring about a marked deceleration of heart-rate and blood pressure, following an initial momentary increase of the generic arousal. The person concerned turns pale, begins to sweat and complains of nausea. Fainting is definitely not exceptional under these circumstances (Cohn, Kron & Brady, 1976; Connolly, Hallam & Marks, 1976: Marks, 1987). Phenomena like these reflect an activity of the parasympathetic nervous system following a preceding "sympathetic" activity. This transition is known as the "diphasic response pattern". The parasympathetic symptoms do not occur when the confrontation with blood lasts only for a short while. Apart from this, "normals" show similar reactions at the sight of blood. The difference between the groups can be found not in the type of reaction but in the seriousness of the symptoms (Carruthers & Taggart, 1973; Öst, 1986). A second distinction that can be made between blood phobia and other simple phobias is that when blood phobia is at issue, reports are mainly about nausea and less about anxiety. All things considered, it is rather doubtful whether the term blood phobia can be regarded as the most suitable name. Obviously, the person in question seems to be more afraid of fainting, which is not always an irrational fear, than of seeing blood.

Differential diagnosis

Discussing the diagnostic criteria, we have already observed that according to DSM-III-R the diagnosis "simple phobia" can be made only after exclusion of some other anxiety disorders. The fear of panic attacks, whether or not combined with agoraphobia, is stated explicitly. Furthermore, the fear of being scrutinized by other persons or of feeling embarrassed is not referred to as simple phobia but as social phobia. The avoidance of contact with certain objects (e.g. doors, chairs, other people) for fear of becoming infected is not classified as simple phobia, but as obsessive-compulsive disorder. To conclude: fear and avoidance of trauma-related stimuli (e.g. avoidance of certain places or looking at photographs) often becomes manifest in post-traumatic stress disorder. In these cases too the diagnosis of simple phobia is scarcely appropriate.

OBSESSIVE-COMPULSIVE DISORDER

John, a 32-year-old single man, had a house of his own but lived with his parents as a consequence of his insecurity. His main problem was a compulsion to write down all kinds of thoughts, because he was afraid of forgetting the things he had seen, felt and experienced. He was very perfectionist. Seven years ago he started writing compulsively without any apparent reason. What began with keeping a diary developed into continuously written reports of his feelings and thoughts. The idea of losing track of things made him very anxious, and as a result of writing them down the tension abated temporarily. He jotted down his feelings and thoughts on scraps of paper which he kept in boxes. He felt he must write down things such as age, bodily sensations, titles of books, memories, and so on. He avoided reading newspapers because he felt compelled to reread and write things down continuously. This daily routine took up hours. Furthermore, he suffered from checking (gas, lights, doors) and orderliness. Everything was kept in the same place, nothing was thrown away (hoarding). Apart from his parents he had no social contacts.

DSM-III-R-criteria

In obsessive-compulsive disorder obsessive thoughts as well as compulsive actions are pivotal. Both symptoms are to a certain extent similar, they manifest themselves in characteristic ways, and often occur simultaneously. In DSM-III-R obsessive thoughts are described as persistent ideas, thoughts, impulses or images which are initially experienced as intrusive and useless. This may be the case when a parent has the recurrent impulse to kill a child which he or she loves or when a very religious person has blasphemous thoughts. The person tries to ignore or suppress such thoughts or impulses or to neutralize them with other thoughts or actions. The patient is able to see that the obsessions are a product of his or her own mind and that they are not imposed from outside (as in the delusion of thought insertion). The content of the obsession must be unrelated to any other Axis I disorder, if present. The ideas, impulses, or images do not concern feelings of guilt, as in the case of a major depression. Compulsions are characterized by repetitive, purposeful and intentional behaviours, carried out as an answer to an obsession, which occurs according to certain rules or in a stereotyped manner. This behaviour aims at either neutralizing or preventing discomfort or tension, or certain feared situations or events. However, the action is not realistically related to what should be prevented or neutralized or is out of proportion. The patient also perceives this behaviour as out of proportion or unrealistic. The latter need not be the case in younger children or in people whose obsessions have developed into delusional ideas. Furthermore, obsessions and compulsions cause substantial trouble because they are time-consuming (cost more than one hour a day) or they are interfering with daily life, with carrying out a profession or the usual social activities or relations with other people.

Clinical picture

Although compulsive rituals and obsessive thoughts are usually distinguishable, about 80% of the people with compulsive problems suffer from both phenomena.

Pure rituals, not accompanied by obsessions, are rare. Generally, obsessions precede rituals but in some cases the sequence is the other way round. The next case presents a good illustration of this point.

David (aged 27) has been suffering from blasphemous obsessions since he was 8 years old. Before being referred to us, he had been psychopharmacologically treated for a psychosis; nevertheless his obsessional complaints remained. His obsessions are "God be cursed", "God is a bastard", "God is crazy", "Fucking God", "I piss on you", and so on. These thoughts were often expressed in German instead of in Dutch to make them less terrifying. He was trying to neutralize these thoughts by kneeling in random places at home about 20 times a day, asking God for forgiveness by praying out loud, moaning, shaking his head, turning to the left, stepping one pace backward, not walking on the lines, and other similar methods. In addition he suffered from obsessional ruminations such as "Am I praying to God or to the devil?" "Am I allowed to look at a beautiful woman, or not?" "Am I allowed to eat cream butter?" "Do I love my wife?" "Am I allowed to buy a car?" "Am I allowed to buy a video?" He also attempted to neutralize these particular thoughts. After having married his wife (his first girlfriend), he had also suffered from harming obsessions. David was raised by parents in a repressive Calvinistic way. From the age of 8 he had been insecure about what is right or wrong because the Bible did not present clear guidelines. The patient was emotionally unable to reconcile his own feelings of anger toward his parents with the commandments he heard every day. The first compulsive thought he remembers was "My parents are cursed". To undo these thoughts he added the word "not", so that he used this word about five or six times. This resulted in "My parents are not not not not not not cursed". The doubting obsessions originated from the time he got married. His mother disagreed with his choice, which put him into serious trouble. His harming obsessions arose from that time as well and pertained to killing his parents-in-law and his wife. Interestingly, in contrast with other patients, this patient did not experience aggravating obsessions during a period of depression.

The most frequent type of obsessions concerns the fear of dirt and contamination. One in four patients has thoughts about violence or harming a person (for example killing one's child). Furthermore, doubting is a frequent obsession (for example asking oneself repeatedly if one has not made a serious mistake). Frequent compulsions are counting, cleaning, washing hands and touching objects. A cleaning compulsion is generally related to the fear of contamination, prompting the patients to clean themselves, their homes, their children, and their partners. When such a person touches something that is allegedly contaminated (for example a doorknob, other people or food), then hands and arms must be washed or one must take a bath or a shower. 'Need to' or 'must' refers to the compulsive nature of the actions. A patient is not able to withdraw because feelings of anxiety and tension increase. Not only actual touching, but also thoughts can provoke washing and cleaning rituals. In checking compulsions patients often check if windows and doors are locked properly and if the gas is turned off. When a person leaves home, he or she returns several times to check if everything is indeed all right. Failing to return results in an enormous amount of tension which can be experienced by a patient as unbearable, while checking reduces the tension. Checking can take many forms, such as driving back in the car to see whether one has caused an accident or returning to the office to see if one has locked somebody in a cupboard. It is noticeable that cleaning compulsions occur more often in women and checking compulsions occur more often in men (Hoekstra, Visser & Emmelkamp, 1989).

Dianne was a depressed 23-year-old teacher who was obsessed by being a lesbian and who had to check all sorts of things. The complaints had started 3 years earlier after she had been approached by a "lesbian" woman. They did not have sexual relations, but she feared becoming a lesbian herself because she liked the attention the other woman paid to her. She thought this discovery to be horrific and became afraid of accidentally telling it to others. After this episode various rituals emerged, such as checking magazines, books and school notes for fear of having written about other people being homosexuals. In addition she repeatedly checked the cupboard in school because she might have locked pupils inside. At home she checked the gas (for fear of fire), the taps and the toilet (for fear of flooding), and doors and windows (for fear of burglary). Finally, she had to make notes on everything she had done during the day to make sure she had checked everything.

People with obsessions and compulsions mostly try to avoid situations and stimuli which provoke such thoughts and actions. This is commonly termed "passive avoidance". Active avoidance, on the other hand, implies the "motor" component of obsessive-compulsive behaviour such as checking and cleaning. Generally, active as well as passive avoidance behaviours are closely related to the content of the obsessive-compulsive disorder. The next example is an illustration of this.

Mrs D. (aged 52) developed her compulsions at an older age. Although she had always been very tidy it was not until 4 years earlier that her compulsive cleansing set in after a hospital admission on account of endometritis. It was about the same time that her dog died of cancer. From that time on she became very anxious about everything connected with disease and possible contamination. This anxiety engendered avoidance of all kinds of situations in which she might become contaminated, among which were shopping areas, crowded stores, and contact with people. She wore a shawl whenever she went shopping to avoid contamination. Should she meet anyone who coughed or looked dirty, she immediately put off her shopping, went home and took a shower; this she did about four times a day. Her laundry was meticulously treated. Nothing should be touched when she was hanging out her clothes. Underclothes especially presented problems. They must be protected and were therefore hung behind other clothing. She nearly always washed them several times and took them upstairs one by one. If anyone observed her in this activity she would perform the whole ritual all over again. She did not allow herself to touch the seat of her underwear with her feet. Her feet were thoroughly cleaned several times and were protected by special shoes. In the event that that particular part of her underwear was touched, it would immediately be washed over and over again. Panties, jeans and pyjama trousers were never worn. The floor also gave cause for anxiety. Nothing must touch the ground (e.g. blankets, ironing, towels), if it did it had to be washed at once. She frequently washed her hands while cooking dinner, and all food (bread, meat, oranges, etc.) was cleaned. Going to the toilet also posed its problems. First, all doors leading to the toilet were opened and then she walked to the toilet holding her hands in front of herself "like a surgeon" as she called it. The door of the toilet always remained agape and toilet paper was used in excessive quantities in a particular fashion. She never went to the toilet in other places. Apart from the symptoms already mentioned, the patient suffered from compulsive checking of the gas, the light switches, the stove, and her car. When leaving home she had to return at least 10 times to check everything over and over again. She also constantly checked her knitting for fear of having dropped a stitch. She badgered the life out of her spouse (who had to reassure her repeatedly) to ask whether he had broken anything, whether he was not dirty, and whether he had checked the house.

Patients with harming obsessions avoid sharp objects (such as knives, scissors, pieces of glass), rope, or being alone with young children. Some, however, are more fearful of harming themselves than anybody else. People with checking compulsions, for example, avoid situations that provoke their rituals, such as being alone, driving a car, using matches, or being the last one going to bed. People with a cleaning or washing obsession take many precautions to avoid contamination. When obsessions are related to death, people avoid all kinds of situations that suggest the notion of death, such as reading papers (obituaries), watching TV, going to a funeral. In such cases, rituals may be very subtle, they may for example consist of touching certain objects, mentioning certain numbers or manners of speech, and repeating over and over again what one was doing. Less usual kinds of compulsions concern compulsive buying or hoarding. Compulsive buying implies that the person has a strong inclination to buy all kinds of things (without needing them) "because they are so cheap". A person who suffers from compulsive hoarding may have cupboards full with old bills, notes, hundreds of pairs of shoes, and underwear. In extreme cases these objects may fill entire rooms. The objects are not used, but the patient is afraid of throwing them away because they may come in handy one day. Hoarding may be considered a serious variant of a doubting obsession. Compulsive counting is a form of obsessive-compulsive behaviour which often accompanies checking and washing. In some patients this counting, however, is the nuclear symptom of the obsessive problems. In these cases a person is compelled to repeat his actions a certain number of times. Some people must stick to a certain number (for example three or five) or must carry out everything an even or odd number of times. When the ritual is interrupted for some reason or another, or the patient does not know whether he has carried out the ritual in the proper way, then everything has to be repeated. Other numbers (for example three or seven or thirteen) may carry a meaning of danger and in that case the patient needs to avoid doing things three or seven or thirteen times. For some people tidiness is the main problem. This, however, should be distinguished from everyday tidiness, which has no compulsive character. These patients have to order objects in a certain way, such as gramophone records, books, clothing in a cupboard, cutlery, furniture, and so on. In extreme cases it takes a patient all day long to organize things in the proper way. Finally, there are patients with a compulsive slowness, who take an extraordinarily long time to carry out routine actions such as dressing and undressing. It should be mentioned that neutralizing thoughts often have the same function as rituals, that is the undoing of the harmful effects of the obsession. One of our patients with a blasphemous obsession ("God is mad") had to think a neutralizing thought every time the obsession occurred ("I will stay Catholic forever"). This reduced the fear caused by the blasphemous thoughts.

Differential diagnosis

Obsessive-compulsive behaviour can be discriminated in several respects from some other disorders. Like agoraphobics some obsessive patients avoid going out. However, the difference between the two states can be deduced from the motive to avoid. Agoraphobic patients are often afraid of having a panic attack or becoming unwell, as obsessive patients are, for example, afraid of contamination. When obsessive thoughts are caused by severe traumatizing experiences, the diagnosis should be post-traumatic stress disorder rather than obsessive-compulsive disorder. Depression is very common in people with obsessions and compulsions. In most cases the depression is secondary to the obsessive-compulsive disorder, which is not surprising considering the severity of the problems. On the other hand, obsessive thoughts are very common in depressive episodes, but they disappear when the depression has subsided; in these cases, the diagnosis of "depression" should be made. If obsessive and/or compulsive behaviours occur during a psychotic episode, this is not diagnosed as obsessive-compulsive behaviour. Certain obsessions are not considered as obsessive-compulsive behaviour. Excessive and obsessive concern related to one's own health is diagnosed as "hypochondriasis", whereas the preoccupation with having an alleged somatic deformity (for example a big nose) is diagnosed as dysmorphophobia (which has been mentioned before in this chapter). Tics are distinguished from compulsions by their involuntary nature, whereas the latter are voluntary. However, a considerable number of people with the Gilles de la Tourette syndrome (characterized by several motor and one or more vocal tics) suffer simultaneously from a compulsive disorder.

POST-TRAUMATIC STRESS DISORDER

One evening while Dominique was cycling through the park, a bald-headed man stopped her. She tried to ride on, but was forced to get off her bike. Dominique struggled for some time but it became clear that the man was many times stronger than she was. Then he raped her in the bushes while holding a knife at her throat. Totally confused and bruised she arrived home later where her friend was waiting. She gave it much thought and finally she decided to go to the police the next day. The days after the rape, she remained very fearful and was shaking all over. At night she dreamt about the scene over and over again, waking up in a cold sweat afterwards. Currently she finds it hard to talk about the event with her friend and dislikes having sexual contact with him. Now she is often extremely anxious when seeing violence and chasing scenes on television, when seeing bald-headed men or photographs with bald-headed men wearing earrings or carrying knives (the perpetrator was wearing an earring). She dare not enter the park alone or even go out when it is dark. The rape has affected her life very deeply.

DSM-III-R criteria

The person in question has experienced an event which is beyond the range of usual human experience and the occurrence is bound to have a significant influence on nearly everybody. Examples of this are serious threats to the person herself or to her partner, children, close relatives or friends; sudden destruction of her own living environment, or the vision of somebody else who is severely wounded or killed in an accident or by physical violence. Three symptom clusters could be discerned, related to re-experiencing, avoiding and increased arousal. The traumatic event is persistently re-experienced in at least one of the following ways:

- recurrent, intrusive and disturbing recollections of the event;
- recurrent, disturbing dreams of the event;
- sudden acting or feeling as if the traumatic event were recurring (including a sense of reliving the experience, hallucinations, dissociations, delusions, even those that occur at the time upon awakening or when the person is under the influence of substances);
- intense psychological suffering when the person is exposed to events which strongly resemble or symbolize the event, including "anniversaries" of the event.

The person shows persistent avoidance of stimuli related to the trauma or a numbing of general responsivity (which was not present before the trauma). This is manifested in at least three of the following aspects:

- attempts to avoid thoughts or feelings related to the trauma;
- attempts to avoid activities or situations which provoke memories of the trauma;
- the inability to remember important aspects of the trauma (psychogenic amnesia);
- a marked diminishing of interest in important activities;

- a feeling of alienation from others or of not belonging;
- a restriction of affect, for example the inability to experience caring and loving feelings;
- a feeling of a diminished future perspective, for example when the person does not expect to have a career, to marry, to have children, or to live long.

The patient complains of at least two of the following phenomena of increased arousal (which were not present before the trauma): difficulty in falling or staying asleep, irritability or outbursts of anger, difficulty in concentrating, hypervigilance, excessive reactions of fright, and physiological reactions upon exposure to events which strongly resemble or symbolize the traumatic event. The diagnosis of post-traumatic stress disorder only applies when the symptoms of the three clusters mentioned above last longer than one month.

Clinical picture

The post-traumatic stress disorder is probably the only anxiety disorder in which the onset is clearly delineated. This is not to say that everybody who experiences a trauma outside the range of everyday experience will react in the same way. The traumata can be very diverse and encompass among other things war, sexual and violent crimes (such as rape and incest), bank robberies, catastrophes, and serious accidents. Research among Vietnam veterans in the United States yielded valuable knowledge about post-traumatic stress disorder. In the literature only very little information is found about victims outside the western world. Only when they are admitted as political refugees does one realize the influence of such a status on their current functioning. Because of language problems in the host-country they are scarcely able to express what it means for them to be tortured or to have seen how their family was murdered or has otherwise died. For many people the disorder starts several hours or days after the confrontation with the trauma. In a number of cases several years pass before problems are manifested in all their severity (problems such as re-experiencing, avoidance and increased arousal). It is known that some concentration camp survivors, for example, began to work very hard after the war had ended, thus repressing all memories of the trauma. One could regard this as a protracted form of avoidance behaviour. When, however, active participation in the labour process has ended, either by pensioning or inability to work, a post-traumatic stress disorder can still be manifested. Sleeping disturbances play an important role in these patients, as well as alcohol and substance abuse, of which excessive smoking is the least severe. Research in the US has revealed an extensive abuse of hard drugs among Vietnam veterans. Addictive behaviour can also be regarded as a form of avoidance: the patient pursues a state of oblivion. Also strong attempts to avoid activities or situations occur frequently in these patients, for instance a war victim who does not want to go to whichever foreign country it was where the trauma occurred. An important characteristic of the disorder is diminished responsivity. In mild cases the person feels alienated from other people and feels that he does not belong among them. In severe cases one can see the inability to experience emotions, especially those of the more intimate kind, such as love, sexuality and tenderness. According to some authors, a severe trauma could even lead to dissociative disorders, such as multiple personality. The post-traumatic stress disorder is often accompanied by phenomena such as depression, suicidal thoughts and actions, phobic fears, unexpected aggressive outbursts and the above-mentioned substance abuse. Furthermore, the disorder may have a great influence on the familial and social relationships of the person concerned, among other things by emotional chilling, or by a preoccupation with the traumatic event, or the avoidance of it. Relational problems, therefore, can be a source of worry similar to the problems in daily activities. In a more general sense, it should be noted that there has been no extensive research into this disorder and many findings are based upon case reports.

Differential diagnosis

Some people relate that they are deeply impressed by events which are in themselves less dramatic. One of our patients, for example, told us that she kept thinking of a scene in her youth when a chicken was slaughtered. This kind of not unusual event along with life events such as divorce, bankruptcy, and the (natural) death of a loved person, are not accounted to the traumata mentioned above. With regard to the differential diagnosis, a distinction should be made between simple phobia (the avoidance of specific situations or objects), obsessive-compulsive behaviour (continuous thoughts about the anxiety-provoking theme), and agoraphobia (in which one could ask what is the reason that a person dare not be in the street, dare not pass a certain point, or dare not travel alone). Depressive disorders often occur as a consequence of post-traumatic stress disorder; therefore depressive patients should be asked about certain themes they tend to avoid. Finally, a distinction should be made between this disorder and pathological bereavement.

GENERALIZED ANXIETY DISORDER

For almost a year or so Marianne, a 34-year-old woman, has been feeling uneasy and restless most of the time. In fact, she cannot understand or explain why this is the case, because nothing special has happened or is going on. On the other hand, worrying and brooding are things she can do very well. When her husband is slightly late home from work, she can picture him lying in hospital because of an accident. When her children are playing outside, she is very jittery, because every now and again she wants to know if they are playing safely. Their vacation became quite an obsession for her this last year, she says, because all the time she was worrying about things that could go wrong, and about accidents that could befall the family. When they were on sunny beaches, she could not feel at ease and continuously tried to observe her husband and her two children and asked if they please would not go too far into the sea or play any wild games. She has been able to contain herself for quite some time now, but currently she is anticipating an anxious summer holiday and she wants to talk about this with a psychologist. Some time before, her general practitioner listened to her kindly, and he told her that she probably was a bit overworked and that she needed a holiday. That advice confirmed her conviction that she was a bit mentally deranged, which in itself became another source of worrying and tension.

DSM-III-R criteria

The diagnosis is made when there is an unrealistic or excessive fear and concern (anxious expectations) about two or more aspects of life. Examples are worries about possible accidents to a person's child (which is not in real danger), or about financial matters (when there is no reason for it). These worries last longer than six months and during that time they are more often present than not. When another Axis I disorder is present, then the concern mentioned above is unrelated to it. The fear or worries are, for example, not related to having a panic attack as in the case of panic disorder. Also generalized anxiety disorder is not manifested solely in the course of a mood disorder or a psychotic disorder. Three symptom clusters are distinguished, that is motoric tension, autonomic hyperactivity, and vigilance and wakefulness. In order to make a diagnosis at least six of the following symptoms should be present when a person is fearful. Symptoms present only during a panic attack must be excluded.

1. Motoric tension, manifested as shaking, trembling, muscle tension, muscle ache, restlessness and fatigue.
2. Autonomic hyperactivity, manifested as shortness of breath or a choking feeling, palpitations or tachycardia, sweating or cold hands, dry mouth, dizziness or lightheadedness, nausea, diarrhoea or other intestinal complaints (hot and cold) flushes, frequent urination, difficulty swallowing or a lump in the throat.
3. Wakefulness or vigilance, manifested as feeling "worked up", exaggerated reactions of fear, difficulty in concentrating, trouble of black-outs caused by fear, difficulty in falling asleep or staying asleep, and irritability.

There is no organic factor (like hyperthyroidism or caffeine intoxication), which causes or maintains the disorder. Furthermore, other disorders in which generalized anxiety often occurs should be excluded before this diagnosis can be made.

Clinical picture

Generalized anxiety disorder is a difficult category, which many authors consider a kind of residual category of the phenomenon of anxiety. Increased arousal is the most prominent characteristic of this disorder. Other symptoms are worrying and brooding about things that might happen, but for which there is no reason to suppose that they actually will happen (fearful expectations). Furthermore, patients report a multitude of bodily tension problems, which are unrelated to specific situations, but seem to be caused by brooding and worrying (that is about what could happen, in contrast with depression, in which brooding often has a retrospective character or is centred around the person's own failing). Butler, Cullington, Hibbert, Klimes and Gelder (1987a) found in 64% of their patients with generalized anxiety disorder a certain extent of phobic avoidance, but this did not have the specific focus that is the case in other simple phobias and agoraphobia. Many patients with generalized anxiety manifest a pattern of irregular and variable avoidance. Of Butler's patients 80% exhibited situational anxiety and 78% exhibited anticipatory anxiety. In the same study, the authors investigated what people themselves were doing to counteract these problems. Excessive use of medications, in particular tranquillizers (benzodiazepines) and frequent use of alcohol are found in 15% of the patients with generalized anxiety disorder. Furthermore, looking for distraction can be regarded as the most important anxiety reducer.

Differential diagnosis

Generalized anxiety and panic disorder are similar in some respects; in both cases there is a longstanding and increased arousal and anxious expectation. The difference between the disorders lies in the fact that anxiety in patients with panic disorder is caused by the threat of a new attack, whereas in a generalized anxiety disorder this is not the case. In the latter disorder, the patient is unable to indicate a specific reason for his anxiety, apart from an excessive worrying and brooding about all kinds of things that might happen, especially thoughts about the fear itself, about loss of control and about possible diseases. This implies that the diagnosis of generalized anxiety disorder can be made only in the absence of panic disorder. Depression is also characterized by an increased tendency to worry. The content of the worries, however, is more depressive than anxious in nature and, among other things, shows a pessimistic outlook on the future and a negative self-image. Similarly, as in the case of panic disorder, in making the diagnosis of generalized anxiety disorder, possible panic should be excluded. Excessive use of caffeine, alcohol and psychotropic drugs has been mentioned.

CONCLUSIONS

Using diagnostic criteria is a less straightforward matter than one is apt to think at first sight. Two important factors play a role, that is the diagnostic skill of the clinician and the clarity of the diagnostic criteria. The delineation of complaints requires an accurate investigation of their precise nature and the circumstances in which they occur. Apart from possessing the usual interview skills, the clinician should possess good insight into the various forms of anxiety disorders and their similarities. An example can illustrate this. A patient is admitted with a fear of using the lift in high buildings. Which diagnosis can one make? Is the patient afraid of enclosed spaces (as in the case of claustrophobia)? Is there a fear of being unable to escape when feeling unwell (as in the case of panic disorder)? Is the patient very tense in the company of complete strangers (as in the case of social phobia)? Is there a fear of being contaminated by touching the lift or the people in it (as in the case of obsessive-compulsive disorder)? Is the lift conveying a traumatic meaning because the patient has been sexually or physically harassed (as in the case of post-traumatic stress disorder)? These and other diagnostic considerations should be made by the clinician before he or she can make a responsible statement. In view of the above it is very important for the clinician to be well informed about the differential diagnoses within the anxiety disorders in particular and psychopathology in general. Novice clinicians especially tend to be quite satisfied with the first bit of information that fits a certain diagnostic picture. Thus they run the risk of investigating only a few of the circumstances of the problems and the patient's motives. A diagnosis is often the starting point for further treatment, such as making a functional analysis or planning and conducting treatment. Another difficulty regarding the delineation of anxiety disorders and making a diagnosis concerns the obscurity of the diagnostic criteria themselves. In the anxiety disorders discussed in this chapter sometimes fear, sometimes avoidance is the most prominent characteristic. In most cases there is more or less a clear object towards which the anxiety is aimed. When one scrutinizes the diagnostic criteria according to DSM-III-R, one can detect a certain hierarchy in the system. Some diagnoses prevail over others, as is the case in panic disorder. It is very important to be sure of its presence or absence before proceeding to the possible social phobia, generalized anxiety disorder, or hypochondriasis. When there is a history of panic attacks, the latter three diagnoses can sometimes be excluded. Furthermore, two diagnoses can be made only by (partial) exclusion of other anxiety disorders. This applies to the diagnoses "simple phobia" and "generalized anxiety disorder", which in a certain way form a "residual category". As the formulation of the latter diagnostic criteria is only of recent date, many clinicians are not familiar with this category and there has also been very little epidemiological research so far.

2 Epidemiology and Aetiology of Anxiety Disorders

EPIDEMIOLOGY

Young children are often afraid of all kinds of situations and objects (such as pets, insects, vacuum cleaners, the dark, and strangers), but generally their fears subside as they grow older (Ollendick, Matson & Helsel, 1985; Verhulst, 1985). Girls appear to be more timorous than boys. Although young children tend to become less afraid of frightening situations as they grow older, an anxiety which is developed after the age of 6 is generally present until adolescence. Fear of natural phenomena (e.g. thunder), social anxiety and fear of sustaining injury or severe hurt are characteristic of this phase in life. Fear of all kinds of situations is quite common in children, however, and we are hardly ever dealing with real phobias at this age. In a study with 2000 children, 10 and 11 year-olds, Rutter, Tizard and Whitmore (1970) found that merely 0.7% of these children were suffering from a clinically significant phobia. School phobia is a relatively rare phenomenon, but the consequences are presumably so serious that parents are obliged to call for professional help for their child. In children, it is the main phobia for which professional treatment is sought. During adolescence social anxiety often prevails and girls start to suffer from it at an earlier age than boys (Abe & Masui, 1981). Epidemiological research among adults in the United States (Myers, Weissman, Tischler, Holzer et al., 1984; Robins, Helzer, Weissman, Overaschel et al., 1984), Canada (Bland, Orn & Newman, 1988) and West Germany (Wittchen, 1988) shows that phobias occur very often. On the basis of these investigations, the lifetime prevalence of panic disorders is estimated to be 2.3% and of phobias 13%. This means that 2.3% and 13% of the interviewees respectively had been seriously suffering from panic disorders or phobias, or were still suffering from them at that time. When the prevalence of psychopathology during the six months preceding the interview is taken into consideration, it appears that it is mostly women who suffer from phobias. With men over 25, phobic complaints are second to alcohol addiction. Furthermore, agoraphobia occurs more frequently than social phobia. One might ask why so many phobics do not seek treatment or are not referred for treatment. It cannot be assumed that most people overcome their fear just like that. In a follow-up study with phobics who had not received treatment (Agras, Chapin & Oliveau, 1972), it emerged that after 5 years only 6% of the phobic adults had rid themselves of their phobic complaints. With 37% of the adults, the phobia had actually worsened, notably with agoraphobics. Although initially obsessive-compulsive disorder was assumed to be relatively rare, it appeared from the above cited epidemiological research that the lifetime prevalence of obsessive-compulsive disorder may be estimated to be 2.6%. During 6 months preceding the interview 1.6% of the population appeared to be suffering from an obsessive-compulsive disorder in terms of DSM-III. The comparatively high prevalence of obsessive-compulsive disorder within the normal population is not manifested in the number of patients who have these complaints and apply for treatment. Many obsessive patients are possibly ashamed of their compulsive behaviour; another factor is that some of them are not actually bothered by their complaints. Many obsessive-compulsive patients apply for treatment only after conflicts with their surroundings and considerable pressure from their families.

Age of onset and sex differences

In Table 2.1. the results are displayed from the main studies of age of onset and sex differences with social phobia, agoraphobia and simple phobia. Emmelkamp (1990b) gives an overview of research into the age of onset of obsessive-compulsive disorders, from which it appears that it starts soon after the twentieth year of life.

Table 2.1. Mean onset age in years of phobic disorders

	Social phobia	Agoraphobia	Simple phobia
Marks and Gelder (1966)	19 (25)	24 (84)	
Shafar (1976)	20 (20)	32 (68)	
Amies et al. (1983)	19 (87)	24 (57)	
Thyer et al. (1985)	16 (42)	27 (115)	16 (152)
Persson and Nordlund (1985)	21 (31)	27 (37)	
Solyom, Ledwidge and Solyom (1986)	17 (47)	25 (80)	13 (72)
Öst (1987)	16 (80)	28 (100)	

Numbers of patients are given in parentheses.

In contrast with agoraphobia, which occurs more often in women than in men, social phobia seems to occur equally in both women and men. The findings of the studies are presented in Table 2.2. Research results show that on the average social phobics are better educated than agoraphobics, belong to a higher social class and have fewer financial problems (Amies, Gelder & Shaw, 1983; Persson & Nordlund, 1985; Solyom, Ledwidge & Solyom, 1986). Thyer et al. (1985) found a mean age of onset of 16 years in a group of 152 patients with simple phobias. It should be noted that the spreading of ages was very large, owing to the fact that the various simple phobias were taken as a whole. The same applies to the study by Solyom, Ledwidge and Solyom (1986), in which a mean age

Table 2.2. Percentages of female patients

	Social phobia %	Agoraphobia %	Simple phobia %
Marks and Gelder (1966)	60 (25)	87 (84)	
Shafar (1976)	55 (20)	87 (68)	
Amies et al. (1983)	40 (87)	86 (57)	
Thyer et al. (1985)	52 (42)	81 (115)	
Solyom, Ledwidge and Solyom (1986)	47 (47)	86 (80)	78 (72)
Öst (1987)	65 (80)	87 (100)	80 (190)

Numbers of patients are given in parentheses.

Table 2.3. Simple phobias: ages of onset

	Numbers of patients	Mean age of onset
Claustrophobia	40	20
Animal phobia	50	7
Blood phobia	40	9
Dental phobia	60	12

From Öst (1987) by permission.

of onset of 13 years emerged in a group of 72 phobics. Öst (1987) managed to break down the different groups in order to be more specific. The results are shown in Table 2.3. As with other phobic disorders, simple phobias occur more often in women than in men (see Table 2.2).

AETIOLOGY

In this section of the chapter, a number of explanatory models will be dealt with concerning the aetiology of anxiety disorders, followed by a more specific discussion of the aetiology of simple phobia, panic disorder and agoraphobia, social phobia and obsessive-compulsive disorder.

Learning theoretical model

The learning theoretical view on the origin of phobias and obsessions and compulsions is founded on Mowrer's two-factor theory of fear and avoidance. According to Mowrer, classical conditioning is held responsible for the acquisition of fear, and operant conditioning for the learning of avoidance behaviour. This model, which was originally developed by conducting animal experiments in a laboratory, has been most influential for theoretical development within behaviour therapy. The first behavioural therapeutic procedures for the treatment of phobias (systematic desensitization and flooding) were based on this two-factor model. In those treatments it was supposed that tackling the aspect of fear by, for instance, systematic desensitization would effect a change of avoidance behaviour. Various experiments showed that a phobia can be adopted by means of classical conditioning. Watson and Rayner (1920) succeeded in changing a healthy one-year-old baby into a phobic through classical conditioning. They conducted the following experiment. Little Albert, who was afraid of nothing except loud noises (which is normal at that age) was allowed to play with a laboratory rat. Albert started to play with the rat without feeling any fear at all. A dramatic change took place when the rat was produced in combination with a loud noise. After this had happened seven times, Albert became anxious just on seeing the rat even without hearing the noise. Watson and Rayner described it as follows: "The instant the rat was shown, the baby began to cry. Almost instantly, he turned sharply to the left side, raised himself on all fours and began to crawl away so rapidly that he was only caught with difficulty before reaching the edge of the table." Moreover, it appeared that the fear had been generalized to neutral objects such as a dog, a fur coat and wool. Little Albert's role was just as prominent for the development of learning theoretical procedures for treatment as was that of little Hans (Freud, 1909) for the psychoanalytic theory. Although Watson and Rayner did indeed show that it is possible to adopt a phobia by means of classical conditioning, it cannot be asserted that all phobias develop through such a learning process. A number of researchers have attempted to replicate this experiment with other children but, generally speaking, there was no result. Also, research into the effects of traumatic experiences shows that such experiences alone do not incite the development of a phobia. Moreover, it appears that phobic patients often do not recall any traumatic experiences. Even though the classical conditioning paradigm may be useful for explaining the development of phobias after a traumatic event, it does not offer an explanation for those cases in which the phobia has developed gradually, as in most cases. The bulk of the research conducted on the development of clinical phobias does not support an interpretation linking classical conditioning with the onset of anxiety (Emmelkamp, 1982). Despite the fact that many agoraphobics develop their phobia as a consequence of a "spontaneous" attack, it does not necessarily mean that classical conditioning can be held responsible for the genesis of a phobia. We will return to this later. However, evidence has been found that classical conditioning plays a role in the onset of simple phobias. From the research by Goldstein and Chambless (1978) it appeared that in 50% of their phobic patients, traumatic experiences were in fact related to the onset of a simple phobia and in the research by Lautsch (1971), in all cases of patients suffering from fear of the dentist, significant conditioning experiences could be remembered.

Biological factors

High arousal level

From various researches it has emerged that patients with panic disorder, agoraphobics and social phobics maintain a high arousal level (Lader, 1967; Lader & Wing, 1966). In a discussion of the outcome of these studies, Lader and Mathews (1968) suggest an interaction between the level of arousal and conditioning. They point out that in agoraphobics and social phobics the chronic state of high arousal is more important than conditioning, whereas in simple phobias conditioning is more likely to be a significant factor, as in this case we are not dealing with a chronic state of arousal. The question remains, however, whether the high arousal levels in agoraphobics and social phobias cause the phobic complaints or whether they can be seen as consequences of the phobia. Beech and his colleagues suggested that a high arousal level might affect the efficacy of the conditioning process. Their investigations revealed that it was easier to acquire a conditioned response in high arousal than in the "normal" state of the organism (Asso & Beech, 1975; Vila & Beech, 1977, 1978). Comparable results were reported by Hugdahl, Frederikson and Ohman (1977).

Genetic factors

Up until now there has been little research into the role of genetic factors in the development of anxiety disorders. McGuffin and Reich (1984) found that members of social phobics' families suffered more often from social phobias than family members of panic patients and "normal people". Although they regarded this as evidence of the influence of genetic factors in the onset of social phobia, certain reservations should be made. Such research offers little evidence of a genetic contribution, in view of the fact that other factors, such as the influence of environment, could be held responsible for the differences that were found. Furthermore, it is not surprising that children should develop the same complaints as their parents because children tend to imitate their parents' avoidance behaviour (compare the study by Windheuser, 1977). Research among twins provides more information regarding a possible genetic contribution, on the basis of the supposition that both monozygotic and dizygotic twins are exposed to more or less the same environmental influences, provided they grow up in the same family. Two studies on monozygotic and dizygotic twins are relevant with regard to social phobia. Research by Torgerson (1979) and Rose and Dilto (1983) revealed a (limited) genetic contribution to the onset of social anxiety. Various investigations have been carried out into a possibly hereditary component of obsessive-compulsive disorder. An overview is given by McGuffin and Reich (1984) and Torgerson (1988). Even although a restricted number of family members of obsessive-compulsive patients also appear to have compulsive symptoms, this fact alone does not mean that we are dealing with a genetic factor. As was said before, it could also be the consequence of common environmental factors. In twin studies, a higher incidence of compulsions was found in monozygotic twins in comparison with dizygotic twins; these studies, however, were far from representative. Information from more recent research does not yet allow any firm conclusions concerning the contribution of genetic factors. Conclusions from research make it plausible to assume that there is no genetic contribution present in the onset of generalized anxiety disorder and post-traumatic-stress disorder. But there are indications of genetic contributions to the beginning of panic disorder and agoraphobia (Torgersen, 1988), although the methodological shortcomings of the studies have made it impossible to make more definite statements. Correspondingly, no genetic factors have been ascertained in connection with most forms of simple phobias. There is, however, one exception to this rule. In blood phobics, notably, a strikingly high percentage of family members were found to have the same complaints, that is 68% (Öst, Lindahl, Sterner & Jerremalm, 1984b). This is a much higher score than that for other phobic disorders (Marks, 1969; Öst & Hugdahl, 1981), which suggests that there is indeed a genetic component present in blood phobia, for instance a hereditarily determined, exceptionally strong reaction of the autonomous nerve system.

Neuro-transmission

In biological psychiatry it is supposed that anxiety disorders are interrelated with disorders in different neuro-transmission systems: the benzodiazepine-GABA-system, the noradrenergic system and the serotonergic system. These suppositions are partly founded on animal experiments, partly on fear provocation tests and partly on the selective working of various drugs in humans. Although it is conceivable that these systems fulfil an important role in regulating fear (Hoehn-Saric & McLeod, 1988; Wamboldt & Insel, 1988), the restricted number of studies which have been carried out so far does not yet confirm any causal relationships.

Psychodynamic view

The defence mechanisms of "suppression" and "displacement" are important for the psychodynamic interpretation of phobias. This means that the original source of fear is being suppressed and that the fear is transferred to another object. In 1926 Freud introduced the concept of "signal fear". The function of the signal fear is to mobilize the defence mechanisms in order to prevent a threatening situation from changing into a traumatic situation (Eagle & Wolitzky, 1988). From this viewpoint, it is seen that emerging thoughts and feelings, engendered by instinctive wishes, lead to signal fear. This fear activates the defence mechanisms and sees to it that the coming thought or feeling remains unconscious. If the defence mechanisms fail, anxiety will be experienced, either in the form of free-floating anxiety, or in the form of panic attacks. From this viewpoint, phobias are regarded as a kind of second-line defence, in which it is attempted to relate the initial diffuse anxiety to specific situations. According to Freud's theory, the anxiety is actuated by an instinctive wish conflicting with the Ego or Superego. Some psychoanalytic authors are of the opinion that there is a relation between the nature of a phobia and the content of the averted fears. In this way, spider phobia has been considered to be an expression of unconscious sexual fears. Abraham (1927) regarded spider phobia as a symbol for the unconscious fear of bisexual genitals. Sperling (1971) maintained that in patients with spider phobia, the key problems are sexual identification and bisexuality. Freud saw the snake as a phallic symbol and it may be obvious how he interpreted snake phobia. Some psychoanalysts regard fear of aeroplanes as fear of sex, in which the aeroplane stands for the womb. A more generally accepted explanation is that flight phobia originates in people with a great fear of loss of control or loss of face. Horney (1950) writes: "The phobia of falling from heights is a frequent expression of the fear of falling from heights of illusory grandeur." The fear of loss of control would also be at the root of claustrophobia. In psychoanalysis little has been written about social phobia. More attention has been paid to a specific form of social phobia, notably erythrophobia or fear of blushing. Several publications on this subject have appeared over the years. Blushing has initially been conceived as a hysterical conversion symptom (displacement of suppressed genital excitement to the face), but also as a fear of unconscious tendencies to expose oneself. The second explanation is supported by Hitschmann (1943), who proposed that shame and shyness serve to replace the tendencies to expose oneself. This replacement is regarded as a victory of the Superego over the Ego, blushing as a proof of obedience to the Superego. Stekel (1924) associated the fear of being caught, which is the consequence of forbidden fantasies, with masturbation. Fenichel (1945) and Bergler (1944) also give very complicated explanations, in which the wish to expose oneself and the fear of punishment are always central.

Cognitive aspects

Over recent years more and more attention has been devoted to (disorders in) cognitive mechanisms of psychopathology in general and fear and depression in particular. Beck and Emery (1985) consider generalized anxiety and panic to be the outcome of so-called "danger" schemata. These schemata contain important information about a person's experiences in comparable situations in the past, also about rules, ideas and expectations concerning future events. These schemata provide the information which the person in question selectively assimilates and interprets as dangerous. In a number of carefully controlled studies, Mathews (1989) showed that anxious subjects perceived threatening stimuli sooner than neutral or positive stimuli, whereas "normal" subjects reacted the other way round. It had been shown earlier (Mathews & MacLeod, 1986) that emotionally threatening words, subliminally presented, interfered with an assignment which the anxious subjects had to carry out, although they themselves were not aware of these words. Similar interference did not occur in the control group. These studies support Beck and Emery's theory.

The aetiology of simple phobias

Developmental factors

In the discussion of the phenomenology of simple phobias, it was mentioned that a slight form of fear of certain animal species and objects regularly occurs in the "normal" population. Probably this has something to do with the fact that some stimuli possess a certain "fear value" for every living being. This seems to be a consequence of the fact that each organism needs a certain environment in order to survive; an environment in which a number of basic needs are satisfied (oxygen, water, food and physical integrity). Stimuli forming a menace to these needs evoke fear and are avoided as much as possible. Fear of heights, for instance, can then be seen as a serious form of the "normal", healthy fear, which can be discerned in all people who are confronted with great heights. Similarly, most people feel uncomfortable in small spaces. Fear of new situations or fear of unknown objects are also well-known phenomena. Equally, the fear of being looked at does not apply exclusively to social phobics; two staring eyes can also evoke a fear reaction in animals, even if the eyes are artificial. Various fears, among them fear of certain animals, often occur in "normal" child development. Usually these feelings of fear develop between the ages of 2 and 4, and disappear spontaneously in the course of time. Only in a few cases do the symptoms persist after secondary school age, although in adults slight feelings of fear are common.

Learning theoretical explanation

At the beginning of this chapter it was noted that classical conditioning appeared to play a part in the onset of simple phobias. With clinical animal phobias patients report the age of onset to be 8 to 10 years of age (Marks & Gelder, 1966; Hugdahl & Öst, 1985; McNally & Steketee, 1985). This is some years later than the phase of a toddler in which the "normal" fears develop. The question remains whether the phobic fear did not originate some years earlier. In addition, it often occurs that patients find it impossible to indicate a clear beginning of the phobia such as, for instance, a conditioning event. In a study by McNally and Steketee (1985) it was ascertained that only 25% of the subjects with animal phobias (snake phobia in particular) could actually remember a traumatic event preceding the onset of the phobic fear. It should be observed that in none of these cases did the animal inflict any physical injury on the person involved. DiNardo, Guzy, Jenkins, Bak et al. (1988) compared two groups of students, one group with a (phobic) fear of dogs and the other without such fear. In the first group 56% recalled traumatic experiences whereas in the second group as many as 66% remembered having them. In more than 50% of the cases the animal had indeed caused actual physical pain. It can be inferred that many individuals do not develop a phobia despite the fact that they have had traumatic experiences, a fact which is also known from other studies (Aitken, Lister & Main, 1981; Goorney, 1970; Lautch, 1971). In various studies corresponding ages of onset are found, at least regarding animal phobias. According to some authors this suggests that children at the age of 8 to 10 would appear to be more sensitive to such fears which disappear at a later stage in life. This suggestion is supported by the fact that persons at an older age suffering from animal phobia are in fact able to recall traumatic experiences. On the other hand, however, it may well be that traumatic experiences are better remembered at an older age. The uniformity in data given by the patients enhances the suggestion that there is indeed a kind of critical age (from 8 to 10) for the development of an animal phobia. A minor traumatic experience at this stage could be sufficient for developing an animal phobia. In toddlers there are hardly any sex differences with regard to animal phobias, whereas the phobias developed later in life occur predominantly in women. This supports the hypothesis that the phobia developed at an older age differs from a phobia of early childhood.

Cognitive factors

Although dysfunctional cognitions play a part in the onset and duration of phobic reactions in general, it seems that the cognitions in simple phobias are less apparent. Considerable research has been pursued on the role of cognitions in phobic reactions to certain animal species. The striking thing is that most animal phobics are not primarily concerned about being hurt by these animals. This particularly applies to spider and snake phobias. McNally and Steketee (1985) found that 91% of the phobics were afraid of having a panic attack, whereas only 41% reported being afraid of pain. In the earlier quoted study by DiNardo et al. (1988), it appeared nevertheless that all the students suffering from dog phobia were indeed afraid of pain or injury.

Agoraphobia and panic disorder

Separation anxiety

Various authors have put forward the theory that there is a relationship between a child's fear of separation and the development of agoraphobia at a later age (Berg, 1976; Casat, 1988). Bowlby (1973) also believes that the cause of agoraphobia can be found in early childhood. Agoraphobics would be afraid to lose the people to whom they are attached. In this context it has often been suggested that agoraphobics have overprotective parents (especially mothers). However, controlled studies on this question do not confirm this thesis. Admittedly, studies by Parker (1979) and Arrindell, Emmelkamp, Monsma and Brilman (1983) showed that the parents lacked affection but they had not been overprotective. It should be noted that both studies were carried out retrospectively. Central to Bowlby's theory (1973) is the concept of attachment. According to Bowlby, anxiety disorders in adults are the results of prolonged and frequent separations during childhood or of the threat of an impending separation. Bowlby's theory gave cause to considerable research. Ainsworth (1984), for instance, pointed out that safely attached children react differently from anxiously attached children when their mothers leave them behind in a strange room. Safely attached children demonstrate explorative behaviour when their mother is present; as soon as their mother leaves them they become tense and when she returns they seek contact and approach. Anxiously attached children, on the other hand, demonstrate some explorative behaviour before, during and after separation from their mother, but often appear to avoid contact when she comes back. It can be assumed that a child uses the adult to whom it is attached as a safe basis from which it can explore the world. If this protective person is no longer present, separation anxiety arises; consequently attachment behaviour is evoked and explorative behaviour is reduced. These phenomena have been found not only in children but also in ducks and monkeys. Bowlby believes that there is a striking similarity between school phobia in children and agoraphobia in adults. In his opinion the fear of leaving home is involved in both cases and both can be regarded as examples of separation anxiety.

The influence of stressful events (life events)

Although no clear relationship has been found between a specific traumatic event in a certain situation and the development of agoraphobia, agoraphobia does often appear to start after a stressful life event. Examples of these life events are the death of a loved one, illness, the birth of a child, increasing responsibilities and problems with relatives. From a study by Kleiner and Marshall (1987) it emerged that 84% of a group of agoraphobics were having relative or marital problems for a long time prior to their first panic attack. Only 15% of Roth's (1959) agoraphobics reported family problems in the period preceding the onset of the disorder, and in the study by Solyom, Beck, Solyom and Hugel (1974) this appeared to be the case with 33% of the patients. Also Last, Barlow and O'Brien (1984) found that one-third of the agoraphobics were having interpersonal conflicts in the period prior to the onset of complaints. In Kleiner and Marshall's study it appeared that all the subjects had experienced various stressful events before the phobia developed. What significance should be attached to the role of these stressful events in the onset of phobic complaints? An important point is that such events are evidently related to a large number of other psychopathological disorders, notably depression, psychosomatic disorders and (relapse in) schizophrenia. The specific relationship between certain stressors and the development of phobias apparently does not matter as much as a general susceptibility to developing complaints in stressful times. The interesting question remains: why do some people develop complaints (such as a phobia) while others do not? Personality factors presumably play an important role in this. The locus of control is possibly one of them. Rotter (1966) suggested that people differ in the extent to which they experience control over environmental factors. Those with a high degree of internal control are inclined to exert control over the events, whereas people with a high degree of external control consider the events to be the result of chance, fate or powerful others. Johnson and Sarason (1978) put forward the theory that the personal reaction to stressful circumstances depends on the extent of internal and external control. They predicted that negative effects of an important (negative) event most deeply affect those people who feel that they do not exercise any control over such events. The results of their study pointed out that locus of control was indeed a moderator variable in the relation between life events on the one hand and anxiety and depression on the other. Persons experiencing considerable stress and at the same time feeling no ability to control these events, appeared to be most vulnerable to the consequences of life events. Emmelkamp and Cohen-Kettenis (1975) found that locus of control correlates with the extent of phobic fear in agoraphobics: the more one externalizes, the more severe the agoraphobia becomes. Elsewhere we have suggested (Emmelkamp, 1982) that persons with an external orientation, suffering from panic attacks during stressful intervals, were sooner inclined to attribute their fear to external sources, for instance pressure, or to a disease such as a heart attack. Others may even interpret the panic attack as a sign of losing their senses. Persons with an external orientation thus perceive the fear as something beyond their control.

The role of panic and hyperventilation in the aetiology of agoraphobia

As was discussed in Chapter 1, bodily symptoms attending panic (such as sweating, trembling, oppression on the chest, fear of fainting and hot and cold flushes) are largely similar to the symptoms attending hyperventilation (Ley, 1985). In a number of studies it was pointed out that it is possible to provoke a panic attack in people suffering from panic attacks in daily life. These manipulations concern among other things infusion with sodium lactate (Appleby, Klein, Sachar & Levitt, 1981), oral application of caffeine (Charney, Heninger & Jatlow, 1985), voluntary hyperventilation (Clark, Salkovskis & Chalkley, 1985) and inhalation of carbon dioxide (Griez & Van den Hout, 1984).

It is very rarely possible to provoke such an attack in patients without panic disorder. For an extensive survey of the literature on this subject the reader is best referred to Ehlers and Margraf (1989) and Van den Hout and Van der Molen (1988). Results from previous studies, together with the notion of a "spontaneous" panic attack, were initially counted as evidence of a biological cause of a panic disorder. There is, however, an alternative psychological explanation. It is plausible that the above-mentioned methods do not directly produce a panic-provoking effect, but arouse panic only if the bodily sensations experienced are interpreted in a certain way. This is the central idea put forward by Clark (1986; Clark & Salkovskis, 1989). The supposition is made that panic attacks are not the direct outcome of bodily processes, but the result of the catastrophic interpretation of these bodily sensations. This means that persons involved are inclined to interpret the sensations as more dangerous than they are in reality (palpitations of the heart for instance, are seen as evidence of an impending cardiac arrest). A vicious circle of fear develops, attending bodily symptoms (notably hyperventilating), subsequent catastrophic interpretation of them, intensifying of fear, followed by an even stronger bodily reaction. This vicious circle can be found in the literature in various forms. Consequently, it is not the symptoms themselves, but the way in which they are interpreted that leads to a panic attack. In the discussion of the treatment of panic in Chapter 6, the model will be dealt with in detail. Up until now research results seem to support this model. On the basis of the cognitive model it would be expected that the thoughts of panic patients are characterized by ideas pertaining to catastrophic interpretations of bodily symptoms. Hibbert (1984a), Ottaviani and Beck (1987), Rapee (1985) and Reiss et al. (1986) found support for this hypothesis in their studies. With regard to the succession of events during a panic attack, a bodily sensation would be expected to be the first perception during a panic attack. Empirical support was also found for this suggestion (Hibbert, 1984b; Ley, 1985).

System theoretical view of agoraphobia

A number of therapists have offered the suggestion that interpersonal conflicts, and particularly marital problems, play an important part in the development and onset of agoraphobia (Goldstein & Chambless, 1978; Hafner, 1982). Hafner related that spouses of phobics were thwarting the positive effects of treatment, or else that they were developing psychiatric complaints themselves. He also believed that a change in phobic complaints in the patient produced negative effects on his or her marriage. These were, however, clinical observations, on the basis of which the suggestion has been made that a system theoretical approach is required in order to comprehend the aetiology and consolidation of agoraphobia. Fry (1962) also hypothesized that the spouses of agoraphobics themselves are having psychiatric problems, notably social anxiety and a sense of inferiority regarding their partner. They supposedly benefit from the maintenance of their partner's phobia, because otherwise their own psychiatric problems would come to light. The patient's phobia will in such a case serve to maintain a balance in the relationship. Hafner (1982) also described similar relationships. Arrindell and Emmelkamp (1985) investigated the psychological profile of partners of agoraphobics. This study pertained to psychopathology, phobias, hostility, neuroticism and a number of other personality traits. On all variables, partners of agoraphobics did not score differently from partners of "normals" or partners of non-phobic psychiatric patients. Consequently, from the results it does not appear that partners of agoraphobics tend to be more neurotic, socially more anxious, more obsessive, or more dependent than partners from the control group. In a follow-up study (Arrindell & Emmelkamp, 1986) the quality of the relationship of agoraphobic couples was compared to that of a number of other groups of couples, that is:

1. couples of which one half was having psychic problems other than phobic complaints;
2. happy couples;
3. unhappy couples who had requested treatment for their relationship problems

On self-report scales of relationship satisfaction and communication agoraphobics appeared to correspond more strongly with the happy couples than with the unhappy couples. The control group of non-phobic psychiatric patients and their partners turned out to be experiencing their relationship in an equally negative way to the group of couples with relationship problems. Naturally, this does not imply that there are no unhappy marriages among agoraphobics. The results of this study do, however, show that this is more an exception than a rule.

Social phobia

Learning theoretical explanation

Öst and Hugdahl (1981) found that in 58% of social phobics the phobia was the result of a traumatic experience and seemed to be explained in terms of classical conditioning. This conclusion seems rather hurried, considering the fact that only two questions were posed. Moreover, the patients were asked only whether their fear had started in a specific situation. It remains unexplained why these persons became anxious for the first time in the situation in which the phobia began. Another possibility is that social phobia develops as a consequence of so-called vicarious learning, that is learning by way of observing other people. According to this paradigm, observing other people who are anxious in a social situation will cause fear in the observer. Other, more indirect evidence in favour of a modelling interpretation of the onset of social anxiety comes from a study by Windheuser (1977), who found that there was a striking concordance between the phobias of phobic children and those of their mothers. This especially applied to social phobia. Also Bruch, Heimberg, Berger & Collins (1989) reported that parents of social phobics were avoiding all kinds of social situations themselves. Öst and Hugdahl (1981) found that in merely 12% of their social phobics, modelling could be held responsible for the development of the phobia. It should be noted that a relationship between the phobias of parents and their children need not necessarily be explained on the basis of modelling. Other processes may be responsible as well, such as genetic factors or exposure to the same traumatic experiences.

Lack of social skills

It is often supposed that a lack of social skills leads to fear in social situations. Results of research on the skills of socially anxious subjects in comparison with non-anxious subjects, however, are ambiguous (Arkowitz, 1977; Beidel, Turner & Dancu, 1985; Dow, Biglan & Glaser, 1985). Research on social phobics shows that poor social skills seem to be less important in the aetiology of social fear than used to be assumed (Edelmann, 1985; Newton, Kindness & McFadyen, 1983). Most people experience social fear not because they cannot act in a socially adequate way, but rather because they believe they do not possess these skills. Hartman (1983) put forward the theory that the "social inadequacy" of socially anxious people resulted from problems of concentrating oneself. In social situations, the socially anxious person must divide his attention between internal cues (negative thoughts and perception of autonomous arousal) and external cues, whereas non-anxious persons are able to concentrate on the interpersonal interaction. Because social phobics are too preoccupied with irrational thoughts ("They probably think I'm weird") and bodily sensations ("I'm trembling"; "I'm blushing") they are paying insufficient attention to the conversation, which may create the impression that they lack some social skills.

Cognitive factors

A number of cognitive-minded clinicians proposed that irrational ideas should be considered to be the cause of fear of social evaluation (Ellis, 1962). Although various researchers indicated that irrational ideas are indeed related to this kind of fear (Golden, 1981; Goldfried & Sobocinski, 1975; Gormally, Sipps, Raphael & Varvil-Weld, 1981; Sutton-Simon & Goldfried, 1979), the relevance of the results from these studies is rather limited. None of the studies included really socially phobic patients. From our own research it emerged that in social phobics there was a clear link between irrational thoughts and fear of social

evaluation (Sanderman, Mersch, Van der Sleen, Emmelkamp & Ormel, 1987).
Even although it might be tempting to think that there is a causal relationship
between the irrational ideas and the fear experienced in social situations, it may
also well be that the increased tension in such situations is liable to make some
persons more susceptible to certain irrational ideas and expectations.

Parental rearing styles

Buss (1980) supposed social anxiety to be the result of negative experiences
as a child or adolescent in the particular situation in which they are judged by
other persons. According to Buss, oversensitivity develops as a consequence
of the way in which a child is raised. Parker (1979) investigated the rearing
methods of parents of social phobics and agoraphobics: social phobics described
their parents as showing little affection and being very overprotective, whereas
the parents of agoraphobics were characterized as parents with little affection.
Parker suggested that a child with overprotective parents, who moreover show
little affection, may experience serious problems in interpersonal situations:
"parental overprotection, by restricting the usual developmental processes of
independence, autonomy and social competence, might further promote any
diathesis to a social phobia" (p. 559). Arrindell et al. (1983) also investigated
the rearing methods of parents of different types of phobics. The results
corresponded with those of Parker. Also in this study the combination of parental
overprotection and lack of affection appeared to be more related to social phobia
than to agoraphobia. Bruch et al. (1989) investigated the extent to which parental
attitudes had affected the fear of being judged negatively in social situations.
In contrast with agoraphobics, social phobics reported that their parents had
isolated them from social situations and that their parents were concerned about
what other people thought of them. In addition, social phobics appeared to
have experienced greater social fear during adolescence and they had fewer
boy- and girlfriends than agoraphobics. In summary, the results of studies on
characteristics of parents can be said to be consistent; rejection and lack of
affection in combination with overprotection may engender anxiety about being
judged in social situations, which is in fact the main characteristic of social
phobia.

Obsessive-compulsive disorder

Learning theoretical explanation

The learning theoretical explanation for the onset of compulsive behaviour
is based on Mowrer's two-factor theory, which was discussed earlier. In
discussing obsessive-compulsive complaints, it seems important to distinguish
between active and passive avoidance. With passive avoidance the person avoids
stimuli or situations which may possibly arouse tension. Active avoidance

usually refers to the behavioural (compulsive) component of the disorder, for instance checking or cleaning (see Chapter 1). However, there is little reason to hypothesize that classical conditioning must play an important role in the onset of obsessive-compulsive behaviour (Emmelkamp, 1982). Although patients often make reference to one or more traumatic experiences in connection with the development of the compulsive behaviour, such a traumatic experience alone hardly ever brings about the disorder. In a number of cases various obsessions and compulsive rituals occur simultaneously. Theoretically speaking, different traumatic events might be expected to be related to the onset of different obsessions. In practice this hardly ever occurs. Consequently, there is little proof that classical conditioning can be held responsible for the development of compulsive problems. More evidence has been found for the second part of Mowrer's theory. From a series of studies it clearly emerged that compulsive rituals reduce fear and tension. Rachman and his colleagues (Rachman & Hodgson, 1980) investigated what happened if compulsive rituals were provoked in the laboratory. With persons having obsessive cleaning as their major problem, contamination in the laboratory led to an increase in fear and tension, while performing the compulsive ritual afterwards induced a reduction in fear and tension. When response prevention was applied (this means when patients were not permitted to wash their hands) it appeared that in the course of time (after approximately half an hour) the tension subsided spontaneously. This did not only appertain to the subjective fear experienced by the patient, but was also observed in physiological measurements. In patients with checking compulsions this relation appeared less unequivocal. In a number of them the confrontation with compulsive situations indeed appeared to induce an increase in tension and fear, and performing checking rituals afterwards also eased the tension, but this did not apply to all patients. Herrnstein's theory (1969) seems more effective than Mowrer's theory in explaining the behaviour of patients with obsessive-compulsive disorder. According to Herrnstein, fear reduction itself does not operate as a reinforcer, but the subjects experience less anxiety after performing a ritual than if they had not done so. Consider, for instance, a patient who must perform certain rituals, such as touching objects in a certain way, as soon as she gets the idea that her children may come to harm. The act of performing the rituals in itself need not precipitate into complete reduction of fear, and may even give rise to an increase in fear. It may, however, be assumed that this fear would be less painful than the fear and guilty feelings springing up if her children should indeed suffer serious injuries. She would then attribute the events to her leaving the rituals undone.

Cognitive disorders

Various researchers have investigated to what extent obsessive-compulsive patients are characterized by cognitive disorders. Research studies in the

1970s pointed out that obsessive-compulsive patients find it difficult to endure ambiguous situations. Studies on assessment tasks, conducted by Beech (1974) and his colleagues, showed that obsessive-compulsive patients on the one hand are sooner in need of a decision than patients without compulsive disorder, but on the other hand, they are inclined to postpone decision-making if the opportunity is found to gather more information. Reed's study (1977) also disclosed that having a hard time making decisions is characteristic for obsessive-compulsive patients. Carr (1974) postulated that patients with compulsive disorder estimate the chances as being extremely high that a decision will lead to an unfavourable course. Results of his study showed that obsessive-compulsive patients regard relatively harmless situations as dangerous.

Premorbid personality and rearing

According to the psychoanalytical theory, compulsive patients are believed to have a compulsive premorbid personality, that is before the onset of the disorder. Black (1974) found that this was indeed the case in 71% of the patients with compulsive disorder. Kringlen (1965) compared the premorbid personality of obsessive-compulsive patients with that of a control group of patients without obsessive-compulsive disorder; 72% of the compulsive patients and 53% of the control group appeared to have a compulsive personality premorbidly. McKean, Roa and Mann (1984) found comparable figures. From this study it emerged at the same time that patients with a compulsive personality had experienced fewer life events before onset of the obsessive-compulsive disorder than had patients without such a personality. This suggests that persons with a compulsive personality tend to develop compulsive symptoms without having a history of stressful life events. The results of the studies by Kringlen (1965) and Rachman and Hodgson (1980) suggested that a premorbid compulsive personality is related not only to the development of obsessive-compulsive disorder, but also to that of other disorders. In summary, there is a clear connection between premorbid obsessional traits and the development of compulsion. The information from the studies in non-obsessive patients conducted by Kringlen (1965) and Hodgson and Rachman (1980) shows, however, that the significance of this relation should be considered as limited. In view of the fact that in a number of patients an obsessive-compulsive disorder is developed independent of a compulsive personality, demonstrates that there is no question of a one-to-one relation. Rachman (1976) postulated that differences in obsessive behaviour arise from differences in rearing practices. According to his theory, checking compulsions develop in families where parents make high demands and are very critical. Patients with checking compulsions try to avoid making mistakes, for fear of criticism and feelings of guilt. On the other hand, Rachman maintains that cleaning compulsions arise in families where parents are overprotective. Hoekstra, Visser and Emmelkamp (1989) tested

Rachman's theory in a large number of obsessive-compulsive patients (n = 122). Following Rachman's theory the supposition was made that patients with checking compulsions would experience their parents as more rejecting than patients with cleaning compulsions, while the latter in turn would find their parents to be more overprotective than the patients with checking compulsions. Moreover, in comparison with normal controls, all patients were expected to rate their parents as more rejecting and showing less affection. Between "cleaners" and "checkers" significant differences were found on the factors "overprotection by the father" and "rejection by the mother". These data only partly support Rachman's theory. Patients with cleaning compulsions regarded their fathers as more overprotective than did patients with checking compulsions. On the other hand, they assessed their mothers to be more rejecting than did the patients with controlling compulsions, which is in contradiction to Rachman's theory. For the time being, there is insufficient support for the hypothesis that a specific rearing style is related to a specific form of compulsive behaviour. The main conclusion of this study, namely that obsessive-compulsive patients judge their parents' rearing style in a more negative way than "normal" subjects, suggests that such negative rearing styles are related to the development of obsessive-compulsive behaviour. It should be noted, however, that the same rearing styles appeared to be connected with other forms of psychopathology such as phobias, drug addiction, development of type A behaviour and depression (Gerlsma, Emmelkamp & Arrindell, 1990). Such negative rearing practices may possibly render children vulnerable to psychopathology in general, and not to one or more specific forms of psychopathology. Other factors should be investigated, in addition to negative rearing styles, that eventually determine which specific form of psychopathology will develop.

3 Functional Analysis and Assessment

The extensive discussion of the diagnostic criteria in the first chapter could nourish the thought that these criteria are determining for the formulation of a treatment plan. But, especially when one departs from behavioural therapeutic principles, after making the diagnosis there is a further round of investigation. In fact, the treatment cannot start while a therapist is still unaware of the factors which cause and maintain the anxiety complaints and also of the consequences of these complaints. Disorders that may be subsumed under the same category are caused and maintained in various patients by quite diverse factors. Therefore it is important to gain insight into the interplay of factors that influence this specific anxiety disorder before commencing treatment. For this reason we begin by discussing the principles of making a functional analysis of problem behaviour. Furthermore, it is often desirable not only to make a functional analysis prior to treatment, but also to monitor the course and results of therapy, using self-report and behavioural measures, as well as (self-) observation.

FUNCTIONAL ANALYSIS

Many consider functional analyses to be the core of behavioural therapy. We can distinguish two levels of analysis, that is the analysis of the functional relationships *within* a specific anxiety disorder and the analysis of these relationships *between* anxiety disorders and other problem areas; Emmelkamp (1982) calls these respectively "micro-analysis" and "macro-analysis". Opinions differ widely on the subject of functional analysis and consequently also on the techniques involved. Although terminology and notation could differ, the actual intentions remain the same, that is the delineation of antecedents, consequences and characteristics of problem behaviours. In general, the information is gathered in an open interview.

Micro-analysis

When a patient has been admitted for treatment, the first thing to do is to analyse the complaints in more detail. In this book we discuss disorders in which fear (or tension or distress) is the characteristic (conditioned) emotional reaction (CR). In the initial interview with the patient, attention is likely to be focused on the onset, the course and the present state of the complaints. Junior therapists in particular do not seem to realize this tripartition and hence go to-and-fro in the first interview.

The onset of the complaints

It is very important to obtain as clear a picture as possible of the onset of complaints. Is there a clear beginning, as may be the case in post-traumatic stress disorder? Or is there a gradual development of complaints as is the case with social anxiety and social phobia? Furthermore, it is important to recognize the circumstances at the time of the onset of the complaints, such as distressing events or the accumulation of a number of small stressors, the so-called daily hassles.

Course of the complaints

Have there been any periods in which the problems have worsened, diminished, or disappeared? Are there any other complaints which, in the course of time, have developed in addition to the anxiety disorders or as a consequence of them? These secondary complaints may pertain for example to depression, alcoholism or medication abuse, or marital problems.

Present state

Before formulating a treatment plan the therapist is most likely to want to depart from the complaints which are currently present.

1. Under which circumstances does the anxiety become manifest? The therapist wants to gain insight into the discriminative stimuli and into the question whether they are restricted to one theme, such as "speaking with strangers", or "being alone in a new situation". When several other themes can be discerned it may be desirable to summarize them in more than one functional analysis (such as one concerning "agoraphobia" and one concerning "social anxiety"). These stimuli can be very concrete (such as situations and objects) or imaginary (such as intrinsically anxiety-provoking thoughts, or thoughts of concrete situations or objects). Furthermore, the concrete stimuli may be bodily in nature, such as blushing and palpitations. Thus, there may be several combinations of internal or external and concrete or imaginary stimuli.
2. Are there any factors that facilitate or potentiate the impact of triggers or the maintenance of the anxiety disorder? One could think of unemployment, intellectual deficits, physical handicaps, failing an examination, and so on. Circumstances which diminish the complaints also deserve attention. One of our agoraphobic patients told us that after she had had a row with her spouse she felt less anxious about going into the street because then she thought "I don't care what happens, if I die, that's just the end of it!" Next, one may ask whether the anxiety is

equally strong under all circumstances. Are there certain days of the week or certain circumstances which make the same discriminative stimuli less or even more fear provoking?

3. What does the patient do when he becomes anxious? In this case the therapist is looking for the conditioned avoidance reaction; in agoraphobia this may be the avoidance of being alone in the street; a social phobic will avoid the presence of strangers; a patient with a compulsion will check whether something is really in order. Furthermore, the patient may use drugs or alcohol or take certain precautions to reduce or prevent anxiety. A social phobic patient, for example, avoided going to parties early in the evening when coffee or tea was being served. He was afraid of trembling while stirring his cup of tea; the noise would certainly attract attention. For this reason he would come later and before leaving home he drank a certain amount of beer to make him feel more relaxed. Other patients feel more relaxed when they take specific comforting objects along when going out, for instance a box of tranquillizers.

4. Which bodily sensations go with the experience of fear? An increase in fear arousal is often evident. This may manifest in ways such as trembling, sweating, blushing or hyperventilation. The extent to which this happens and a person's tolerance level differs strongly among people. For one patient a slight feeling of distress may be difficult to bear, whereas someone else in the course of time has become used to one great panic attack a day.

5. What are a patient's thoughts before and after a period of anxiety? A characteristic feature of anxiety is the general preoccupation with thoughts of imminent threat. In the clinical descriptions in Chapter 1 we discussed specific characteristic cognitions of various anxiety disorders. According to our experience it is often difficult to elicit cognitions from the patients. The question: "What do you think when you're in situation X and you are feeling anxious?" does not always yield the desired information. Alternative questions are, for example: "What went through your mind?", "What did you think could happen?", "How did you think it would end?", "What were you afraid of?" It also helps to have the patient close his eyes, imagine a situation, and think aloud. The latter technique in particular enhances the chance of obtaining a detailed picture of the anxiety-inducing situation.

6. What are the short-term consequences of the avoidance behaviour? We should discern between desired and aversive consequences, which in turn may increase or decrease. Most patients mention reduction of tension as a relatively immediate effect of their avoidance behaviours. This does not imply that there are no other emotional reactions following the avoidance of the feared stimulus. When the patient realizes that he has given in to avoidance, being overcome by fear once again, he may become rather

depressed. One of the negative consequences, amongst other things, is that the patient has not been able to reach his or her goal, such as shopping, paying a visit or having a hobby.

7. What are the long-term consequences of the avoidance behaviour? An example is the development of a continuously enhanced arousal in patients as a consequence of anticipation anxiety in which no confrontation with the feared situation takes place. What are the advantages and disadvantages of this behaviour? Some patients derive certain privileges from their "sick-role", such as extra attention and consideration from other people. Disadvantages in the long run could be becoming dependent on others, or the threat of being unfit to work. For a person with an elaborate checking compulsion the urge to check is a very time-consuming practice which determines his or her whole daily life. Agoraphobics and social phobics run the risk of becoming more and more isolated from their social environment.

It should be borne in mind that a phenomenon can play more than one role in a micro-analysis. Palpitations can be regarded as a physiological component of anxiety, but they can also be seen as an interoceptive stimulus that triggers anxiety. The next case illustrates the formulation of a micro-analysis.

One of our patients had developed agoraphobic complaints in the course of time. She was afraid of leaving the house on her own, of taking a bus or train or of going to the supermarket or other big shops. In these places she suffered from various somatic symptoms such as wobbly knees, pressure on the chest, feeling that she was not quite in control of herself. At such a moment she was very much preoccupied with the thought that she would become unwell, faint and that afterwards people would stare at her. She gradually began to avoid situations in which these bodily sensations and thoughts could emerge. This avoidance behaviour resulted in a decrease of tension and anxiety. Her husband had to go with her when she wanted to visit friends or relations. In the course of time, the patient was becoming more and more dependent on other people whenever she wanted to leave home.

In Figure 3.1 the micro-analysis of the complaints is depicted. The basic scheme of this patient's complaints is quite straightforward. Several discriminant stimuli lead to the conditioned emotional reactions and to avoidance behaviour, which in turn yields anxiety reduction.

Macro-analysis

Patients often present with more than one complaint. In most cases there are functional relationships with other more or less clearly defined problem areas. In a macro-analysis these relationships are delineated in order to establish where treatment should commence in the first place.

In the patient described above a number of other factors played a role in the onset and maintenance of her agoraphobia. Since her early adolescence she had felt

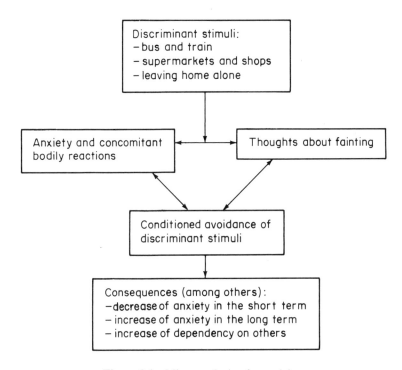

Figure 3.1 Micro-analysis of complaints

increasingly insecure in the company of people. She often felt that they were watching her, and she believed that others considered her a weird person. Mostly during the night, she was brooding over these disturbed relationships with others. As a consequence she became less interested in having sex with her husband. She dared not tell him straightaway, so she often feigned having a headache, and lay awake at night feeling very tense. She could not fall asleep, which caused her to have a bad temper the next morning. Her husband in turn hardly understood anything about her rejecting attitude and after some time reacted quite coolly to her. On the other hand, the patient needed him to get her out of the house because she dared not do so on her own.

It is clear that the agoraphobic complaints of this patient form part of a complex of mutually influencing factors. Relationships between the problem areas of the case are schematically presented in Figure 3.2. A successful treatment outcome remains doubtful when information is lacking on the interaction between the anxiety disorder and other antecedent or consequent factors. When formulating a treatment plan, it is therefore desirable to include other problem areas in the choice for a specific intervention. This issue will be addressed in more detail in the chapters on treatment. When the treatment plan is based

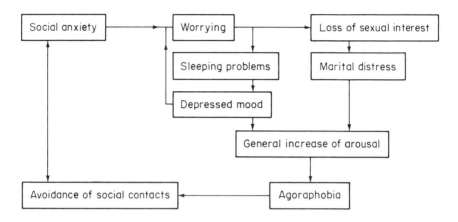

Figure 3.2   Macro-analysis of complaints

on a macro-analysis of the problem behaviour, the risk of symptom-substitution (once an often heard critic on behaviour therapy) will decrease. The formulation of a micro- and a macro-analysis, however, is not a unique occasion restricted only to the first interview. Moreover, later on in treatment, when the therapist has obtained more or new information, it is quite wise to make additional analyses or to improve the original one. When we regard a functional analysis as a hypothesis, it should be tested by means of the application of treatment interventions. When specific interventions do not produce the desired effect, then either the treatment strategy has been inappropriately chosen or carried out or the functional analysis is inadequate. In the latter case the time has come to reconsider, and to gather new information on the patient and his or her environment.

DIAGNOSTIC METHODS

The formulation of the functional analysis of problem behaviour often leads to gathering more specific information. In clinical practice it is therefore useful to have instruments that complement a clinical impression of the unstructured interview. In such cases it may be desirable to use standardized diagnostic instruments. In general, the use of standardized methods increases the reliability of the assessment procedure. In the next sections we briefly discuss the semi-structured interview, observations, self-report questionnaires and self-monitoring. Diagnostic methods may be used for various goals, such as:

- detecting problem areas which have been insufficiently dealt with in the admission interview—here the standardized assessment has a general screening function;

- the quantification of clinical impressions (e.g. the establishment of the *degree* of avoidance behaviour);
- the evaluation of treatment, by administering an instrument before and after the application of an intervention;
- tracing the course of treatment by frequent administration of process measures (e.g. the continuous registration of compulsive behaviour).

Interviews

The clinical interview is undoubtedly the method clinicians feel most acquainted with. The conversation between patient and therapist is the most frequently used form of data gathering. In clinical practice, the frequently used method is the unstructured open interview in which the clinician tries to get a clear picture of the complaints and the reason for the patient's seeking help. In the previous section on functional analysis, we pointed out the specific information that is of relevance to the behaviour therapist. Therefore the direction of the conversation is not randomly chosen, but is determined by the theoretical framework of the clinician. In a number of areas of application, one may feel the need for a more formalized diagnosis of anxiety disorders. This is the case when one wants to compose more homogeneous groups in order to conduct research into the effectiveness of treatment. The choice of standardized interviews primarily aimed at anxiety is not very large.

Anxiety Disorder Interview Schedule (ADIS)

The ADIS-R of DiNardo, Barlow, Cerny, Vermilyea, Vermilyea et al. (1985) is a semi-structured interview, primarily aimed at the diagnosis of anxiety disorders departing from DSM-III-R criteria. The interview begins with a short introduction and explication of its purpose. Next, the patient is questioned about the nuclear symptoms of the specific anxiety disorders. When these nuclear symptoms appear to be present, more detailed manifestations of the complaint are investigated in terms of specific DSM-III-R criteria. In addition, a short description of the current problems and their history is obtained. The ADIS-R, therefore, gives more information than is formally necessary to establish a DSM-III-R diagnosis. Apart from questions on anxiety disorders, other information is obtained on depressive phenomena, somatoform disorders (such as somatization disorder and hypochondriasis), and substance abuse. DiNardo et al. (1983) conducted research into the interjudgement-reliability of the precursor of the ADIS-R, the ADIS, yielding a satisfactory level of agreement.

Observation

Unstructured mutual observation forms an integral part of the interview with the patient. The therapist may include several aspects in the interview record:

the way in which the person presents himself, speaks, moves and dresses may reveal signs of his or her well-being or problems. Unfortunately, there are only a few standardized instruments for recording the various aspects of behaviour. In some interview schedules, such as the Present State Examination (PSE), the interviewer is required to fill in questions about the observed behaviour. Observation also takes place during the treatment session itself, in which the therapist takes notice of the patient's characteristics regarding formality and content of speech, bodily posture (a tense person sitting on the edge of his chair), mobility (as an expression of nervousness, wringing hands), eye-contact (its avoidance in social phobia), breathing pattern (irregularity in the event of hyperventilation), the urge to touch or not to touch objects (in obsessive-compulsive disorder). Some of our patients, for example, decline the offer of having tea or coffee. In one of them this was prompted by the fear of trembling. Another patient was afraid of having to use a strange toilet afterwards. In addition, the therapist may obtain a great deal of information outside the walls of the treatment location by means of structured or unstructured observation. One example is a house call on an obsessive-compulsive patient in order to gain insight into the way in which the patient has arranged his household. In agoraphobic patients a "diagnostic visit" may give valuable impressions of the real distances and the specific characteristics of the environment.

Self-report questionnaires

In the past decades many self-report questionnaires have been published pertaining to global as well as specific aspects of anxiety. Their standardized form and their ease of administration have made them extremely popular. In the next sections, we present a brief overview of some of the most popular instruments used within the realm of anxiety. It should be emphasized, however, that none of the scales mentioned have been developed for the assessment of a specific DSM-III-R category. Most self-report questionnaires are basically an indication of the *severity* of the complaints; they do not serve to make a discrete diagnosis. In some events the authors of the test, however, use an arbitrary cut-off score to facilitate a distinction between pathological and non-patient groups. Being arbitrary, such a distinction, however, does not have the status of a discrete diagnosis. An extensive overview of instruments used in the Anglo-Saxon language area is provided in the *Dictionary of Behavioural Assessment Techniques* edited by Hersen and Bellack (1988). A few examples of self-report questionnaires are given below.

Anxiety scale

This self-report scale has been developed to measure specific situational patterns of the behaviour of agoraphobic patients. The original version by Gelder and

Marks (1966) and a later improvement by Watson and Marks (1971), consisted of idiosyncratic items which could vary over patients. Emmelkamp, Kuipers and Eggeraat (1978) formulated five items relevant for the majority of agoraphobics. These five situations are:

- a crowded street (alone);
- drinking coffee in a crowded café or a restaurant;
- walking from the hospital to the town centre (alone);
- shopping in a supermarket or department store (alone);
- travelling by bus (alone).

Symptom Check List (SCL-90)

The SCL-90 of Derogatis (1977) is a multi-dimensional checklist, consisting of 90 items. In answering the items the patient himself judges on a five-point scale the extent to which he, during the past week including the current day, has been bothered by a specific complaint, such as anxiety, agoraphobia, or obsessive thoughts.

Fear Survey Schedule (FSS)

Basing their work on earlier scales, Wolpe and Lang (1964) designed an elaborate scale for the measurement of various phobic complaints. The phobic themes pertain to, among other things, animals, social situations, harm, illness, noise and other phobias.

Fear Questionnaire (FQ)

The Fear Questionnaire was published in 1979 by Marks and Mathews as a short questionnaire to measure the extent of avoidance. The Fear Questionnaire consists of three parts: the first is concerned with the respondent's most important phobia; the second, the Fear Questionnaire proper, consists of 15 questions (divided into three subscales, i.e. Agoraphobia, Social Phobia, and Blood and Injury Phobia); the third contains five questions assessing the degree of anxiety and depression.

Maudsley Obsessive Compulsive Inventory (MOCI)

This scale was developed by Hodgson and Rachman (1977) to delineate various forms of obsessive-compulsive behaviour (rituals in particular). Thirty questions yield five subscales: checking, cleaning, slowness, doubting and general obsessive-compulsive behaviours (i.e. a total score).

Behavioural measures

This method implies that the patient is asked to perform a series of actions in a way structured by the therapist. In this sense behavioural measures are distinct from verbal or written reports of the patient and from observation by the therapist.

In vivo *measures*

An example is the "behavioural walk", frequently applied in the assessment of agoraphobic avoidance. The procedure consists of a previously determined route that should be walked by the patient (Emmelkamp, Kuipers & Eggeraat, 1978). The standardized instruction is as follows: "You're asked to walk a route, and to return to our clinic immediately once you feel tense." The patient is provided with a map on which the route is drawn. The route is divided into a number of segments (e.g. 20). The therapist records both the time spent on this test as well as the distance the patient has covered. High correlations (in the 0.90s) have been found between this measure and the scales for avoidance and anxiety. Although this behavioural measure is rather time-consuming and, in the opinion of some critics, adds little to the assessment of agoraphobia, it is particularly interesting because of the extra information it provides. The therapist obtains an actual impression of the way the patient handles a task situation. When debriefing this task the therapist has the opportunity to ask specific questions on task performance, or to administer a specific questionnaire.

Hyperventilation provocation

The elicitation of bodily symptoms can be considered a behavioural measure. In discussing the treatment of panic and agoraphobia in Chapter 6, a detailed picture is given of the way this provocation is introduced to the patient.

Self-monitoring

Both in the assessment phase and during treatment, a patient's self-registration can be of great value for gaining insight into the (course of) anxiety complaints. During the admission interview the information is gathered retrospectively, and therefore is subject to distortion of memory, selective perception, social desirability, and so on. As a consequence, the therapist may have gathered superfluous or insufficient information. In itself, self-registration or self-monitoring seems to be rather a simple procedure, but this is only partly true. It is important to select the proper behaviours, emotions or cognitions for registration. "Proper" means that information is of direct importance for treatment. It should be noted, however, that self-monitoring has a psychometrically unclear status;

measures often possess no more than face validity. This means that one should be cautious in one's interpretations and generalizations. Self-monitoring can be performed if a certain problem behaviour should occur, but also can serve as a form of continuous registration. In the former event, the clinician has the frequency and the intensity of the complaints monitored (e.g. of obsessions, compulsions, avoidance behaviours, panic attacks). This method is particularly useful in behaviours and phenomena with a relatively low frequency. Second, the patient can be asked to monitor a certain high-frequency phenomenon at fixed times (behavioural sampling), for example, to investigate the course of anxiety over 24-hour periods. The nature and frequency of complaints and the aim of monitoring determine the choice for specific or global measures. A clinician may consider the following options:

1. *Discrete measures*, such as a tally of the number of times an action has been performed.
2. *Scales* frequently occurring in questionnaires can be adapted to the individual problems. In our own clinic, for example, we use blank versions of the anxiety scale (see above), in which the patient records fear-provoking situations prior to treatment. This idiosyncratic scale is completed after treatment as well, allowing an estimate of the amount of change over treatment.
3. A *Visual Analogue Scale* (VAS) is a scale in which the intensity or severity of a phenomenon can be indicated. For example, the degree of anxiety can be indicated by putting a dot on the line from 0 to 100. This type of scale can be used for various applications.
4. *"Thought listing"* is a widely used method before and during a cognitive therapy. The patient receives the instruction: "Write down what you're thinking in situation X." During the therapy this method can be used to record alternative (i.e. rational) thoughts in addition to spontaneous (often irrational or catastrophic) thoughts. Apart from being collected in writing, these thoughts can also be gathered with the use of other media. Williams and Rappoport (1983) had agoraphobic car drivers speaking into the microphone of a tape recorder while driving their car.

Applications

Very often it will so happen that a therapist is not particularly interested in just one (aspect of) behaviour; he or she will then prefer a combination of behaviours and even various parameters. The next example serves as an illustration.

At the admission interview Mr. Baldwin indicates that he is often bothered by panic attacks during which he is completely at a loss. When the therapist inquires about the nature and intensity of the symptoms (according to DSM-III-R; see Chapter 1), the patient is able only to indicate that he has them at all times. He cannot remember time and place. Even recent panic attacks are hard to describe in

Date: . . . . . . /. . . .   Did special things happen today ?
                            If yes, please describe them briefly

---

How anxious/tense did you feel today in general ?

   0. . . .10. . . .20. . . .30. . . .40. . . .50. . . .60. . . .70. . . .80. . . .90. . . .100
   not at all   extremely

How many **panic attacks** did you have today ?   None / . . . .

Which symptoms: I situation   II situation

   1 Shortness of breath   1
   2 Palpitations   2
   3 Choking sensations   3
   4 Chest pain or discomfort   4
   5 Sweating   5
   6 Dizziness   6
   7 Feeling unreal   7
   8 Nausea   8
   9 Hot flushes or chills   9
  10 Trembling or shaking   10
  11 Numbness / tingling   11
  12 Fear of dying   12
  13 Fear of going crazy or   13
      losing control

Severity of each attack (0 – 100)

Which **thoughts** went through your mind during the attacks ?

Attack I: . . . .
. . . .
Attack II: . . . .
. . . .

Figure 3.3   Example of a panic diary page

detail, because the anxiety during and after the attack seems to have affected his memory. In order to provide more clarity, the therapist instructs the patient to monitor every attack for the next 2 weeks, paying attention to the individual symptoms, the degree of anxiety, his thoughts at the moment of the attack, as well as its time and place. Figure 3.3 is an illustration of the page of the diary this patient was completing. This diary leaves enough space for the patient for symptom rating, to describe discrete events, for a visual analogue scale, and for thought listing. After the monitoring period, both the patient and the therapist are provided with a more detailed picture of the frequency, the intensity and the content of the panic attacks. Next, this information is used in the formulation of a specific treatment plan.

Finally, it should be remarked that this form of monitoring may be used not only by the patient but also by the therapist. In such an event the therapist records his own estimation of certain behaviours, thoughts or emotions of the patient.

CONCLUSIONS

Particularly in goal-oriented treatments, such as behaviour therapy, it is of the utmost importance to obtain as clear a picture as possible of the patient's problems. This holds both for the initial diagnostic phase and for the assessment of the course of treatment. It may be superfluous to remark that assessment methods will only produce the desired information if a clinician has been adequately trained in their use. A more elaborate description of designs and methods in individual applications can be found in, for example, Barlow and Hersen (1984).

4 General Treatment Principles

DESCRIPTION OF SOME STRATEGIES IN BEHAVIOUR THERAPY

This chapter aims at presenting recent insights into the treatment of anxiety disorders. Various forms of psychotherapy have been employed in the treatment of phobic patients, but only the efficacy of behavioural interventions (notably exposure *in vivo*) has been established convincingly. For this reason the emphasis in this chapter is placed on cognitive and behavioural methods to reduce anxiety. Psychoanalysts have regularly reported on the treatment of phobics (for a review, see Emmelkamp, 1979). These reports consist of theoretical essays, illustrating the descriptions of the analysis of one or more patients. However, the effectiveness of the treatment is rarely examined. Only a few studies show that the effectiveness of psychotherapy was investigated in a methodologically responsible way. On the whole, these studies showed that insight-oriented psychotherapy produced less effect than behaviour therapy. Interesting is the fact that Freud himself (1947) also questioned the use of exclusively psychoanalytical treatment of phobics. As he wrote down:

> Man wird kaum einer Phobie Herr, wenn man abwartet, bis sich der Kranke durch die Analyse bewegen läßt, sie aufzugeben. Er bringt dann niemals jenes Material in die Analyse, das zur überzeugenden Lösung der Phobie unentbehrlich ist. Man muß anders vorgehen (...), hat nur dann Erfolg, wenn man sie durch den Einfluß aer Analyse bewegen kann, sich wieder wie Phobiker des ersten Grades zu benehmen, also auf die Straße zu gehen und während dieses Versuches mit der Angst zu kämpfen.

This means that Freud actually asked his phobic patients to enter difficult situations to overcome their fear. This strongly resembles the behavioural method of exposure *in vivo* in which assignments are given in a more systematic way. Behaviour therapy is, among other things, to be distinguished from other psychotherapies by its emphasis on systematic evaluation of the effectiveness of treatment. Since Wolpe introduced desensitization as a treatment for phobias, research has been conducted at different locations into the efficacy of various behavioural methods for phobias. Before discussing the treatment of various anxiety disorders in greater detail in the following chapters, this chapter will provide a brief overview of the theoretical backgrounds of the procedures applied, after which attention will be given to some general issues that are important in the implementation of treatments.

Systematic desensitization

Until recently, systematic desensitization (Wolpe, 1958) has been the best known behavioural therapeutic procedure. In systematic desensitization the patient is first taught how to relax. Subsequently, a hierarchy of anxiety-provoking situations is constructed and successively offered to the patient, who is trying to stay relaxed. The patient will move on to the next item only if the previous item can be handled without any fear at all. Thus it is the patient himself who actually determines the pace at which treatment is conducted. Although systematic desensitization can be performed both imaginarily or *in vivo*, the former procedure is the one which has been applied most frequently. In this strategy, the patient is instructed to imagine the situations of the hierarchy; actual confrontation with fear-provoking stimuli does not occur. Even though the effects of systematic desensitization can be explained in terms of reciprocal inhibition and conditioning, little evidence has been found in research (Emmelkamp, 1982) to support this thesis. In a large number of studies it was pointed out that relaxation need not necessarily form a part of systematic desensitization. From Wolpe's point of view the fear should subside before the avoidance behaviour can change. Research into *in vivo* procedures has, however, indicated that fear reduction is not a requisite for a change in avoidance behaviour. In the 1970s the idea caught on that the effects of systematic desensitization could be better explained in cognitive terms (Emmelkamp, 1975). An important role was the notion of expectancy. Research indicated that systematic desensitization produced more effect when patients had been informed about treatment procedures. Systematic desensitization appeared to be more effective when patients were told that they were being treated for their phobic complaints, rather than when they thought they were participating in some physiological experiment. Despite the fact that this interpretation was sharply criticized initially (Wilson & Davidson, 1975), it has now gradually become endorsed. Also Wolpe's statement (1963) that "there is almost invariably a one-to-one relationship between what the patient can imagine without anxiety and what he can experience in reality without anxiety" has not been supported by research. Goldfried (1971) developed a variant of systematic desensitization, in which the emphasis is put not on "deconditioning" of fear, as in the procedure of classical systematic desensitization, but on acquiring active coping skills. In this variant, systematic desensitization is not considered as a process to which a patient should be submitted passively; instead, the patient is given a much more active role, active application of relaxation techniques in order to control fear in actual phobic situations being emphasized. There are some indications that this procedure is more effective than classical systematic desensitization and that the results generalize to untreated phobias (Emmelkamp, 1982). It should be noted that no research was conducted in patient groups; subjects were mostly students with less serious problems.

Flooding

Flooding is based on the work of Stampfl and Levis (1967), who developed the "implosion therapy". In this procedure patients are told to imagine the most terrifying scenes continuously over a long period of time. In doing so the therapist wants patients to become as anxious as possible. During a single session the implosion is to be continued until the fear has substantially subsided. Stampfl and Levis started from the principle of extinction: they assumed that classically conditioned fear would extinguish when stimuli were presented continuously. During this implosion they also offered psychodynamic cues, assuming that they were interrelated with the phobic complaints. Themes under discussion were, for instance, aggression, guilt, punishment, rejection, and loss of control. Prochaska (1971) showed, however, that it is superfluous to offer these psychodynamic themes in implosion therapy. Behaviour therapists have conducted much research into the effects of the implosion technique, while excluding psychodynamic themes from therapy. This variant is usually called imaginary flooding. The most important variable in flooding has been found to be the duration of the exposure. A presentation which is too short may trigger an increase instead of a reduction of fear. Comparable studies in the 1970s pointed out that imaginary flooding is less effective than flooding *in vivo*. In the latter procedure the patient is confronted with the most difficult situations right from the start until the fear has subsided. Therapists initially had the impression that during flooding the fear should be as intensified as possible, but very soon it became clear that this was not necessary and often even disadvantageous (Hafner & Marks, 1976).

Gradual exposure *in vivo.*

In the early 1970s Leitenberg and his colleagues (Leitenberg & Callahan, 1973) developed a treatment programme for phobic patients, based on the principles of operant conditioning. Patients were given instructions to try gradually to stay longer in the phobic situations; as soon as they became anxious they were allowed to leave the phobic situation. Every time they managed to stay longer in the situation the therapist reinforced them by paying them compliments. If no progress was made, the therapist reacted in a more neutral way. In a series of single case studies this method proved to be effective. Although Leitenberg and his colleagues believed that improvement should be attributed to the reinforcement given by the therapist, results of another study showed that this reinforcement was in fact redundant (Emmelkamp, 1974; Emmelkamp & Ultee, 1974). In a series of investigations it appeared that gradual exposure *in vivo* brought about effective changes in fear and avoidance behaviour without explicit reinforcement by the therapist. The different kinds of this type of exposure will be discussed extensively in the following chapters.

The process of exposure in vivo

One of the most important challenges for researchers in the field of phobias is offering a theoretical explanation for psychological mechanisms which allow exposure treatments to produce their therapeutic effect. Although it may be apparent that most behavioural therapeutic procedures contain exposure to phobic stimuli, it does not explain why they lead to a decrease in anxiety and avoidance behaviour. Exposure is merely a description of what is going on during treatment and not an explanation of the process. Exposure is usually considered to be a passive process; tension (subjective as well as psychophysiological) generally decreases gradually during continuous exposure in a single session (Emmelkamp, 1982). This process of fear reduction as a function of continuous exposure can be explained in terms of "extinction" or "habituation". Cognitive-oriented theorists (for instance Bandura, 1977), on the other hand, do not regard exposure as a passive process, but assign an important role to cognitive processes occurring during exposure. Unfortunately, practically no research has been conducted in this area. In a study by Emmelkamp and Felten (1985) an attempt was made to investigate the influence of self-statements on subjective fear, behaviour and physiological reaction during treatment with exposure *in vivo*. This research was conducted on persons suffering from serious fear of heights. In order to monitor the influence of cognitive processes, half the group of subjects were instructed to substitute positive thoughts for negative thoughts, whereas the other half received exposure *in vivo* alone. The treatments

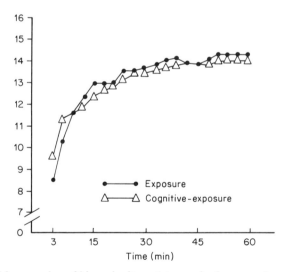

Figure 4.1 Mean number of hierarchy items (stages of a fire escape) performed during the exposure session. Ground level is 0, highest floor is 16. (Reprinted with permission from *Behaviour Research and Therapy*, **23**, Emmelkamp & Felten, The process of exposure in vivo, copyright 1985, Pergamon Press Ltd.)

consisted of climbing a fire-escape. Every 3 minutes the subjects had to indicate their feelings of fear on an eight-point scale, and their pulse rate was registered during the whole session. Figure 4.1 shows that during exposure the subjects in both conditions were able to climb the steps of the fire-escape higher and higher. The addition of positive thoughts did not affect their achievements. Despite the fact that the subjects were climbing higher all the time, pulse rate and subjective fear decreased only gradually. After 60 minutes heart-rate appeared to be reduced to baseline level. The addition of self-statements did not affect the heart-rate, but did affect the subjective experience of fear at the end of the session (see Figure 4.2). Changes in subjective fear during treatment did not precede the changes in heart-rate, which contradicts a cognitive explanation of habituation processes. This information offers some support to the notion that fear reduction by means of exposure *in vivo* is a process to which a person is subjected passively, generating more or less synchronous changes in subjective fear and psychophysiological arousal.

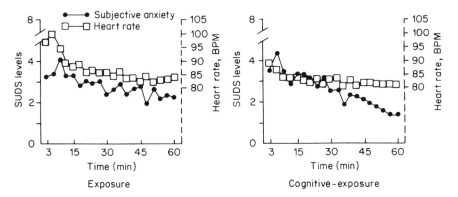

Figure 4.2   Mean heart rate and mean subjective anxiety every 3rd minute during the exposure session. (Reprinted with permission from *Behaviour Research and Therapy*, **23**, Emmelkamp & Felten, The process of exposure in vivo, copyright 1985, Pergamon Press Ltd.)

Cognitive therapy and anxiety management

Cognitive procedures have been more frequently used in anxiety disorders. One of the earliest developed cognitive strategies is Ellis's Rational Emotive Therapy (RET). Ellis (1962) started from the so-called ABCDE-model, the letters standing for:

- *Activating event*: an objective description of the event;
- *Beliefs*: the irrational, tension-evoking thoughts;
- *Consequence*: the emotional consequences (feelings) of the thoughts;
- *Discussion*: questions which are raised to test the thoughts under B to reality;
- *Evaluation*: the more rational thoughts resulting from the challenge under D.

In this therapy the (irrational) thoughts which bring about the fear are traced, and these thoughts are subsequently challenged by the therapist. In doing so, special attention is devoted to the "musts", which means changing the idea of most patients that they "must" do all sorts of things. Ellis himself has a rather persuasive style, and as a therapist he likes to lecture. Homework assignments often consist of entering difficult situations (in fact exposure *in vivo*). A practical guide for executing rational emotive therapy is the book by Walen, DiGuiseppe and Wessler (1980). This treatment is discussed more elaborately in Chapters 6 and 7. Beck and Emery (1985) also start from the principle that emotions, fear being one of them, are generated by disorders in cognitive processes. They do, however, emphasize faulty perceptions, erroneous conclusions and disturbed processing of information. Beck and Emery regard cognitive therapy as an experiment: the patient is invited to find out whether his or her ideas fit in practice. This means that exposure *in vivo* is essential for most people having this kind of treatment. This strategy is illustrated in Chapter 6. In contrast with Ellis and Beck, who both try to modify underlying cognitive structures, the aim of self-instruction training (SIT, Meichenbaum, 1975) is only to teach patients to attach other labels to phobic situations. Meichenbaum believes that the fear experienced by patients in phobic situations is generated by negative self-statements. Self-instruction training aims at teaching patients to replace their negative, fear-provoking self-statements by positive, coping self-statements. Different stages are distinguished, the three most important being preparing for an anxious situation, confronting the anxious situation, and coping with anxious feelings. During therapy sessions patients are taught to change their thoughts in the situations by means of imaginary exercises. They are instructed to imagine the situations in which they usually become anxious, to monitor the attending negative self-statements and to try consequently to substitute positive self-statements for the negative ones, after which a reduction in fear can be expected. Even though cognitive therapy proved to be successful in research among volunteers (students) having less serious fears (a review is given by Emmelkamp, 1982), until now cognitive therapy has yielded less favourable results in phobic patients. We will return to this in the discussion of the treatment of the separate anxiety disorders. Anxiety management is a compilation of techniques used by patients in order to master their fear. Important components are relaxation and self-statements. In relaxation it is essential for patients not to remain passive but to acquire active skills enabling them to control their fear in anxiety-provoking situations. Patients learn to recognize physiological signs of tension and to relax as soon as tension is perceived. Relaxation training is often applied in the treatment of generalized anxiety disorder, and therefore the practical implementation will be discussed in Chapter 9. In addition, applied relaxation during exposure *in vivo* may help some patients to remain in the phobic situation. Changing self-statements may also serve as an important expedient for patients with generalized anxiety disorder. The techniques of self-instruction have been discussed above. Coping self-statements are expected to generate a decrease in the level of anxiety. "Rational" alternatives are preferable but not requisite. If rational self-statements fail to engender a reduction in fear while less rational self-statements do succeed, the latter are to be preferred. Anxiety management should be distinguished from rational emotive therapy, in which emphasis is placed on acquiring insight into irrational ideas supposedly lying at the root of the problem. Anxiety management is, in fact, more "eclectic", in the sense that those coping strategies are chosen which are believed to be effective for the individual patient. Gaining insight into the problems may be desirable for patients, but it is not necessary. When patients are able to control their fear in imagination by means of coping self-statements, they are instructed to enter *in vivo* situations in order to learn to control their fear using these self-statements. In employing anxiety management procedures it is essential that the patient does not make spasmodic attempts to prevent the fear. While teaching the patient to apply relaxation it is important not to raise unrealistic hopes about the effect of relaxation techniques in actual situations. Even if patients are able to relax completely at the therapist's office and at their own homes, it does not mean that they will be able to do so in fear-evoking situations. Having too high expectations may lead to failure and eventually to giving up treatment.

Other interventions

The treatments described so far are limited to directly tackling anxiety symptoms by means of fear reduction. In addition, or even instead, it might be sensible to use other interventions. Some examples will be discussed in this book. Social skills training is not only useful in the treatment of social anxiety, but is also frequently employed in other anxiety disorders (see Chapters 7 and 8). In the case of relationship problems, it often occurs that these problems have to be dealt with during treatment. Patients' partners may possibly affect the therapeutic process adversely, particularly with agoraphobia and obsessive-compulsive complaints. During therapy it sometimes appears that the partner is resisting change in the patient. However, it does occur less often than suggested (Arrindell, 1987; Emmelkamp, de Haan & Hoogduin, 1990). Sometimes the partner feels less needed and less important as the patient grows more and more independent. If problems arise resulting from this kind of situation, it may be wise to involve the partner in the treatment. In Chapter 8 an elaborate discussion is devoted to a treatment in which several interventions were needed before permanent improvement could be established.

CONDUCTING TREATMENT

Before treatment commences, the therapist draws up a functional analysis of the problem (see Chapter 3). After this initial phase for defining the problems, the treatment goals are set. These goals may be relatively simple or more complex. An example of a limited goal for an agoraphobic patient is the reduction of fear when travelling by bus, walking in the street or visiting public places. A more complex treatment goal is "becoming independent". Even when a limited goal has been set, it is necessary to describe the desired final result precisely, for instance "going out shopping in the neighbourhood on my own" or "going abroad on holiday alone". Usually a simple goal is chosen first and after this has been accomplished a new goal is often set. When agreement on the objectives has been reached, it can be ascertained how the treatment will be evaluated. This can be accomplished by using questionnaires and more specific measuring instruments (rating scales). With the use of these measurement scales of fear the patient is given the opportunity to judge difficult situations before, during and after treatment. During treatment, general fear level, panic attacks and obsessions can be registered daily. These measurements have been discussed in Chapter 3. Generally speaking, psychophysiological measurements are not useful for clinical practice. They cost considerable time and money and hardly make a contribution to decisions concerning treatment plan and evaluation of treatment. Exposure can be performed in two ways: imaginary exposure, patients being asked to imagine themselves in the difficult situations, and exposure *in vivo*, in which patients are actually exposed to the situation. In most cases exposure *in vivo* is more effective than imaginary exposure. Important variables in exposure treatments are the extent of fear and the duration of exposure sessions. The exposure can either be controlled by the patient, allowing him to determine when to move on to the next item, or it can be controlled by the therapist as with flooding or prolonged exposure *in vivo*. Sometimes certain components, such as relaxation strategies, are added to the exposure. However, up to now it has not been proven that relaxation is indispensable for a successful treatment. Modelling, with the therapist showing approaching behaviour in difficult situations, also appears to contribute little to the effect of exposure, although it may be useful in some cases (notably in simple phobias). The most successful exposure programmes are consequently those which are carried out *in vivo*, during a longer, uninterrupted period of time (prolonged) and in which escape and avoidance are prevented (Emmelkamp, 1982). It is often possible, sometimes even necessary, to administer the exposure treatment with the help of homework assignments. The important thing for patients is to understand the rationale perfectly, to receive specific assignments, to practise the assignments at fixed times (during a consecutive period of at least 2 hours) and to discuss their homework with their therapists (after one or two sessions of practising) and receive new assignments. If treatment is actually carried out by means of exposure assignments, it is most important that the exposure should take place gradually. In consultation with the patient, the therapist draws up a hierarchy of situations avoided by the patient. This hierarchy forms the starting point of treatment and it should therefore be designed carefully, bearing in mind "the more concrete, the better". First, the principle of the fear thermometer is explained. Patients are asked to judge certain situations in which they feel fearful or which they avoid on a scale rising from 0 (no fear) to 100 (panic). A number of homework assignments are written down on cards, each card containing a task concerning a difficult situation. Next, the cards are sorted out according to a progressive scale of fear-provoking situations. The assignments of the hierarchy can be determined by therapist and patient during the session, but drawing up this list can also be given as a first homework assignment. The practical implementation of these exposure programmes for simple phobias is described in Chapter 5, for agoraphobia in Chapter 6, for social phobia in Chapter 7 and for compulsive-obsessive disorder in Chapter 8. With a number of complaints (for instance obsessions, fear of thunder and post-traumatic stress-disorder) it is difficult or impossible to carry out exposure *in vivo*. For this purpose it may be useful to employ imaginary methods. These treatments are illustrated in Chapters 8 and 9.

Therapeutic relationship

Many psychotherapists hold the view that the therapeutic relationship in behaviour therapy and cognitive therapy should be less important than in other therapies such as experiential and psychodynamic therapies. This idea is incorrect. Although behaviour therapists have tended to devote little attention to the therapeutic relationship, it is our considered opinion that this relationship is vitally important. Without a warm relationship it would be impossible to gather the information that is essential for drawing up a treatment plan. The therapeutic relationship is also essential for the implementation of treatment. If a therapist does not gain the confidence of his patients, and is more or less considered as a stranger, his patients cannot be expected to speak frankly. In exposure, the therapist's attitude should be warm and resolute. If a certain treatment strategy is decided upon, the therapist should keep a strict hand upon this strategy. Even though it may be important for the patient to discuss other problems, this will be discouraged during exposure exercises. Should other problems demand immediate attention, then they will have to be discussed shortly before the end of the session. The therapist should certainly not only be interested in his patient's progress during the exposure programme, he must also pay ample attention to his or her feelings. From research it has emerged that ambitious therapists striving for achievement are regarded as inconsiderate, which may bring about therapeutic failure (Emmelkamp & Van den Hout, 1983). In the meantime it has appeared from various studies that the therapeutic relationship does indeed affect the outcome of behaviour therapy (Emmelkamp, 1986; Schaap & Hoogduin, 1988; Schindler, 1988).

During treatment a therapist devotes a considerable amount of time to non-technical aspects, such as increasing the patient's motivation, explaining the

therapeutic model and preparing for certain techniques and homework assignments. From a study by Schindler (1988), it followed that the first sessions
were crucially important for further development of therapy. The most essential
dimension appeared to be "support", which is a general term for diverse
therapeutic interventions such as giving positive feedback, confidence and
encouragement and positive relabelling. It is important for the therapist to
be perceived as an expert. This does not involve any unnecessary exposure
of one's achievements, such as an ostentatious display of diplomas in the
therapy room, but the therapist should prove his expertise by his attitude and
behaviour. Another important dimension is respect. The therapist should always
be punctually on time for his appointment with the patient. In the event that the
therapist should be prevented from coming, his patient must be notified well
before the time of the appointment. This respect should also appear from the
way a therapist is dressed. A therapist wearing shorts in the summertime does
not show respect for his patients. We do not advise our therapists to wear a
three-piece suit, but we are pointing out that it is necessary to present a well-
cared-for appearance. Within this scope it should also be considered whether
it is appropriate to be on familiar terms with patients. A 30-year-old therapist
calling a 50-year old woman by her first name, even though the intention is
to make her feel more comfortable, may easily be viewed as patronizing. It
goes without saying that respect is also shown by a thorough preparation of the
therapy sessions. The suggestions given above are aimed at cutting out adverse
effects on the treatment process resulting from aspects of the therapist which
are irrelevant to the therapy. It is futile to react in an unfriendly way to hostile,
unfriendly patients. Meeting a friendly and helpful person often strikes these
people as an eye-opener (Schaap & Hoogduin, 1988). In these cases it will
also be useful to make a functional analysis of the patient's (and therapist's)
behaviour. Questions which may be raised are: Why is this patient reacting in an
unfriendly way? Is the therapist's behaviour provoking certain reactions from the
patient? To what extent does the patient also assume a hostile attitude towards
persons resembling the therapist? A similar analysis may cause the therapist to
alter his attitude or even the plan of treatment. It is often wise for the therapist to
show some pliability when a patient constantly resists therapeutic instructions.
The therapist can, for instance, suggest that the patient is not yet prepared for
this assignment and can ask the patient to come forward with some suggestions
himself. Such a strategy will prevent the therapist from becoming too insistent.

Mr Johnson is a dominant, somewhat opinionated man, who is being treated for
obsessive behaviour. He persists in not carrying out his homework assignment
because he believes that he is "not getting rid of his obsessions in this way".
Moreover, he thinks it is perfectly normal to check the heating, lights and doors
a dozen times and he sees no reason why he should change this. The therapist
admits that he has doubts whether this is the right strategy for his complaints
and asks the patient to think about another solution for the next week. On return

the following week it appears that the patient has not thought about it yet. The therapist remains amiable and proposes to break off the session and make a new appointment after the patient has been able to think about a possible solution. He stresses that the task is rather difficult and proposes to wait a fortnight for the next appointment. Mr Johnson protests that a week's time will be sufficient and the appointment is set for the following week. In the next session Mr Johnson says that he has reflected on his problems for a long time and that he has come to the conclusion that he is always running away from his problems. He comes up with the idea that it would perhaps be best at present to carry out the former homework assignments.

Criticizing patients who have not completed their assignments will usually have no effect and may even be counterproductive. The therapist had better instead find out why the patient has not done his homework. In some cases it is even sensible for the therapist to lay the blame on himself for "not having fully explained the purpose of the assignment". Schaap and Hoogduin (1988) provide a number of useful guidelines.

Resistance

There are various reasons for a patient's resistance. Resistance may be engendered by the fact that the therapist has failed to give a clear and full explanation of the therapy. In that case the therapist had better take ample time to discuss the therapeutic model. It is also possible that patients have developed their own ideas about the cause of their complaints, or have specific expectations of a treatment. If a patient believes his complaints are hereditary "because my mother and my sister suffer from the same complaints", it is not surprising if he strikes us as less motivated because he does not expect any cure from therapy. When a patient presumes that his fears will in fact be dispelled in a couple of days by means of "a little pill", his commitment to a protracted therapy, implying going through all kinds of fearful situations, will be minimal. Some patients calling on their general practitioner with anxiety complaints are not (yet) ready for therapy. They may have managed to strike a reasonable balance in their lives, so that any kind of change, including therapy, may upset this balance. Practice teaches us to acknowledge that not all patients can be motivated for treatment. Another adverse factor may be that the patient also gains some advantage from his complaints. Although one should be careful not to make a rapid judgement of secondary gain, with some patients it does indeed play a role.

Tackling obstacles during treatment

In the course of treatment many patients gain self-confidence through overcoming their fears and perceiving progress. It is, however, inevitable that patients will experience "a relapse". They are afraid of relapsing into the old feeling of losing control of themselves and will interpret this as a sign of having to start all over again. A sensible strategy for the therapist is to redefine the relapse as a good opportunity to put into practice what patients have learned: "Such a relapse needs to be restrained". Discouraging ideas about relapse are often prompted by the assumption that a continuous improvement of one's functioning is to be expected. In most cases there are fluctuations in positive and negative directions, yielding gradual improvement on the whole. Also in these cases, positive labelling of temporary relapses will prove to be a profitable technique. Another obstacle which occurs regularly is when patients appear to function worse than before the therapy began, for example being more anxious or more depressed and sleeping more badly. Sometimes this may be explained by the fact that they are being exposed to situations which they have avoided for a long time, consequently triggering an increase in arousal and a keen awareness of the present dysfunctioning. Another complication occurs when treatment is broken off prematurely. In order to minimize drop-out, several precautions must be taken: a thorough assessment, a thorough explanation of the rationale of the treatment and a description of the content of the therapy (also mentioning the fear to be expected). Particularly with prolonged exposure, patients should be notified beforehand that their problems will only get worse if they give up treatment. It may sometimes be useful to draw up a written agreement clearly indicating what can be expected from both therapist and patient. Lastly, patients should be informed about the nature of their expected progress and the time it will take, allowing them to form realistic expectations. Not all treatments are, of course, equally successful. If the treatment should fail, the function analysis and various treatment variables must be studied critically. Starting from the assumption that the treatment procedure has been carried out correctly, two possibilities have to be considered: the technique employed is not suitable for that particular patient or the function analysis is not correct. The function analysis is in fact a hypothetical construction of the patient's problems and the treatment can be considered as an experiment testing this hypothesis. The problem may appear to be more complex than was initially believed. For instance: phobic behaviour appears to provide the patient with reinforcers which were overlooked at the outset of therapy (such as receiving attention, or not needing to accept the responsibility for a job) A new analysis of the problems may lead to another treatment programme.

Finally, some critical remarks have to be made about the use of psychotropic drugs. Research into the effectiveness of psychopharmacological therapy is described in Chapter 10. Many patients applying for treatment with anxiety complaints have been using psychotropic drugs for many years, notably benzodiazepines. If possible, it is always advisable to discontinue the use of medication during treatment, the main reason being that whatever has been learned in a drug-state is not likely to be generalized to a non-drug-state. As an illustration, it emerged from a recent study by Reich and Yates (1988) that patients who had been treated with a combination of exposure *in vivo* and alprazolam fell into relapse as soon as medication was terminated. Relapses after discontinuation of tricyclic anti-depressant drugs and monoamine-oxidase inhibitors were also frequently reported. In treating anxious patients who also have depressive symptoms it might seem expedient to combine the exposure treatment with tricyclic anti-depressant drugs. If this treatment proves to be successful, the medication will have to be tapered gradually; particularly in this phase the patient should still be given behaviour therapy and a number of booster exposure sessions in order to prevent relapse. With benzodiazepines it is advisable to taper medication gradually before starting an exposure programme. This certainly applies to patients using drugs with relatively short metabolic turnover. It should be realized that patients may subsequently suffer from severely disturbing sensations as a result of this abstinence and may also experience a rebound of fear and panic. This means that patients' fear may become (temporarily) greater than before prescription of the medication. Patients need to be well informed about this possibility. For this reason we advise against tapering medication during an exposure programme. Patients will be likely to attribute phenomena due to abstinence and rebound to exposure and for this reason they might stop treatment prematurely. Naturally, the termination of medication will have to take place in consultation with the doctor who has prescribed the drug.

5 The Treatment of Simple Phobias

EMPIRICAL RESULTS

Controlled research into differential treatment effects with simple phobias requires adequate numbers of patients with similar complaints. Although simple phobias are very common in the "normal" population, requests for professional help are relatively rare. The main reason could be that the phobia does not, or barely does, interfere in one's daily life. Simple phobias as secondary complaint can be found in a number of patients. In such cases the treatment is first of all geared to the principal complaint (e.g. social phobia or panic disorder), while the simple phobia can be dealt with afterwards, if desired. Groups of volunteers, especially students with minor phobic complaints, have actually been examined in several studies. Research, however, proved that in some respects this population is different from phobic patients, particularly regarding the severity of complaints, concomitant psychopathology (Emmelkamp, 1986) and cognitions (Last & Blanchard, 1982). It is very doubtful whether the available outcome can be generalized towards truly phobic patients. The first behavioural treatments of simple phobias widely applied imaginary procedures, such as systematic desensitization and flooding. Systematic desensitization turned out to be more effective than other therapeutic procedures such as insight-oriented group or individual psychotherapy (Gelder, Marks & Wolff, 1967; Gelder & Marks, 1968). As for simple phobias, systematic desensitization and imaginary flooding appeared to equal each other in effectiveness (Marks, Boulougouris & Marset, 1971; Gelder, Bancroft, Gath, Johnston et al., 1973). *In vivo* treatments were first introduced in the early 1970s. With regard to simple phobias, the results were unambiguous: in all studies exposure *in vivo* proved to be more effective than imaginary procedures (Barlow, Leitenberg, Agras & Wincze, 1969; Crowe, Marks, Agras & Leitenberg, 1972; Dyckman & Cowan, 1978; McReynolds & Grizzard, 1971). Mathews observed in 1978 that the available evidence suggests that direct exposure is always superior with simple phobics. In this respect no fundamental changes have occurred since. Bourque and Ladouceur (1980) and Williams, Dooseman and Kleifield (1984) studied whether exposure *in vivo* was more effective when the therapist demonstrated the desired behavioural attitude (modelling) or when he or she assisted in other ways during the session (e.g. preventing the patient from escaping). The results of these studies were contradictory. Bourque and Ladouceur did not find any difference between the two approaches, whereas the study by Williams, Dooseman and Kleifield showed that additional support on the part of the therapist seemed to heighten the effect of the treatment. This latter study was partly set up on the basis of the self-efficacy model as formulated by Bandura (1977). The principles of this model are that the patient's phobic complaints will disappear when a specific self-perception is induced and strengthened. That is to say: the idea that he or she will be capable of handling phobic situations effectively. Certainly, it is not so much the exposure as such that is emphasized during treatment, but the quality and the amount of efficacy-enhancing information, supplied in confrontation with the phobic stimulus. Several studies made it clear that changes in phobic behaviour are connected with changes in self-efficacy (Bandura, Adams & Beyer, 1977; Biran & Wilson, 1981; Williams & Watson-Newhouse, 1985), which certainly means a marked support to the model as such. The effects of cognitive strategies for simple phobias were evaluated in five studies. Without discussing these studies in detail the conclusion may be that, in general, cognitive therapies make hardly any contribution to the effectiveness of exposure *in vivo* treatments (Biran & Wilson, 1981; Girodo & Roehl, 1978; Ladouceur, 1983; Emmelkamp & Felten, 1985). One study, however, reported positive results from the addition of cognitive procedures to exposure. This was a study by Marshall (1985) who, with a group of 20 patients with fear of heights, compared exposure *in vivo* with a treatment combining exposure *in vivo* and the acquiring of cognitive coping strategies. Öst, Johansson and Jerremalm (1982) studied the interaction between treatment factors and individual characteristics of patients. Claustrophobics were divided into two groups according to different response patterns: behavioural and physiological reactors. In each group half of the patients received either a more physiologically or a more behaviouristic oriented therapeutic method (relaxation versus exposure *in vivo*). Results showed that for behavioural reactors exposure *in vivo* was superior to relaxation, whereas for physiological reactors the reverse was found. The outcome of this study suggests that—when drawing up treatment strategies for simple phobic patients—it may be important to consider individual response patterns.

Summary

Exposure *in vivo* proved to be an effective method for treating various types of simple phobia. There is little or no evidence that cognitive strategies are of any use for this population. When he or she shows a strong physiological reaction, it may be wise to teach the patient how to relax and apply this during exposure *in vivo*.

CONDUCTING TREATMENT

Practical use of exposure *in vivo* with simple phobias requires observance of a few rules. First, prolonged exposure gives better results than brief exposure

(Marshall, 1988); second, frequently practised exposure (e.g. daily) is superior to exposure with long intervals in between (one or two weeks); third, self-controlled exposure is just as effective as therapist-guided exposure. Although no convincing argument in favour of modelling by the therapist himself could be produced, it is quite possible to use this technique during exposure *in vivo* sessions. The treatment can be roughly described as follows. As is the case with other behavioural therapies, treatments should be preceded by detailed functional analyses. They should include information about the problem behaviour as such: what are the characteristic features; which situations and stimuli elicit the fear. Other questions of major importance are: what are negative (and positive) consequences in daily life, which cognitions play a role, what are the maintaining factors (for example avoidance behaviour) and how and when did the fears start. Another crucial question is: do other problems also play a part and how are they related to the simple phobia? During the formulation of the functional analysis the aim of the treatment is established in consultation with the patient. For example: a person with a dog phobia can set himself the target of walking in the streets without allowing himself any deviation for strange dogs and also of being able to stroke his friend's (slightly familiar) dog. He does not need, however, to acquire the ability to spontaneously pet all sorts of unfamiliar dogs in the street. As the treatment is usually short and intensive, a good deal of "overlearning" will be useful in preventing relapse. In view of this it is highly desirable for patients to learn to handle situations that largely exceed reality in level of difficulty. Strictly speaking these situations should surpass all that is necessary to achieve the aim of treatment. In our experience it is not always sensible to tell patients before treatment exactly "what is in store for them". Things can be made unnecessarily difficult when patients get information prior to treatment; if it comes to that there is a real danger that patients will drop-out. As a matter of fact, nothing will happen against the patient's will during exposure *in vivo* sessions. At the beginning of the treatment the therapist explains how phobias are kept alive; he emphasizes the role of the patient's avoidance behaviour and cognitions that exist about the phobic stimuli. The therapist then explains the principles of exposure *in vivo*. He makes it clear that the treatment will take place in a limited number of prolonged sessions, maybe even in one session. The patient is instructed to keep practising in daily life after the therapy has ended, to steady the changes. He will be asked to stick to the troublesome situation during the session until the anxiety settles down and not to run away under any circumstances. Moreover, it is stressed that the treatment is a joint venture of patient and therapist. The therapist has committed himself never to do anything without explanation, to demonstrate procedures when the occasion arises and never to forget to ask the patient's consent before taking more difficult steps. The next step is confrontation with the feared stimulus. Now, the patient is repeatedly encouraged to approach it as close as possible and to stick to that point until the anxiety has eased. This is followed by renewed efforts to approach the object even closer. The session will not be finished before the anxiety level has come down substantially. This also means that the patient should not be confronted with new, more demanding tasks just before the end of the session. If possible and if necessary, the therapist can show the patient how to handle the feared object, for example having spiders crawl along one's arms, and fondling dogs or cats. It is difficult to estimate in advance how long a session will take: two or three hours will normally suffice. The instructions at the end of the therapy are of great importance. They tell the patient to stop avoiding in daily life and to try to consider each confrontation with the feared stimulus as an opportunity to put the acquired knowledge into practice. Besides, patients have to do individual assignments at home which they are expected to carry out as soon as possible. These may include taking spiders home for practice, using lifts, listening to audio tapes of thunderstorms or walking along galleries of flats. Illustrative of such treatments is the example below.

Kim, a 35-year-old secretary, and her husband live in a "dog-ridden" residential area on the outskirts of their town. Some years ago Kim began to develop a phobia about dogs, a reason for staying indoors most of the time. She has figured out a roundabout route to go to work on her bike. By doing so she hopes to minimize the chance of coming across dogs. She dare not call upon people with dogs. She has never liked dogs and her parents "didn't think much of dogs" either. She has never had traumatic experiences with dogs or any other problems. On our listing the fear-provoking stimuli it becomes clear that young, lively dogs that jump up against people on every occasion, make quite unexpected movements and bark, are the most fear-provoking. She is less anxious if the dog is accompanied by its master. She is not in the first place afraid of being bitten and the size of the dog seems unimportant as well. Kim is treated with exposure *in vivo* in three sessions of one and a half to two hours, spread over 10 days. The first session takes place in a room with a big dog and its master. In spite of her intense anxiety, on the therapist's insistence, she can bring herself to sit down beside the dog after a while. When after an hour and a half the fear (at a scale of 0 to 10) has sunk from 10 to 4, it is decided to end the session. During the second session the same dog is used for training, this time without its master and on unknown territory. It does not take her long to summon up enough courage to stroke the dog, to sit down on the floor next to it and to take it out, first together with the therapist and later on her own. In two hours time the fear has fallen from 7 to 2. The third session is spent in playing and walking with young, brisk and barking dogs. She even manages to take two middle-sized dogs into her lap; it barely arouses feelings of anxiety. At the end of the session Kim receives instructions for homework spread over the next few weeks. They run as follows: "meet people with dogs as often as possible, and play with your neighbour's young bouvier a couple of times a week". She is also told to take the shortest route to her office. Some weeks later, at follow-up, Kim appears to have successfully (and joyfully) carried out these tasks. The anxiety has disappeared almost completely.

Öst (1989) evaluated the effects of a similar treatment among 20 patients. In his study the therapy was limited to one exposure session. In most cases the treatment proved to be very successful. The patients involved needed exposure sessions of well over 2 hours on average. Broadly speaking, patients with animal phobias appeared to take more time than people with an injection phobia. Öst observed that in principle the described treatment is suitable for all simple phobias, at any rate all animal phobias, fears of darkness, of height and blood and injury phobias. He had some reservations about fear of flying and claustrophobia. In the first case the patient's lack of knowledge of aeroplanes and flying is likely to play a part, and it may be wise to spend some time on this aspect first. In the second case (claustrophobia) the phobia is often not very specific and occurs in a variety of situations. In fact, many patients with claustrophobia suffer from panic disorder, which generally needs a more elaborate treatment. Hence, major criteria for a successful treatment are: the phobia must have no connections with other complaints; the phobic stimulus must be well-defined; and above all, patients must be sufficiently motivated to free themselves from the complaint and be prepared to endure short periods of strong anxiety. Our own experience with this method, however, proved that more exposure sessions are needed before patients can give evidence of real habituation. This goes in particular for patients suffering from storm and thunder phobias, noise phobias, extensive claustrophobia, as well as those with blood or injury and swallow phobias. Another example shows that not every treatment of simple phobias can be concluded after one or two sessions.

Mrs Baker (42, married 15 years, no children) has suffered from fear of swallowing for some years. At first she only felt anxious when she ate certain kinds of vegetables, but over the years a growing number of different kinds of food caused trouble. At the time of our first interview she can eat only fluid food, mainly porridge and yoghourt. This has lasted for well over 6 months, causing a substantial loss of weight. On our making a functional analysis the following points present themselves. She cannot remember any event that could have provoked her fear of swallowing. Because of the problems it is impossible for her to eat with other people present, apart from her husband, or outside the house either. Apart from the fear of swallowing she seems to be hindered by symptoms of hyperventilation. As both phenomena interact they form a vicious circle and exert a negative influence on the swallowing problems. It is evident that, when under stress, the patient begins to hyperventilate and primarily to gasp for breath, causing a total immobility of the chest muscles. She tries to relax by gulping. By doing so she inhales extra amounts of air, which results in fits of coughing and feelings of severe oppression. She tells us that she has problems at her work (she has a full-time job as secretary/coordinator at an office). These problems are chiefly in the sphere of unassertiveness and in her relationship to her husband as well. Although unassertiveness seems to be the central problem, the fear of swallowing has become "functionally autonomous" after all. For that reason we decide after two exploratory sessions to focus the treatment primarily on the latter problem (of course, in consultation with Mrs Baker). This is done by means of exposure *in vivo*, that is to say by starting a process of eating problem foods in order of difficulty. The exposure is carried out with response prevention (no coughing, spitting or drinking of water during the meals) and with cognitive therapy, with an eye to the fear of swallowing. During the first session particular attention is given to the vicious circles, to explanation of the principles of exposure *in vivo* and to drawing up a hierarchy for problem-posing foods. In this context it is strange to see how "illogically" things are arranged. Very important is the character of the food, referred to by her as "slimy", "stringy" or "gritty". The hierarchy ranges from gritty via stringy to slimy. Bread gives fewer problems than hot food. The easiest task is to eat white bread with butter only, the most difficult is to eat spinach. The fear of swallowing is dealt with in twelve exposure sessions. At first the patient practises on her own by means of home assignments. After a few sessions the exposure is carried out in the therapist's presence, partly because of the necessity of introducing a social stimulus but also in order to deal with the response prevention more effectively. The sessions take place at the patient's home. After eight sessions Mrs Baker can bring herself to eat white as well as brown bread with all sorts of fillings, in the presence of the therapist. Taking hot meals is also getting better, but only if she takes them slowly. Spinach and certain kinds of food still cause great problems. From the twelfth session onwards she practises again without her therapist but now in the presence of other people. On our discussing the assignments, it becomes perfectly clear that there is a connection between the general level of stress (e.g. owing to problems at work) and the problems of swallowing. After spending sixteen sessions on the fear of swallowing, the therapist gradually switches over to the sources of stress, that is unassertiveness and marital problems. These issues require another fifteen sessions, including cognitive therapy and social skills training. On completion of the treatment, after thirty-three sessions in all, the fear of swallowing has almost disappeared and the unassertiveness has improved substantially.

The treatment of blood phobia

As discussed before, di-phasic response patterns are characteristic of blood phobics. Most striking is the dramatic fall in blood pressure and heart-rate after a short increase of both in the first minutes upon confrontation with a stimulus involving blood. It raises the question as to whether the usual treatments for phobic complaints, exposure *in vivo* in particular, serve the purpose adequately. Up to this moment hardly any research has been done in this field, in spite of the fact that blood phobias are fairly predominant among the population (Agras, Sylvester & Oliveau, 1969; Costello, 1982). In a study by Öst et al. (1984b) exposure *in vivo* proved to be more effective than an active form of relaxation (applied relaxation, see Chapter 9). The latter method teaches patients to relax when they are confronted with phobic stimuli. At follow-up both methods proved to be equally effective. This is not really surprising as the majority of the patients had meanwhile become blood donors, thus factually continuing exposure *in vivo*. In view of the specific characteristics of blood phobia, namely the increased parasympathetic activity, some points concerning the realization of exposure *in vivo* in practice may be important. The treatment should not be aimed at bringing down the arousal; on the contrary, the arousal should be heightened, back to a "normal" level. Confrontation with a blood stimulus, however, can bring about an initial sharp drop in heart-rate or even a total heart block for some time. Marks (1987) described the case of a 25-year-old man who had an asystole (heart block) for 25 seconds during the initial exposure trials. For this reason it is necessary to attend to the patient during exposure *in vivo*, so that fainting, if it should occur, cannot cause injuries. It is therefore advisable to ask patients to sit down, especially during the first sessions. Treatment of blood phobia by means of relaxation cannot be recommended, as this method stimulates fainting by reducing blood pressure. A case study which, for the first time ever, took into account the di-phasic response pattern was described by Kozak and Montgomery (1981). They applied, instead of relaxation, a tension technique to raise blood pressure and heart-rate. The promising first results of this approach motivated Öst and Sterner (1987) to work out a procedure, referred to as applied tension, describing this technique in detail. The applied tension technique teaches patients to tighten their muscles in order to raise their blood pressure. They learn to become aware of tiny signals that announce a drop in blood pressure which in turn must be counteracted by tightening the muscles. The treatment as described by Öst and Sterner (1987) includes five sessions held on the basis of an elaborate functional analysis. In the first session the rationale of the technique is explained, followed by a demonstration of muscle-tightening. Patients are instructed to do the same and to hold the tension for 15 to 20 seconds. This is repeated about five times. Patients are then told to practise at home: five consecutive tightenings, five times a day. During the second and third session patients are shown slides of all kinds of more or less seriously injured people. There is a dual concept behind this: patients learn not only to become aware of the first signals of drops in blood pressure, but also to implement the tension technique. In the fourth session patients go to the blood bank of a hospital to be able to practise in a real-life situation. After they have been taken round and given the necessary information a nurse takes the patient's blood. Of course, patients have ample opportunity to watch how other people's blood is taken. If patients have proved to be acceptable as blood donors they are advised to sign up as regular donors, thus enabling them to put the therapy lessons into practice. In the final and fifth session patients, accompanied by their therapist, visit the operating room of the thorax surgery department to watch an open-heart or a lung operation at a distance of about 5 metres from the operation table. On these occasions also patients must continue practising the applied tension. If patients should happen to faint, the therapist has to see to it that they come round as soon as possible. However, there is minimal chance of that happening, according to the authors' reports. In any case, exposure needs to be combined with the technique of applied tension. The session is concluded with a summary of the current progress to that moment. The instructions to patients cover the following 6 months and include individual exposure assignments, for example, watching films about bloodshed and killing, talking about blood-related topics and paying regular visits to a blood bank.

6 The Treatment of Panic Disorder and Agoraphobia

Until recently, no systematic mention has been made in the literature on the treatment of agoraphobia of the presence and severity of panic attacks. DSM-III-R discerns panic disorder without agoraphobia, panic disorder with agoraphobia, and agoraphobia without panic disorder (see Chapter 1). There are, however, indications that the majority of agoraphobics have at one time had one or more panic attacks. The patients' persistent avoidance behaviour obscures the relationship between panic and phobia, although the fear of recurrence of an attack is the maintaining factor in the elaborate avoidance of situations. For this reason one should be careful in the interpretation of the results of less recent studies and in the treatment of this particular group of disorders. In this chapter a brief overview is first given of research into the effects of treatment of both agoraphobia and panic disorder. In the second part, case studies are used to demonstrate the actual application of two types of treatment procedures, that is exposure *in vivo* in agoraphobia and cognitive therapy in panic disorders.

EMPIRICAL RESULTS

First, studies on the treatment of agoraphobia will be discussed, with a particular emphasis on exposure *in vivo* and cognitive procedures. Next, recent developments in the treatment of panic are summarized.

Exposure with agoraphobia

Over the past decades the effectiveness of treatments based on exposure to feared situations has been extensively studied with regard to agoraphobia. The findings lead to a number of conclusions.

1. *Exposure* in vivo *is more effective than exposure in imagination.* In the 1970s especially both variants of exposure were investigated, yielding the most favourable results for exposure *in vivo* (e.g. Emmelkamp & Wessels, 1975).
2. *Prolonged exposure is more effective than brief exposure.* Stern and Marks (1973) found two sessions of an hour produced more improvement than four sessions of 30 minutes each.
3. *Fast exposure is more effective than slow-paced exposure.* The study by Yuksel, Marks, Ramm and Ghosh (1984) showed that exposure at a fast

rate results in earlier improvement than slow-rate exposure. On the other hand, at the end of treatment both groups were equally improved.

4. *Massed practice is more effective than spaced practice.* Ten frequently held sessions resulted in greater improvement than ten sessions at longer intervals, as was demonstrated by Foa, Jameson, Turner and Payne (1980b) in a cross-over design.

5. *Group exposure and individual exposure are about equally effective.* On the whole, no clear differences seem to exist between individual and group treatment (e.g. Emmelkamp & Emmelkamp-Benner, 1975; Hafner & Marks, 1976). In some instances group treatment is more efficient since it saves the therapist's time, and group members may be good role models for each other.

6. *Treatment can be conducted as a self-help programme.* The first self-help programme, developed by Emmelkamp (1974), implied that the patient exposed himself gradually to the fear-provoking situations (gradual exposure *in vivo*). During every 90-minute session the patient recorded the time spent in the particular situation. The therapist received the patient's notes after each session. The effects of this approach did not differ from those of therapist-guided treatment. A similar self-help programme has been developed by Mathews, Gelder and Johnston (1981), in which the partner plays an important role; according to Mathews' instructions the patient has to remain in the situation until the anxiety has decreased.

7. *The effects of exposure treatment are long lasting.* Follow-up results generally show treatment results to remain stable 4–9 years after treatment; in some cases there is even further improvement (see Emmelkamp, 1990a, for a review of recent literature).

8. *Individual response patterns do not influence the effectiveness of exposure* in vivo. Exposure *in vivo* is as effective in cognitive reactors as it is in non-cognitive reactors (Mackay & Liddell, 1986), and in behavioural and physiological reactors (Öst, Jerremalm & Johansson, 1984a).

Cognitive therapy with agoraphobia

The past decade has shown an increasing interest in cognitive therapy. Cognitive theorists assume that anxiety reactions are cognitively mediated by non-rational cognitions or fear-inducing self-instructions (Beck & Emery, 1985). Anxiety reactions are assumed to originate from inadequate interpretations of certain situations or sensations. Cognitive interventions are aimed at changing the patient's fear-inducing cognitions into more adequate thoughts. In Chapter 4 the principles of some variants of cognitive therapy are discussed, such as rational emotive therapy (RET) and self-instructional training (SIT). A number of these cognitive procedures in the treatment of agoraphobia have been compared with each other and with exposure *in vivo*.

• *Exposure* in vivo *is more effective than Rational Emotive Therapy and Self Instructional Training.* In a number of studies, patients were randomly assigned to either cognitive or exposure conditions. Emmelkamp, Kuipers and Eggeraat (1978) found prolonged exposure *in vivo* to be more effective than cognitive therapy, on behavioural measures as well as on phobic and avoidance scales. In a subsequent study (Emmelkamp & Mersch, 1982) a third condition was added, that is a combination of exposure and cognitive therapy. The exposure component proved to be responsible for improvement. In a third study (Emmelkamp, Brilman, Kuiper & Mersch, 1986) cognitive interventions did not lead to clinical improvements on measures of anxiety and avoidance. Other researchers also reported that a cognitive approach adds little to the effects of exposure *in vivo* (e.g. Michelson, Mavissakalian & Marchione, 1988). Some of the studies mentioned above showed an improvement in cases of depression and unassertiveness in the cognitive condition at follow up, which is in contrast to the results in the exposure condition.

Furthermore, problem solving interventions do seem to add to the effects of exposure *in vivo*, although they are not effective when used on their own (e.g. Cullington, Butler, Hibbert & Gelder, 1984). As with the application of assertiveness training in non-assertive agoraphobics (Emmelkamp, Van den Hout & De Vries, 1983), problem-solving therapy appears to prevent post-treatment relapses.

Partners and the treatment of agoraphobia

Many clinicians and researchers have devoted attention to the role of (intimate) relationships in the maintenance of patients' complaints. Studies show, however, that the cooperation of the partner is not necessary for treatment: the spouse's aid does not increase treatment effectiveness (Cobb, Mathews, Childs-Clarke & Blowers, 1984; Emmelkamp, 1990a). In Chapter 2 we discussed the absence of a causal relationship between the quality of (marital) relations and agoraphobia. Arrindell, Emmelkamp and Sanderman (1986) found marital satisfaction not to be a predictor of treatment success with exposure *in vivo*.

Cognitive therapy with panic disorders

For several years therapeutic programmes have incorporated cognitive views. Former research into the effects of RET and SIT showed that agoraphobics benefited less from these cognitive methods than from exposure *in vivo*. A recent model directed at the interpretation and treatment of panic disturbance has been formulated by Clark (1986). He describes a panic attack as the consequence of a faulty interpretation of unharmful bodily sensations, which may, for instance, have been triggered by hyperventilation. There emerges a positively accelerating vicious circle resulting in a panic attack (see Chapter 2).

The treatment advocated by Clark consists of three parts: first, an explanation and a discussion about the role of hyperventilation in panic attacks, then the prescription of breathing exercises and the redefining of bodily sensations. Several studies show that this approach leads to a decrease in the number of panic attacks (Clark, Salkovskis & Chalkley, 1985; Salkovskis, Jones & Clark, 1986a; Clark, 1991). The decrease occurred particularly in the persons who had experienced concurrent symptoms with both a panic attack and a hyperventilation provocation. Bonn, Readhead and Timmons (1984) compared exposure *in vivo* alone with exposure *in vivo* in combination with breathing exercises. At the end of treatment both groups had made the same progress. After 6 months, however, it appeared that the group with combined treatment had improved more. Furthermore, there is evidence that cognitive therapy is at least as effective as tricyclic antidepressants (Clark, 1991). A more behavioural approach to panic was demonstrated by Griez and Van den Hout (1986) who exposed the panic patients to CO_2 inhalation. The result after repeated exposure was a decrease in fear for interoceptive stimuli. It is noticeable that many strategies contain an exposure-component; exposure can be applied to external situations as well as interoceptive stimuli (such as palpitations or the feeling of fainting). More research is needed, however, to establish the specific position of the cognitive component in the therapy.

CONDUCTING TREATMENT

The remainder of this chapter will be devoted to the discussion of two types of treatment strategies, the first directed towards avoidance behaviours by the agoraphobic patient, and the second towards learning to cope with panic attacks.

Exposure treatment in agoraphobia

At the beginning of this chapter it was stated that exposure *in vivo* can be considered the most effective method in the treatment of agoraphobia. There are several variants of this technique. In the first place there is a difference between gradual and prolonged exposure. It is also possible to call in the help of the partner, who is to act as co-therapist (described extensively by Mathews, Gelder & Johnston, 1981). In some approaches the therapist plays an active role in carrying out the tasks, whereas in another approach the patient is expected to "do his homework". The following case concerns the latter variant (homework with prolonged exposure *in vivo*). As the reader may know, treatment starts only after an assessment phase in which a functional analysis is made. Basically, the procedure followed is rather simple at face value. What it boils down to is that the patient actually exposes himself to anxiety-provoking situations. In spite of this apparent simplicity, it is still prerequisite to have a therapist with sufficient training conducting this kind of treatment. In consultation with the patient, the therapist draws up a list of increasingly difficult situations (fear hierarchy).

Next, all situations must be practised by means of home assignments; the patient should remain in the feared situation for a certain period of time, agreed upon beforehand. The objective is to reduce the patient's initial intense fear in the situation to an acceptable level after a period of exposure. In this way the patient will gradually overcome the avoiding and fear responses and learn a coping response. After one situation has been exercised satisfactorily (i.e. the fear no longer increases when the patient is confronted with the situation), the next situation is given as homework. The procedure followed contains three elements:

1. Explaining the rationale to the patient.
2. Constructing a fear hierarchy.
3. Carrying out and discussing exposure tasks.

The course of an exposure *in vivo* treatment will be illustrated by the case of Mrs Gerard.

Mrs Gerard (aged 45) is married and has no children. Over the last 5 years she has become more and more afraid to go into the street; walking in the street makes her feel nervous, she is afraid of becoming sick or faint. She found her job as a saleswoman rather exacting and her problems started at a time when she was overstressed. At first she found it difficult to go to work by bus because she often felt the urge to get off. She remembers her first moment of great fear when she was sitting in the back of the bus, short of breath and feeling dizzy and anxious. After the incident she reported sick regularly and since then she has been declared unfit to work. At the beginning of treatment it appears that she hardly ever gets out of the house unless her husband accompanies her, and even then she goes exclusively by car. Her social contacts are very limited since she is afraid to pay a return visit after someone has come to see her. Mrs Gerard makes a rather gloomy impression and she is convinced that there is little point in going on in this way. Moreover, she and her husband often quarrel. During the initial interview her husband seems to understand little of his wife's complaints. Even though he tries to help her as much as he can, his wife shows no improvement. Because his wife insists on his presence at home after work he feels restricted in his movements. Whenever the two are together at home the atmosphere is tense.

   After the admission phase it seems that exposure *in vivo* will be the most appropriate treatment for this strong avoidance behaviour. On the basis of the functional analysis the therapist concludes that the depressed mood, social isolation and marital problems have resulted from the agoraphobia. Her husband's supporting role seems to function as a maintaining factor of the phobic complaints.

Explaining the rationale to the patient

When the therapist decides to offer the patient an exposure treatment for the agoraphobic complaints, he must be certain of counting on the patient's full cooperation. It is therefore an important condition for the patient to understand the principles of treatment. For that reason the therapist will explain the working of exposure *in vivo* as soon as possible. This is illustrated by a fragment from the second session of Mrs Gerard's treatment (T: Therapist; P: Patient).

T: "Last time we discussed all kinds of difficult situations. This time I want to talk to you about the treatment itself. You told me that in the course of the last 5 years you have become more and more afraid to go out. First you were afraid to go by bus, so you went by bike; later on you stopped going by bike and then you hardly walked anywhere far from home. Your husband accompanied you more often and he did the shopping as well. The striking thing is that your circle has become smaller and smaller. Let's therefore try to figure out how your phobia has come so far. Could you tell me why you stopped going by bus in the first place?"

P: "Well ...I was afraid of what would happen in case I couldn't get off."

T: "And then you started to avoid the bus?"

P: "Yes, you might put it that way."

T: "Did the avoidance make it easier or more difficult for you to take the bus the next time?"

P: "More difficult, that's for sure."

T: "Let's see now, after you have avoided a fearful situation, it becomes more difficult to face the same situation the next time. You also told me last time that you have become less daring, and that as soon as you feel unwell you want to go home. The avoidance has become a habit because it yields something in the short term, that is, you feel less anxious. In the long run this strategy of avoiding has caused even greater problems: by escaping all fearful situations, you hardly ever go out by yourself now. For this reason we are going to apply another strategy in the treatment. You also told me that it has gradually become more and more difficult to go far away. Well now, in the treatment we will proceed to work in the same way: you are gradually going to extend your radius again, starting with less difficult situations. In order to do so we'll draw up a list of situations in which you feel anxious, moving from a little anxious to extremely anxious. After the list has been completed you are to practise the situations as homework assignments. The object is to stay in each situation for rather a long time, about 90 minutes, and not leave. In doing so, you will learn to experience that you will become less anxious. After a period of practice, when you are no longer afraid in this situation, the idea is to move on to the next situation on the list. Is it clear how the treatment works?"

P: "Yes, I think so. But...will the anxiety just disappear? I'm always worried about fainting."

T: "Now that's just the avoidance behaviour we were talking about. What did that lead to in the course of time?"

P: "Indeed, that I had less nerve to do anything."

T: "You might say that the strategy of avoidance has incited the agoraphobia. You have never given fear itself the chance to subside, because you have constantly pulled the emergency brake by escaping, or by staying indoors. Now we're going to work the other way round."

P: "I think it's going to be very difficult."

T: "Indeed, it's going to be tough work. But there's another way of seeing it: if it would be no trouble at all, you wouldn't be afraid to do it, and then we wouldn't be spending our time on it."

P: "No, I suppose you're right."

T: "If it's a great effort, you should realize that you're working on something worthwhile. After some time practising you will find that it gets easier all the time."

In this phase it is important to emphasize that much will be expected from the patient, and that his self-activity will to a great extent determine the effect of the treatment. After this explanation the therapist asks Mrs Gerard to describe in her own words how the treatment will work. At home she can fill her husband in on the principles so that he will become informed and she may have the opportunity to rehearse the procedure.

Constructing a fear hierarchy

After the therapist has explained the rationale to the patient, and the patient clearly understands it, the next step will be the start of the exposure treatment: constructing a hierarchy of situations in which the patient is afraid and of situations avoided by the patient. This hierarchy forms the starting point of the treatment, therefore it should be formulated with care and be very specific. First, the principle of the "fear thermometer" will be explained.

T: "We are now going to compare several situations regarding the fear they evoke. It is therefore helpful to make use of a 'fear thermometer' on a 10 point scale. Zero means that you have no fear at all, and 10 means that you experience the greatest possible fear. Most situations discussed so far can be indicated somewhere on this fear thermometer. So, the higher the mark, the greater the fear you have in the situation. The situations will be written down on a number of cards and subsequently be arranged according to the extent of fear they arouse. It is important for us to check exactly whether the fear decreases during the treatment. Consequently, it is necessary to describe the situations as accurately as possible. Only then will we know which situation we're dealing with. Let me give an example. Let's say we write down the situation 'Going to the shop'. Does this seem specific enough for you?"
P: "No, because you don't know which shop."
T: "Exactly, but will it be entirely clear if you mention the shop?"
P: (Pause) "I don't think so, because it also depends whether it's busy or not."
T: "Fine, this means we'll have to write down several things on the list about each situation, what we're dealing with, what time; it may also matter if someone goes with you (this can occur in the beginning) and the means of transport, walking, by car, on the bike. Furthermore, it is important to note the object of the excursion: is it because you want to cover a certain distance or is it because you want to buy something or post a letter?"

After briefly discussing the principles of the fear hierarchy, the patient will be instructed to summarize the principles in his own words. During the session it is possible to lay down the elements of the hierarchy, but writing down these situations can also be given as the first homework assignment. Since geographical aspects often play a major part in the agoraphobia, it will be useful for the patient to bring along a map of his or her relevant surroundings. This helps to make the talks more specific. In view of the temporary contact between therapist and patient, and the limited number of sessions, it is important to formulate a final goal which can be attained within a reasonable time. In the case of serious agoraphobia, for instance, the patients may be able to carry out their daily activities again, such as work, housekeeping, hobbies and raising children. It should be remembered that the hierarchy should be practised by means of daily exercises. This implies that we should be dealing with situations which occur frequently and are preferably relevant for the patient's daily life. Suppose a patient is strongly restricted in his possibilities and one of the items on the list is a trip to the zoo, then there will be considerable doubt about its relevance for the patient's daily life (it may, however, prove to be a very useful assignment for a zoo employee). If the patient hardly ever leaves home, the first items may be exercised in the company of others. The same situations will return higher in the hierarchy, but will then be practised alone.

After the therapist has explained the treatment principles, he and Mrs Gerard formulate a final goal. In her opinion the important goals are being able to do the shopping by herself, paying her neighbour a visit and passing through the town without fear. This means that all the situations take place in town. Since the therapist is not familiar with the surroundings, Mrs Gerard has brought a map, so that the distances and the important routes can be established. At home she consults her husband in order to select the situations in the hierarchy. During the third session she and the therapist agree on the composition of the hierarchy and its theme: enlarging the radius within the town. Before the next session she has to exercise the first assignment, which is walking around the house according to a defined route. The therapist gives her a registration form for carrying out the instructions (Figure 6.1) on which is to be registered time, the fear, the company and the means of transport (walking, by car, on the bike).

On the one hand, a registration for doing homework serves as a reminder for evaluating the course of the assignment and on the other hand it shows how the fear has decreased. This last point especially, can be a strong point of feedback, just as marking on the map the distances which have been covered can be. In this way both therapist and patient can clearly see what the improvements are. For some patients the registration form is the push to make them work, because they dare not appear with a form partly filled in.

Carrying out and discussing exposure assignments

It is sensible for the patient to spend 1.5 to 2 hours on carrying out the instructions in order to experience sufficient amelioration. Sometimes the exposure is too brief because of too short distances covered. An insufficient decrease of fear in these situations can be prevented by giving several

Date	Time from - to	Anxiety 0 – 100*	Route (which way ?)	Company (with whom ?)	Transport**

*0 = No fear at all 100 = maximal fear
**Walking, by bicycle, by car, by bus or train ?

(Behavioural diary ———————— Name: ——————)

Figure 6.1   Behavioural diary for exposure exercises. Based on a list in Mathews, Gelder and Johnston (1981)

consecutive instructions. It should be emphasized that the patient is to remain in the situation until the fear has subsided. Ample time should be taken to make the patient fully aware of this principle.

At the next session Mrs Gerard reacts moderately enthusiastically. The walk in the neighbourhood has been quite exacting. The first few days before going outdoors she had felt nervous, but after a week the period of anticipatory fear had gradually become shorter. In the street she had felt very uneasy and thought that her neighbours were watching her all the time. She had kept up a stiff pace and had come home feeling very tense. Actually, she is not satisfied about her progress. The therapist wants to know where her discontentment lies. Mrs Gerard replies that she wants things to go faster. Going out and walking used to be a matter that went without saying. In answer to this the therapist says: "It strikes me that you have only paid attention to what has not happened. You have hardly given thought to what actually did happen. What you have done is something that has not happened for a long time. For the first time you have gone out and walked all alone." They also discuss the way in which Mrs Gerard has taken the route, feeling chased and walking very fast. The therapist advises her to go more slowly next time. In doing so she will come closer to her goal, that is, walking about and feeling at ease.

Mrs Gerard and many other patients are inclined to neglect the progress they have made. In this respect it can be useful to label the efforts positively. In this way the therapist serves as a model for an alternative way of interpreting events, a method that proves to be more productive than negative labelling.

In the next session the patient is much more enthusiastic. She had taken heed of her pace, stopped to look around and she even deviated from her route. She was more aware of her surroundings and the consequence was that she felt less tense. During one of her walks she suddenly felt quite dizzy. According to the exposure paradigm she suppressed the inclination to go home, she stopped to sit on a bench, and proceeded with her walk later on.

Naturally, it sometimes does occur that the assignments have not been carried out satisfactorily. When things do not work out the therapist tries to find out why: perhaps the instructions are believed to be too difficult, too easy, or irrelevant.

Mrs Gerard devoted fifteen sessions to working through the hierarchy. First, she went through the town on her bike, then she went walking; next, she visited the small shops and the supermarket; and then she and her husband went for a spin in the countryside. Mrs Gerard's husband did not attend the sessions, but she told him how he could be helpful. Currently, Mrs Gerard is becoming less dependent on her husband. She dares to go out alone and does most of the shopping. Both of them consider their relationship to have improved in the course of time after treatment. For the first time in years they are making plans for their holidays, even although the idea still scares her. Mrs Gerard no longer feels depressed; she engages in all kinds of activities, visits her sister in town and even thinks of working as a volunteer in a home for the elderly. The gains in the latter area support the functional analysis the therapist made at the start of treatment.

Exposure in the form of homework assignments has a number of advantages over exposure with the help of the therapist. Homework assignments can easily be carried out by the patient himself and therefore cost less of the therapist's time, and also a greater generalization can be expected in the home situation. There are, however, also contraindications. It may, for instance, be very annoying for the patient to pass his neighbour's house, especially when they live in a small town. This problem may be solved by having the patient practise from a different starting point, for instance, the place of treatment. Another problem involving this type of exposure is that the patient can spend his time avoiding the difficult situation. Regarding the homework variant, the frequency and intervals of contact between patient and therapist differ, depending on the patient. For some agoraphobics, only one or a few sessions may be sufficient before the assignments can be carried out. Other patients need more help and encouragement before they can do it on their own. Even patients who are perfectly capable of carrying out the procedures will benefit from some encouragement given by the therapist through regular telephone calls. The exposure treatments we are dealing with here may seem rather simple, but they are not carried out that easily. It is very important for the patient to experience a prolonged exposure to anxiety-provoking stimuli, without having the chance to avoid or escape them. Inexperienced therapists often instruct their patients to go for a short walk, then to take the bus for a short period, and so on, until the session is over. Although this can be considered a prolonged session, the actual exposure to each situation remains brief. It is not surprising that this kind of exposure often fails, because the patient is still anxious when leaving the situation. It is vitally important for the patient to remain in the situation until his fear has subsided before proceeding to the next situation. These guidelines imply that exposure *in vivo* should be tuned to the individual needs of the patient, even when we are dealing with a group. As was mentioned before, it is not necessary to maintain the highest possible level of fear. Prolonged exposure can be carried out with the help of a hierarchy of fear-provoking situations. It is essential, however, that all situations during one session should evoke the same degree of fear. It is wrong to assign a difficult task first and then an easy one, because this will prevent habituation to the fear-provoking stimuli. Patients will feel relieved when they receive an easy task which arouses no fear. The important thing is to find out exactly which stimuli excite the patient's fear. Although most agoraphobics are afraid of crowds, every patient has his own fears. For some patients quiet streets may be frightening; for others, places near water or unknown places.

For one of our social agoraphobics the exposure did not produce the desired extinction of fear. When discussing the course of the exposure it appeared that the patient had continually avoided making eye-contact, and in doing so he had escaped the real exposure. In the next session the patient was asked to walk the same route again and to make eye-contact with passers-by. Even though the exposure initially caused much more anxiety than the first time, the fear eventually became less.

Other subtle forms of avoidance behaviour may be carrying medicines, wearing sunglasses, having a chat with passers-by, carrying a bag, or running in the street. Also, real exposure can be prevented by cognitive avoidance, for instance by thinking: "there is a hospital"; "my sister lives there"; "the doctor lives nearby, at least there will be help if something goes wrong". It is often very difficult to trace these subtle forms of avoidance behaviour since many patients themselves are not aware of them. During the exposure *in vivo* sessions, the therapist gradually withdraws from the practice situation in order to make the *in vivo* exercises increasingly difficult for the patient. For most agoraphobics, real exposure to fear-provoking situations does not take place when they know that the therapist is around.

Cognitive therapy with panic disorders

The aim of this treatment is to replace catastrophic cognitions by more rational or realistic ones; interventions directed at correcting the way of breathing have a function within this scope. According to the procedure put forward by Clark (1986), the principle is to break through the circular process. Figure 6.2 shows that an internal or external stimulus is perceived as a threat which evokes fear. The consequence of the fear is that the patient will breathe too fast. As a result the CO_2 percentage in the blood will drop and the pH level will rise. The acidity changes to basic (this phenomenon is called respiratory alkalosis) and this leads to all kinds of bodily sensations. The panic patient experiences these symptoms and interprets them as catastrophic, meaning that they are interpreted as more dangerous than they really are. The consequence will be the experience of panic. We finally come full circle when the panic itself provokes more bodily reactions of anxiety. It can be observed that the way of interpreting bodily symptoms, not the symptoms themselves, is responsible for the panic attack. The treatment developed for patients with panic attacks is based on the model described above. Many others have designed strategies of treatment which are variants of this procedure. Cognitive therapy, just like every other treatment, is preceded by a detailed inventory of the complaints and setting up a functional analysis. During the admission interview an inventory is to be drawn up of the patient's possible physical afflictions (such as asthma, bronchitis, heart troubles, and epilepsy) and of his experiences with physiotherapy (many of our patients received physiotherapy). If a patient makes use of a plastic bag for breathing control, let him demonstrate how he uses it; only by seeing it done can you find out whether he uses it correctly. Often a patient covers only his mouth and breathes through his nose or only partly covers his nose and mouth for fear of suffocation. In the latter case the patient can be reassured by making a small

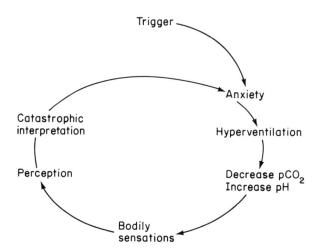

Figure 6.2 A panic attack according to a cognitive perspective. Based on a figure in Clark (1986)

hole in the plastic bag, so that he will not become unduly anxious and will still be able to inhale enough CO_2-enriched air. In the treatment the following steps are to be distinguished:

1. Inventory of bodily symptoms and cognitions.
2. Evaluation of the hyperventilation provocation.
3. Discussion about the role of hyperventilation in panic.
4. Training of abdominal respiration.
5. Learning non-catastrophic cognitive responses.
6. Behavioural experiments.
7. Identification and modification of panic provokers.

The next case illustrates the various steps in this procedure.

At the advice of a company doctor, Henry (aged 31) comes to us with severe complaints of anxiety. For several years he has been working as an administrator in an office. He is satisfied with his job and is known to be a hard and conscientious worker. Some 8 months ago after the summer vacation his complaints started. When he was taking a relaxing stroll in the woods he was seized by great anxiety and felt such a terrifying pain in the heart that he believed that he was going to die. The general practitioner examined him thoroughly, but could find nothing out of the ordinary. On the one hand Henry felt relieved, but on the other hand he kept feeling worried about the cause of his symptoms. According to the doctor his troubles were psychic, he was working too hard and was too meticulous. He still kept worrying that it would happen again and indeed, he did have some recurrent attacks. His girlfriend, with whom he lives, is not able to give him any support when he has an attack. On account of the severity of the complaints, Henry dare not go far from home. Because he has lost control of his behaviour he has become considerably depressed, he cannot concentrate, sleeps badly and has withdrawn from social life. The situation persists and eventually he submits a request to us for treatment. From the initial interview it can be concluded that Henry is suffering from a panic disturbance with mild agoraphobia and that he makes high demands on himself. His greatest fear is that he will die from a heart attack. Since Henry is able to rationalize this fear in between attacks, the diagnosis "hypochondria" does not apply. In view of the temporal relationship between panic and depression, it is decided to treat the panic disturbance rather than the depression; the therapist hypothesizes that his mood will improve as the fear subsides.

Inventory of bodily symptoms and cognitions

After the admission interview we offer Henry a treatment for his complaints. In the second session an inventory is made of the bodily sensations and thoughts experienced just before, during and after a panic attack. In order to gather clear information, Henry is asked to describe a typical (preferably recent) panic attack. The therapist records both Henry's thoughts and his bodily sensations during the attack, with the intention of returning to them later on in the session.

Hyperventilation provocation

In principle, verbal information can give a distorted picture of the actual circumstances during a panic attack. Therefore, the next step of the treatment will be to provoke hyperventilation. The aim is to gain insight into the similarities between the sensations of a "spontaneous" panic attack and the sensations of an artificially provoked panic attack. In particular the similarities and differences between the cognitions occurring in both situations are of great importance for the course of treatment. For that reason the therapist should introduce the provocation test as neutrally as possible, in order to prevent induction of fear or specific expectations as to the effects. It is better to speak of a "diagnostic test" than of "hyperventilation provocation". The patient is asked to breathe through his nose and mouth deeply and quickly (about 30 intakes of breath a minute) for a period of 2 minutes, although he is allowed to stop sooner if he cannot maintain it. Before conducting the test for the first time, the therapist should practise the breathing test himself either alone or with his colleagues. The therapist will learn which phenomena will occur and at which rate. Careful preparation will produce an optimal effect with the patient during the therapy session.

The therapist introduces the test to Henry as follows:

T: "I would like to ask you to do a diagnostic test. This test is quite easy and it may provide us with much information about the complaints we have just discussed. I would like you to breathe deep and fast through your mouth for 2 minutes. I will tell you when to stop. All right, is this clear? Let me show you first how to do it."

(Therapist demonstrates the breathing test for 2 minutes.)

T: "During these 2 minutes you may possibly feel certain sensations. Some people experience them as pleasant, others do not. As soon as you feel different from the way you do now, raise your hand while continuing with the test. After the 2 minutes we will return to it."

Henry wants to know what he can expect to happen in the test, but the therapist suggests it would be better to talk after the test. It is best not to raise expectations or induce fear. If Henry should want to stop before time is up, he can do so by resuming normal breathing. Should he want to stop more quickly, it is best to cover the nose and mouth with a plastic bag in order to rebreathe the expired air. The therapist shows him how to do it and asks whether he has any more questions about the test. All other questions will be discussed after the test. The therapist presses the stopwatch and for a few seconds he breathes together with the patient to help him keep the right rate and depth of breathing. The patient continues on his own while the therapist makes some encouraging remarks, such as "good", "fine" and "keep it up". When the patient raises his hand to indicate that he has noticed the first symptom, the therapist records the time which has elapsed from the beginning of the test. After 2 minutes the patient is asked to stand up, close his eyes, and mention all the bodily sensations he feels at the moment.

Evaluation of the provocation

After the test, the point is to gain an impression about the similarities between these provoked symptoms and those of a "spontaneous" panic attack. It is helpful to use a list of symptoms on which a patient can indicate the severity of the symptoms (see Figure 6.3). Subsequently, the therapist marks the similarities between these symptoms and those of a panic attack on a scale from 0 (no accordance) to 10 (perfect accordance). The two checklists form a starting point for discussing the similarities to and differences from a real panic attack. The following three questions are dealt with: "What symptoms did you have in both situations?", "What symptoms did you have during the test and did not experience during a panic attack?" and "What symptoms did you have during a real panic attack alone?" A characteristic dialogue follows:

T: "Please, tell me what symptoms you have during a panic attack which didn't occur during the previous test?"

P: "Well . . . as a matter of fact I didn't feel so anxious this time."

T: "Right, not so anxious." (Writes it down.) "Are there any more symptoms you didn't have this time? "

P: "Another thing is that I wasn't perspiring that much, and I was feeling less insecure."

T: "Hmm . . . less perspiration and less feeling of insecurity." (Writes this down as well.) "Are there any more differences?"

P: . . . "No, I don't think so, only that the symptoms were less serious."

T: "Let me recapitulate: you were feeling less anxious and insecure just now, you perspired less and the symptoms were less severe."

P: "I believe that's right."

T: "It's quite remarkable, isn't it? Can you explain these differences?"

P: (Pauses.) "I don't think I can."

T: "It seems hard to explain. Let's try to find out. When you made the test, what made you feel less anxious?"

P: "I'm not sure, perhaps I was aware that it was only a test."

T: "Only a test. . . . Was there anything else you were thinking of?"

P: "Well . . . I reckoned that if something might go wrong, I would be in good hands."

T: "So that's what you were thinking just now. What are your thoughts when you have a panic attack?"

P: "I only feel terribly frightened!"

T: "All right, you feel frightened, but what goes on in your mind when the attack comes?"

P: "What I think of then . . . I always think that I'll faint, that I'll collapse, and that when I come to, people will just stand there staring into my face. It makes me sick just to think of it."

Symptom List					

Patient:..............   Session:..............   Date:..../..../....

To what extent did you notice an increase in the following sensations during the diagnostic test?
Please tick the appropriate box.

	Not at all	A little	Some	Much	Very much
Muscle pain	( )	( )	( )	( )	( )
Sweating	( )	( )	( )	( )	( )
Lump in throat	( )	( )	( )	( )	( )
Trembling	( )	( )	( )	( )	( )
Drowsiness	( )	( )	( )	( )	( )
Numbness	( )	( )	( )	( )	( )
Dry mouth	( )	( )	( )	( )	( )
Sense of unreality	( )	( )	( )	( )	( )
Heart racing	( )	( )	( )	( )	( )
Nausea	( )	( )	( )	( )	( )
Stinging	( )	( )	( )	( )	( )
Fear	( )	( )	( )	( )	( )
Shaking	( )	( )	( )	( )	( )
Earache	( )	( )	( )	( )	( )
Anxiety	( )	( )	( )	( )	( )
Choking	( )	( )	( )	( )	( )
Headache	( )	( )	( )	( )	( )
Palpitations	( )	( )	( )	( )	( )
Faintness	( )	( )	( )	( )	( )
Tension	( )	( )	( )	( )	( )
Tingling	( )	( )	( )	( )	( )
Pins and needles	( )	( )	( )	( )	( )
Cold limbs	( )	( )	( )	( )	( )
Dizziness	( )	( )	( )	( )	( )
Muscle tension	( )	( )	( )	( )	( )
Breathlessness	( )	( )	( )	( )	( )
Blurred vision	( )	( )	( )	( )	( )
Other sensations:					
....	( )	( )	( )	( )	( )
....	( )	( )	( )	( )	( )
....	( )	( )	( )	( )	( )

Figure 6.3 Symptom checklist for a breathing test. Based on a checklist mentioned in a treatment manual used by Clark et al. in Warenford Hospital, Oxford

T: " . . . and the symptoms you had here strongly resemble the symptoms of a panic attack, don't they?" (Looks at his notes, patient nods.) "You were also just saying that you gave them seven points on the scale from 0 to 10, concerning their similarities. You also told me that you believed you were in good hands here, whereas in the panic attack situation you were afraid of fainting and being embarrassed. What do you make of that difference?"
P: "I'm doing this to myself, aren't I? It's the way I think that makes me afraid!"

Although most patients need more time before they arrive at the same conclusion, the principle of the discussion remains the same. The therapist wants the patient to find out for himself what the difference is between a panic attack and the provocation. This technique is called the Socratic dialogue, after the Greek philosopher Socrates. By asking his interlocutors rather simple, sometimes silly questions, Socrates provided them with knowledge and insight not known to them before. Some consider the Socratic dialogue to be one of the main components of cognitive therapy. In this approach it is important not for the therapist to collect information, but rather to make the patient think in a different way. The more actively and self-reliantly the patient works, the more successful the treatment will be. At face value this method may seem time-consuming and digressive: it would be much easier and faster just to tell the patient about the role of cognitions during a panic attack. However, there is the danger that the patient will not grasp the essence and (most importantly) will miss the opportunity to exercise with an alternative, non-catastrophic way of thinking. Trower, Casey and Dryden (1988) wrote a book on the practical approach of cognitive therapy, and Walen, DiGiuseppe and Wessler (1980) elaborate on the practice of RET and the Socratic dialogue. At this stage of the therapy it is vitally important to construct the vicious circle as displayed in Figure 6.1. The therapist and the patient recapitulate the course of an attack. While talking the therapist takes down notes and constructs the circle step by step. With each step the therapist checks whether the patient recognizes the description ("Am I right when I say that you are feeling dizzy then?", or "Correct me if I'm wrong when I say that you mostly think of fainting during a panic attack?"). This active questioning is meant to set the patient thinking and to clarify the course of the panic attack. For people who are unfamiliar with the phenomenon of hyperventilation this phase can be quite enlightening. The patient is encouraged to acquire the model fully by, for instance, talking it over with his or her partner or friends at home. Complete understanding is a *conditio sine qua non* for the treatment because the model will be returned to in future sessions.

Discussion about the role of hyperventilation

There is, however, one part of the procedure that should be elucidated through a didactic explanation, that is an explanation of the phenomenon of hyperventilation. The patient's foreknowledge and intellectual sophistication determine how detailed this explanation should be. It goes without saying that the therapist must be sufficiently informed on this phenomenon in order to explain it clearly. Lum's article (1976) provides much information on chronic hyperventilation. There are several essential points that certainly should be discussed. One of them is the obvious presence of disturbed breathing, the subsequent decrease in CO_2 level and the consequent bodily sensations. To illustrate this, a fragment from one of Henry's sessions follows.

T: "From the test just now it appeared that your overbreathing triggered a number of complaints quite similar to the complaints you have during a panic attack. What do you make of this?"

P: "That the cause is my breathing?"

T: "Your overbreathing is indeed an important factor in your complaints. We call it hyperventilation. Is the term known to you?"

P: "I've heard the word before, but I can't tell exactly what it is."

T: "Let me explain. Hyperventilation means that one's breathing is too strong in comparison to the needs of the body. When you're exercising your body in sport, you need to breathe faster. The reason for this is that the body needs to get rid of a lot of waste gases, mostly carbon dioxide (CO_2). When you hyperventilate, you also exhale a great deal of this gas without any physical exertion. In doing so, the level of carbon dioxide in the blood will drop and consequently change the acidity: the blood becomes less acid. This causes a number of bodily sensations, some of which you have experienced during the test. Hyperventilation therefore has almost nothing to do with a lack of oxygen. Many people actually think that this is the cause of hyperventilation and of the choking sensations. Hyperventilation is a decrease in carbon dioxide level, let's say expired air, and therefore it helps to rebreathe it in a plastic bag so that an attack can be prevented."

After this explanation the therapist asks the patient some questions in order to check his amount of understanding of the mechanism of hyperventilation. This can be done by asking, for example, "Imagine you would want to explain hyperventilation to a member of your family, how would you do that?" In this active way (maybe even role playing) the information will be better assimilated and the therapist is able to correct potential misunderstandings. When the patient fully understands the principle of the vicious circle, the attention is then focused on the panic complaints themselves. This discussion concentrates on breathing correction and the non-catastrophic interpretation of bodily sensations.

Training in abdominal breathing

One of the conclusions from the previous discussion is that the patient should adopt a different breathing pattern. In the case of hyperventilation the muscles of the thorax are used strongly, whereas the abdominal muscles are too tense and do not play a role in breathing. The aim of the breathing exercises is to acquire a relaxed abdominal breathing pattern. Clark (1986) recommends a rate of 8–12 breaths per minute, in which the (nasal) inhalation is as long as the (nasal) exhalation. It is useful if the patient uses an audiotape on which the words "in" and "out" are recorded at the required rate. Homework consists of breathing training three times a day for about 20 minutes. One hand should be placed on the stomach and the other on the breast while practising. When the patient breathes correctly, only the hand on the stomach will move. After several days the tape may be stopped every now and then, while the patient keeps on breathing at the same rate. The therapist demonstrates the correct breathing and asks the patient to do the same. For many patients it is quite difficult to use their abdominal muscles in this way; in such cases this becomes the first goal. The homework should be done in complete peace and quiet, without any obstructive items of clothing. In the next session the therapist checks the progress in breathing correction. To do this specifically the patient is asked to overbreathe for a short time (approximately 15 seconds), after which he is encouraged to perform the newly acquired breathing pattern. This procedure makes it possible to suggest technical improvements.

The acquisition of non-catastrophic cognitive responses

The main aim of cognitive treatment is to teach the patient to adopt adequate (i.e. non-catastrophic) cognitions. The list of cognitions which the therapist has obtained before the provocation test is the point of departure. The patient's misinterpretations are challenged by asking him to give evidence of the imminent catastrophe. More specifically, the discussion starts with the bodily sensations and the interpretations the patient attaches to them. Patients often appear to be very preoccupied with the possible consequences of a panic attack, and seem to disregard the triggering events of the mechanism of panic. To obtain specific information on a specific panic attack, it is often worthwhile asking the patient to close his eyes and to concentrate on this attack.

Henry tells the therapist that he has had another panic attack the evening before the session: just like that, apparently without any cause. He was sitting on the couch, watching television, enjoying a drink and expecting his girlfriend to come home half an hour later.

    T: "What happened then?"
    P: "I felt terribly bad, my heart was pounding like mad and I felt dizzy, nauseous, as if I were going to faint any minute. I don't understand how it could happen, I was just watching television."
    T: "What is it exactly you don't understand?"
    P: "Well, that such a thing can happen without reason. All was well at the office, no stress at all."
    T: "What was the next thing you were thinking of then?"
    P: "Then I started to wonder whether there was something wrong with my heart after all!"

T: "It really unsettled you, didn't it? Let's try to use this attack to your advantage and see what we can make of it. Let's start at the beginning: try to recollect what happened as precisely as possible, what you were doing and what you were thinking of. You may close your eyes if you like."

P: (Closes his eyes.) "I was watching television and wasn't worrying about a thing."

T: "What were you watching?"

P: "All kinds of programmes, I think, nothing in particular."

T: "And what programme was on just before the panic attack?"

P: "I think it was a detective series on channel 2... yes ... . it was exciting this time ..."

T: "So it was exciting? ... indeed ... did you get carried away?"

P: "Yes, I suppose so."

T: "What happens normally when things get exciting?"

P: (Hesitates) "Well ...you get involved, is that what you mean?"

T: "That's exactly what I mean...how do you notice this involvement?"

P: "What do mean?"

T: "Can you describe your bodily reactions when you're watching something exciting?"

P: "Oh well ...I sit tight and get carried away. If it's really thrilling, my heart starts pounding in my throat... it's as if I'm actually there."

T: "Your heart starts pounding in your throat...what was it like yesterday evening?"

P: (Reflecting.) "Yes... now you come to mention it, I believe it was exactly the same way."

T: "What did the panic attack begin with?"

P: "With heavy beating of the heart."

T: "What crossed your mind then?"

P: "I was thinking ... oh my God ... I'm all alone now ... What will happen if I have a heart attack?"

T: "How were you feeling then?"

P: "Frightened to death, wouldn't you be?"

T: (Imperturbable.) "How did your thinking affect your breathing?"

P: "I started to pant like a steam engine."

T: "And then?"

P: "Everything went wrong, I panicked completely."

T: "What can we conclude after retracing the course of your so-called 'spontaneous' panic attack? It seems to me that you have misinterpreted a normal fast heart-beat due to an exciting film, and thought you were going to have a heart attack. This catastrophic view in turn triggered a fear reaction and the attendant bodily sensations." (The therapist illustrates this point by showing the vicious circle which he has drawn in the mean time.)

P: "I believe I got so worked up that I had this attack... was it really because of a film?"

T: "That's a very good question indeed: was it because of the film or was it your own doing?'

P: (Reflecting.) "I think it was my own doing. I've been worrying about ordinary palpitations."

This type of dialogue can be considered characteristic for cognitive reorganization and for reinterpreting the provokers of panic as well as the panic attack itself. At first, patients will find it difficult to recognize this mechanism because they will still be experiencing fear or tension by talking about the panic attack. The therapist and the patient have to rehearse this line of reasoning so that eventually the patient will be able to reason for himself. The therapist will refer many times to the model of the vicious circle and ask the patient to fit in his experiences. Keeping an accurate diary may be helpful for the reinterpretation, because the patient will feel encouraged to put down on paper the details and situations of panic attacks.

Henry's homework assignment is to write down what he normally thinks as soon as the first symptoms of the panic attack set in. Beside each catastrophic thought he is to put down a realistic and reassuring thought. In the following sessions he notices more and more his ability to challenge the catastrophic thoughts by conceiving alternative non-catastrophic ones. In the course of treatment he improves this skill. Every now and then he is bothered by annoying bodily sensations, but in contrast to earlier periods he is now capable of handling them, thus preventing undue anxiety and situational avoidance.

Identification and modification of panic triggers

Often panic triggers are only minor and hardly noticed at first sight. One of our patients reported having had a limited symptom attack while wearing high-heeled shoes to which she was not accustomed. When discussing this event she discovered that she automatically associated this unsteady feeling with one of the first symptoms of her panic attacks, that is the feeling of faintness. Another patient thought he noticed the first symptoms of a panic attack when he wore a friend's glasses with strong lenses, although he himself did not wear spectacles. The blurred vision made him nearly panic. These examples illustrate that panic attacks may be triggered by seemingly minor bodily sensations. The problem is, however, that patients are preoccupied to such an extent with the phenomena of the actual panic attack and the associated anxiety that the actual onset of the attack becomes totally obscured. In the course of treatment, in which the detection of triggers is an important issue, the causes of panic are gradually revealed. Careful questioning of the patient brings the triggers to the foreground and stimulates the patient to look for these triggers himself. In this way thoughts that panic attacks just come out of the blue or that they are being caused by some serious disease, eventually disappear. Identification of panic triggers is facilitated by the use of a diary, in which the patient records the occurrence and intensity of the (limited) attacks on a day-to-day basis. Cognitions existing during an attack should also be noted. The therapist and the patient use the diary to discover triggers and catastrophic cognitions, in order to modify both of them. After a number of sessions, the patient himself becomes more and more aware of the discovery of the onset of panic; its "spontaneous" nature will then be seen in a different light.

Behavioural experiments

Both Beck and Emery (1985) and Clark (1986) consider behavioural experiments to be a substantial part of cognitive therapy. Basically, the patient is stimulated to perform certain activities aimed at the verification or falsification of his catastrophic interpretations. Critics say that these experiments are in fact equivalent to exposure to feared stimuli, thus making cognitive therapy less cognitive; and indeed many experiments do have the character of exposure assignments. The patient is asked to test his catastrophic cognitions in a realistic situation. This implies that he has to expose himself to something that may at least be considered exciting or fear-provoking. In a discussion after the experiment the therapist and patient agree on which of the hypotheses are actually supported by the experiment: the patient's catastrophic hypothesis or the therapist's more realistic one. It is neither necessary nor likely that a patient should abandon all of his irrational cognitions, but rather that a gradual shift takes place towards the desired non-catastrophic direction. In clinical practice, behavioural experiments can be a powerful tool to induce the patient to discover that his catastrophic thoughts are not tenable. It is of great importance that the experiment is designed in such a way that it is fruitful to therapy and that it cannot be considered by the patient as a failure. The patient's mere performance of the experiment is of use in therapy. Behavioural experiments should be tailor-made and are carefully chosen by the therapist to fit the patient's complaints.

Henry devoted several sessions to breathing exercises and reinterpretation of his bodily symptoms. Yet he still worries about going into the street alone, for fear of becoming sick or fainting. When he tells the therapist of his fears, the therapist finds it a good opportunity for a behavioural experiment. The following week Henry is to go to town several times on his own and find out what happens. He has learnt the breathing correction well and it is likely that he will get the chance to practise with it during the experiment. Henry is not very keen on carrying out the experiment but still agrees to proceed. At the next session it appears that he has been in town twice. The first time he felt dizzy, insecure and anxious; after a short while he went home. He considered it a failure. On the next occasion he pulled himself together and went again. After 20 minutes the first symptoms of panic occurred, after which he applied his breathing correction and encouraged himself to keep it up ("Just continue to breathe normally and everything will be all right. I won't faint and even if I do, so what?"). The therapist believes that the experiment has demonstrated much. Henry has shown himself how to cut short an attack and he has discovered that no catastrophic things happen. Similar experiments are repeated several times and increase Henry's belief that he has only harmless symptoms in which he himself can intervene instantly.

In the patient's manner of speech the therapist actively seeks elements which betray catastrophic thoughts. Because many patients are strongly inclined to absolutist reasoning, the therapist can be a model for a different cognitive style. For that reason an experiment does not go "right" or "wrong", but something in between. In the above example strategies are sought which make it easier to cope with panic sensations.

The context of panic

At the admission interview Henry indicated that he was very meticulous at work, and was easily annoyed when things went wrong. After some time his panic has subsided and Henry has learned to cope adequately with what is left of it. In this phase the therapist suggests having a closer look at his more structural sources of stress. In general Henry appears to make high demands on himself. This is shown in his work (he does not allow himself any mistakes at all), as well as in social respects (he wants to be friends with everybody). This causes great stress and tension in his daily life. The next couple of sessions, therefore, are devoted to RET. The therapist explains that Henry's panic attacks evidently do not come out of the blue, but are directly or indirectly influenced by his own life style and personal rules. During each of the subsequent sessions they pick a particular theme or situation and make a rational analysis in which the Activating event (A), the particular Beliefs (B) and the behavioural or mood Consequences (C) are specified. Homework consists of rational analyses of recent events. In the third session, for example, they discuss Henry's tendency to try to be friends with everybody. This implicit rule means that he hardly opposes anyone even if he does not like the way things are going. When a colleague at work took a few days off in a busy period, Henry dared not say anything about it, although it annoyed him very much. In his mind he was very angry and swore at his colleague, but he was outwardly very friendly every time they met. The therapist investigates the advantages of being good friends with everyone. After some thought Henry remarks that in the case of his colleague, it was only Henry himself who was bothered, whereas his colleague did not seem to be aware of any of Henry's annoyance. In challenging this irrational thought "Everybody must like me", the therapist asked if Henry would want to stick to it for the full 100% and under all circumstances. Well, 100% does seem a bit exaggerated to Henry, so he will be satisfied with 50% of the people, some of the time. His annoyance towards his colleague belongs to those cases in which he does not necessarily want to be liked for the full 100%. The costs exceed the benefits in this event, because avoiding a confrontation with his colleague gives him a lot of stress and tension. In sum, wanting to be liked by everybody under all circumstances appears to be an irrational wish preventing Henry's adequate functioning. He decides to adopt the thought that it is not absolutely necessary to be liked by everybody. An immediate consequence of this new rule is a row with his colleague. During the next session Henry reports this somewhat shakenly, because he is not used to such less pleasant ways of associating with other people. Henry told his colleague he did not like his absence in very busy times; he found it annoying. His colleague replied to Henry that this was none of his business. Although this argument did not yield a direct benefit, Henry seems quite pleased and even a little proud that he has behaved assertively. In a similar way attention is paid to the high demands Henry makes on himself. By very much wanting to prevent any mistakes, he becomes tense to such an extent that he cannot concentrate well on his tasks. This makes him slower and less accurate. "Should I deliberately make all kinds of mistakes?", Henry asks the therapist. "No", the latter says, "But you should look at what it brings you when you keep telling yourself everything must be done perfectly."

After challenging this irrational thought Henry comes to the (obvious) conclusion that even he himself, as a simple mortal being, cannot rule out the possibility of making mistakes every now and then. However, by clinging to his demand to be perfect and do his job without any mistakes he only makes more mistakes. This strengthens his conviction that failures should be avoided, thus making a full and vicious circle. After five sessions both Henry and his therapist agree that he is quite capable of making his own rational analyses. His mood has improved considerably and he feels more cheerful, without having paid any particular attention to this. Six months after termination of therapy the therapist receives a letter from Henry in which he reports having had only a few panic attacks, with which he was able to cope by using his breathing exercises and cognitive modification. Furthermore, he says his attitudes toward his job have changed, making him more productive and even eligible for promotion.

The example of Henry's treatment once more emphasizes the necessity of a good functional analysis of the problem behaviours, on both micro- and macro-levels. The high demands can be regarded as a more structural problem, although they were dealt with later in therapy. It would not have been very strategic to have started with this problem area, because Henry would probably have remained very afraid of panic attacks, thus preventing a full consolidation of rational cognitions. Furthermore, treatment results support the therapist's estimation that the depressed mood was only secondary to the incapacitating effects of panic. The patient's failure to meet his own high demands also can be considered depressogenic. In a number of patients the treatment of panic must be followed by additional treatments, as was shown in the above case illustration. When anxiety is related to relational dysfunctioning, partner-relationship therapy may be considered. A phobia of one of the partners may have disturbed the relational balance, which means that tackling the problems implies a restoration of that particular balance. In a substantial proportion of agoraphobics an important maintaining role is to a certain extent played by social phobia. We consider it to be a therapeutic mistake if this social phobia is not dealt with, because it may, after some time, trigger another agoraphobic or panic episode. A good functional analysis made at the start of treatment and updated every now and again gives indications for a next step in treatment.

7 The Treatment of Social Phobia

EMPIRICAL RESULTS

In the discussion about the aetiology of anxiety disorders it has already been mentioned that three different models have frequently been used for explaining the origin and maintenance of social phobic complaints. During the 1960s emphasis was laid on a lack of social skills, assumed to be a consequence of faulty socialization processes during childhood. Fear of social situations was considered to be a result of aversive reactions from other people, provoked by the individual's awkward behaviour. According to this skills deficit model, teaching adequate skills is still the first, and maybe the only object of treatment. Although at first the model seemed appropriate for many patients, several social phobics soon appeared to possess adequate social skills in therapy sessions or laboratory settings, but were too inhibited to use them in real life situations as a result of their anxiety. Other patients reported remaining anxious, in spite of their ability to behave in a socially adequate manner. In the second model, centred around conditioning processes, emphasis is put on the fear and anxiety itself, likely to be caused by one or more traumatic experiences in social situations, and generalized to other social settings. According to this model the aim of treatment is a direct reduction of anxiety instead of teaching adequate social skills. Currently, lavish attention is being paid to several kinds of cognitive processes which can lead to fear and anxiety. In the models generated in this area—summarized to denominator cognitive inhibition model—irrational, non-realistic expectations and attitudes of the individual are assumed to be responsible for the development and maintenance of social anxiety. Based on the different aspects emphasized in the models, over the years several therapeutic strategies have been developed: social skills training for teaching adequate skills, flooding, systematic desensitization, relaxation strategies and exposure *in vivo* for direct reduction of anxiety, and cognitive strategies, such as rational emotive therapy (RET, Ellis, 1962), cognitive behaviour therapy (e.g. Beck & Emery, 1985), and self-instructional training (SIT, Meichenbaum, 1975) for changing the irrational cognitions. In this context, the number of studies on the effectiveness of such strategies in the treatment of social anxiety has largely increased. However, it was not before the introduction of DSM-III (1980), that some agreement was reached about social phobia as a clinical phenomenon in its own right and about its features. Until that time the patient groups treated were rather heterogeneous, which is a major drawback when comparing different studies. The groups studied consisted of volunteers (often students) with social anxiety, or of patients with various psychiatric problems, social anxiety being often a secondary problem. Only recently have studies been published with respect to treatment of more homogeneous groups with clinically relevant social phobia. As was said earlier, over the years several therapeutic strategies for easing social anxiety have been tested, some being successful, others not. In the past decade exposure *in vivo*, social skills training and cognitive strategies have been emphasized. Before we give a description of the use of these procedures for social phobics, the results of their effectiveness will be briefly reviewed. A consideration of the literature about treatment of social phobia shows that, until now, relatively little research has been carried out and what is more, that the reported results are contradictory. As a consequence, it is difficult to summarize the findings in unambiguous conclusions. For that reason, the following paragraphs must be hedged with some caveats.

1. *Systematic desensitization is not very effective with social phobics.* During the 1970s in particular systematic desensitization was popular among behaviour therapists, this technique being used in several studies, for clinical as well as for non-clinical populations (students). A marked difference in effectiveness for these populations was found. In contrast to the observation that this treatment produced a significant decrease in anxiety among volunteers, the improvement among patients appeared to be limited or absent (Hall & Goldberg, 1977; Marzillier, Lambert & Kellett, 1976; Shaw, 1979; Trower, Yardley, Bryant & Shaw, 1978; Van Son, 1978).

2. *Flooding seems to be of no use in the treatment of social phobia.* Only one study compared the effects of flooding with those of systematic desensitization and social skills training on social phobics (Shaw, 1979). At the end of treatment, patients in all conditions showed minor improvement, but no different responses to the various strategies were observed. Due to methodological shortcomings the relevance of this study is limited. Given the small results achieved and the fact that flooding is an upsetting and aversive procedure for patients, we do not recommend its use with social phobics.

3. *Relaxation methods may be useful for some social phobics.* Alström, Nordlund, Persson, Harding and Ljungqvist (1984) found relaxation therapy to be only temporarily effective and far less so than exposure *in vivo*. In studies by Öst, Jerremalm and Johansson (1981) and Jerremalm, Jansson and Öst (1986) a specific relaxation strategy (referred to as applied relaxation) was used in the treatment of social phobics. A review of these studies follows later in this chapter. For the moment there is some reason to say that applied relaxation can be considered an adequate treatment for patients who suffer from strong physiological arousal in social situations.

4. *The effects of social skills training are rather divergent.* Based on the

skills deficit model mentioned before, the effectiveness of social skills training has been evaluated in several studies, with divergent results. Marzillier, Lambert and Kellett (1976) compared the effects of social skills training, systematic desensitization and a waiting list control period. At post-test the treatment groups appeared to have improved to the same extent, but did not differ significantly from the untreated control group. At 6 months follow-up, only the social skills training group showed a lasting improvement. Similarly, Van Son (1978) found that social skills training gave better results than systematic desensitization. In other studies, however, no differences were found between these two strategies (Hall & Goldberg, 1977; Shaw, 1979; Trower et al., 1978). Finally, in one study social skills training appeared to be more effective than group therapy (Falloon, Lindley, McDonald & Marks, 1977).

5. *Exposure* in vivo *is an effective method of treatment for social phobia.* Exposure *in vivo* has been widely and successfully used for treatment of anxiety disorders. In social phobics, surprisingly, to date the effects of exposure without addition of other techniques, such as social skills training or cognitive restructuring, have been only sparsely studied. Studies that compared exposure *in vivo* with other strategies, such as cognitive procedures, or a combination of exposure and other techniques, have been conducted by Butler, Cullington, Hibbert, Klimes and Gelder (1984), Emmelkamp, Mersch, Vissia and Van der Helm (1985), Mattick and Peters (1988) and Mattick, Peters and Clarke (1989). Generally speaking, exposure produced significantly more improvement than no treatment, and its effects were comparable with those of cognitive therapy.

6. *Cognitive procedures are effective treatments for social phobia.* In many social phobics irrational cognitions seem to play a crucial part in the development and continuation of the complaints. Therefore, cognitive procedures can be expected to reduce the fear. However, a study by Biran, Augusto and Wilson (1981) did not support the use of cognitive procedures for patients with writing anxiety, a discrete form of social phobia. Two patients with this complaint were first treated with cognitive therapy, which did not change baseline level. In contrast, five sessions of exposure *in vivo*, given subsequently, were successful. The third patient, who received exposure *in vivo* immediately following the baseline, improved to the same extent. On the other hand, with cognitive therapy good results were achieved in reducing test anxiety, public speaking anxiety and interpersonal anxiety in volunteers (Rachman & Wilson, 1980).

Recently, some studies have been conducted with more homogeneous groups of patients (Emmelkamp et al., 1985; Mattick & Peters, 1988; Mattick, Peters & Clarke, 1989). It may now be concluded that cognitive therapy and exposure *in vivo* are equally effective for social phobia.

7. *There is only little evidence that a combination of different strategies should be preferred over a single treatment.* Up to now, several studies on the effectiveness of combined treatments have been conducted; in some of them the combined treatment was superior, in others no differences were found. A combination of social skills training and cognitive therapy was not superior to a single social skills training (Frisch, Elliott, Atsaides, Salva & Denney, 1982; Hatzenbühler & Schröder, 1982; Stravynski, Marks & Yule, 1982). Results of the more recently conducted studies on social phobics (Butler et al., 1984; Mattick, Peters & Clarke, 1989) have suggested but not clearly supported the use of a combination of strategies. The study by Butler et al. (1984) investigated whether anxiety management (a cognitive procedure) conduces to the effects of exposure *in vivo* alone. At post-test, both treatment groups showed improvement compared to the waiting list control group. In addition, the combined treatment group had gained larger progress with regard to the cognitive measures. At 6 months follow-up, the superiority of the combined treatment was also reflected on the other measures, although the differences were small. Mattick, Peters and Clarke (1989) compared three conditions: therapist-guided exposure *in vivo*, cognitive therapy, and a combination of both. All treatments were given in small groups. At post-test, all treated patients had improved compared to the non-treated control group. The differences among the treatment conditions were small, which was in line with the results of Emmelkamp, Mersch et al. (1985) who had found that exposure *in vivo* and cognitive therapy were about equally effective. The results at follow-up were interesting. The cognitive therapy group had further improved since the close of treatment, while the exposure group had slightly deteriorated. This fact, that cognitive therapy effects changes after the treatment has ended, has been reported in other studies as well. The effects of the combined treatment had not changed since post-test.

8. *If several procedures are used, it may be wise to use them successively, rather than at the same time.* Scholing and Emmelkamp (1989) treated nine social phobics in a multiple baseline design. Each patient received exposure *in vivo*, cognitive therapy (RET) and social skills training, but in different order. Each of the treatments consisted of six sessions, spread over 4 weeks, while 4 weeks of no-treatment were planned between each two treatment-blocks, in order to assess possible delayed treatment effects. The results showed that the treatments were equally effective. Irrespective of kind of treatment, the first treatment block yielded the largest improvement, which was enhanced by the treatments in the following blocks, suggesting that a combination of strategies is desirable. However, the results raise the question of how to combine techniques most effectively. Until now, no study has been published in which a combination of strategies at the same

time is compared with application of the same techniques consecutively.

9. *Treatments are to be attuned to individual characteristics.* The results described thus far showed only minor differences in effectiveness between several treatment strategies, which is in contrast with the findings for agoraphobia or simple phobia, where exposure *in vivo* has been repeatedly found to be the treatment of choice (see Chapter 6). It is generally agreed that social phobics form a rather heterogeneous group of patients. Some patients complain of strong psychophysiological reactions, but show adequate social skills, while others show reverse patterns. The so-called individual response pattern is strongly different, which raises the question whether this variability relates to the inconsistency of findings in studies on treatment effectiveness. It is of course presumable that, when comparing groups, it is impossible to find between-group differences as the within-group differences are too large. This would imply that careful assessment of the individual response pattern should precede the choice of the treatment strategy. Based upon the hypothesis that different response patterns can be distinguished among social phobics, several studies have been started to match response pattern and treatment (Trower et al., 1978; Fremouw, Gross, Monroe & Rapp, 1982; Turner & Beidel, 1985; Öst, Jerremalm & Johansson, 1981; Jerremalm, Jansson & Öst, 1986; Mersch, Emmelkamp, Bögels & Van der Sleen, 1989). For the sake of brevity we limit our discussion to the latter three. In these studies the anxiety dimensions as proposed in the three-systems model (behaviour, cognitions and physiology) were used to form different groups of social phobics. In each study two dimensions were chosen. Öst, Jerremalm and Johansson (1981) used somatic complaints and behaviour, and Jerremalm, Jansson and Öst (1986) used somatic complaints and cognitions, yielding somatic versus behavioural reactors and somatic versus cognitive reactors respectively. Treatments consisted of applied relaxation and cognitive therapy or social skills training respectively. It was hypothesized that a treatment attuned to the individual response pattern would give better results than the other treatment. All patients were treated individually. The first study partly supported the hypothesis, the second study did not. Mersch et al. (1989) divided patients into groups of behavioural versus cognitive reactors. All patients were treated in groups. In this study also no differences were found.

10. *Individual treatment may be as effective as group treatment.* It can be expected that, especially with social phobia, group treatment is clearly advantageous, mainly because group therapy offers a continual exposure to one of the most feared stimuli: a group of other people. Advantages and disadvantages of group treatment will be discussed later in this chapter. A direct comparison between group and individual treatment for social phobics has hardly been made until now; however, social inadequates (Van

Son, 1978) and unassertive women (Linehan, Walker, Bronheim, Haynes & Yerzeroff, 1979) showed no differences between both modalities.

In conclusion, we have seen that during the last decade more research has been carried out on treatment of social phobia; unfortunately, the results are not as yet unequivocal. At first the studies were mainly aimed at evaluating the effectiveness of social skills training. The results appeared to be precarious and, moreover, it became clear that many social phobics possessed adequate skills but were inhibited in using them because of anxiety and irrational cognitions. In recent years attention has shifted to exposure *in vivo* and cognitive strategies, which seem to be about equally effective. Treatment with special attention to individual response patterns has given disappointing results until now: all treatments were about equally effective for the different groups. It is unclear whether group and individual treatments have differential effects. Although the need to take into account the often reported heterogeneity of the social phobics seems self-evident, additional research is needed to specify more precisely how to optimally match patient characteristics and treatment.

CONDUCTING TREATMENT

Chapter 1 gives a description of Alex, who was referred to us with a generalized, serious social phobia. Alex was treated with behaviour therapy, consisting of separate blocks of social skills training, cognitive restructuring and exposure *in vivo* (in this order), each applied during six one-hour sessions spread over 4 weeks. The practical implementation of the treatment of social phobia will be illustrated by means of the course of this therapy. Emphasis will be on aspects of the social skills training, because this technique has been specifically developed for problems in social situations, and is only briefly discussed in the remaining chapters of this book. Before we give a description of the treatment, it should be noted that a treatment plan ought to be based on a functional analysis of the complaints, which may imply that other problems have to be treated first.

Illustrative of this approach is the case of a 45-year-old woman who was referred to us because of a social phobia. During the first interview she showed signs of an acute anxiety in social contacts which was a severe setback in daily life. However, working through the admission interviews prior to treatment, it became apparent that she had had to endure sexual assaults by her brother from her ninth to her fourteenth year. Thus many problems seemed to be a direct consequence of those traumatic experiences in the past. This made us invite her to choose between two possibilities: treatment directed at either her social phobia or her incest experiences. She opted for the latter. After a long-lasting and difficult but reasonably successful treatment, a short treatment of her social phobia concluded our programme.

Social skills training

Proceedings of Alex's treatment

During the first session of the social skills therapy block the intention of the treatment is explained to Alex. For a better understanding we shall give a full account of the most important parts of the explanation. "You have applied to us because you feel tense and uncertain in situations that compel you to mix with other people, in short in 'social situations'. This anxiety is therefore called 'social anxiety'. You also told us what situations are causing you trouble and how long they have been harassing you. This feeling of uncertainty can have different origins. One of them may be that you don't exactly know how to deal with certain situations; for example, you don't know how to criticize somebody or how to start a chat. Maybe you've never learned it or have indeed been able to manage those situations in the past but forgotten how to do it. Now you've reached a point of forgetting all about the moment when you first felt anxious. Really important is that you've learned to feel anxious, but that you can also learn to be less anxious. Thus, people can feel anxious because they don't know how to behave. It is important to keep in mind that your behaviour has effects on people around you. To give an example: imagine you're in company and want to join in a conversation. Yet you feel insecure, afraid that nobody will take notice of you. You speak softly and rapidly with your head bent down. As a result you may be sure that the other party doesn't pay any attention to what you're saying. That makes you feel more and more uncertain and will surely wear away your self-confidence. Just try to imagine the importance of somebody's behaviour. When people speak in a loud and clear voice and look into other people's eyes, the person addressed will soon get interested in what is actually being said. And that's good for one's self-confidence. The treatment in the coming sessions is aimed at making you feel less insecure by teaching you how to get certain social skills well under control. Important skills are: to begin, to keep going and to end a conversation, to give your opinion, to express or accept criticism or compliments and to make requests or to refuse something. The treatment includes the practising of various skills, especially the ones that cause you a lot of personal trouble. Of course, general skills that are important for everybody won't be forgotten."

The rationale having been given, and if desired extended with some examples from the patient himself, it is explained that skills will be taught by means of role-play, to be immediately followed by a short practical example wherever possible. It is desirable to do this in the first session, in the first place to make clear what will happen during the sessions, and second to help the patient cross the threshold to conducting role-play as quickly as possible. In addition, several points need to be stressed. First of all treatment sessions will be highly structured, most attention being spent on exercises. Next, it is useful for the patient to keep a diary of difficult situations, which will be used for role-playing. The therapist should warn the patient that training in skills may be a somewhat artificial task, especially in the beginning, and that the patient may feel role-playing is very different from reality. It is explained that the primary goal is to learn certain skills, and that acquiring new behaviour is often accompanied by feelings of clumsiness. Consequently, difficult situations and inherent skills are inventoried in agreement with the patient. If possible, it is advisable to make a hierarchy of situations and skills, which facilitates practising increasing grades of difficulty. When too-difficult skills are taught patients may be blocked, which can unnecessarily diminish their self-confidence. Nevertheless, it must be borne in mind that fear of critical examination is a central theme for all social phobics. Hence, it makes sense to practise reacting to criticism early in the treatment, no matter if it is difficult for the patient. The therapist can explain that responding to criticism is difficult for most people, and that it is one of the most important skills in interpersonal contacts, which makes it sensible to spend considerable time on it. Experience has taught us that many sessions should be dedicated to this skill. Generally speaking, in individual skills training one particular skill is discussed per session. The first step is a discussion about how the patient usually reacts in the relevant situation. It is often sensible to ask the patient to show his behaviour in a role-play. Next, it is discussed how the patient would like to react in reality, and which reaction would be most effective. It is important for the therapist to take this step carefully. Social skills training carries the risk that, although the therapist has a clear opinion about which behaviour is the most socially adequate, the patient might not share this idea with him. Practising skills will be useless if these differences are not noticed and discussed, since in that case it is quite possible that the patients, non-assertive as many social phobics are, might seem to follow the therapist's suggestions, whereas generalization of skills to daily life situations does not occur. The general rule in social skills training is that patients learn to behave in a way that balances between sufficiently standing up for themselves on the one hand, and taking into account other people's wishes and feelings on the other. After reaching agreement about the desired behaviour, the stage is set for practising. It may be useful if the therapist first demonstrates the skill (modelling). Consequently, the patient is offered the opportunity to practise in role-play, which may be monitored by videorecorder if desired, so that the patient can judge his own behaviour afterwards. Caution is required at this point: some patients are frightened at confrontation with their own behaviour to such an extent that they disappointedly drop out of treatment, having acquired a more negative self-image than they had at the start of treatment. Besides, the use of video is time-consuming. Although it is advisable to spend considerable time on skills that are labelled important by the patient himself, it is always useful to review a number of basic skills such as:

- attention-giving behaviour;
- opening, maintaining and closing a conversation;
- asking or refusing a favour;
- criticizing or reacting to criticism;
- stating one's opinion;
- self-disclosure.

During the review it will soon become clear which skills need improvement, so that more attention can be spent on them. The effectiveness of social skills training is highly dependent on the way role-plays are prepared, carried out and discussed. During the preparation important information is gathered about the situation that will be practised, which can be partly taken from the diaries. This phase can be kept short. It is not necessary for the therapist to know exactly what patients have gone through; he needs only to form a picture of the patients' (lack of) skills. In doing so, he has to keep in mind that patients might not have problems with situations as they actually occur, but with situations they are afraid will happen. This is illustrated by the next example.

One of our patients, a 23-year-old man, has been troubled by anxiety in social situations since he first attended secondary school. Although he did reasonably well at school (general A-level education), he left at the age of 16 because of his anxiety. Looking back he is ashamed of it now. Since then he has been out of work. During the first interview he mentions in particular his fear of walking in the streets of his home town and his aversion to going shopping, because he is afraid of meeting people and being obliged to strike up a conversation. During the social skills training, however, it turns out that having to have a chat with somebody is not actually the point. In reality he is scared stiff that one day he will run into one of his old schoolmates or, even worse, some of his teachers who will ask him how he is doing, what is his job and so on. Our patient knows for sure that such a situation will make him completely tongue-tied. He is afraid of saying that he has not got any diploma at all and has been out of work for years, in short, that he has rather serious problems. On the other hand he hates the idea of telling lies, as he knows that the mere thought of it can make him blush at once.

Here the problem concerns a situation that has never yet occurred, but that can be practised in role-play as well. It may be obvious that the time role-playing will take depends on the skill in question. Opening or closing a conversation, making or receiving a compliment, can be practised in one or two minutes, and repeated in several variants, while learning to maintain a conversation needs more time. The role-play is discussed afterwards. First, it is highly important that the therapist gives patients the opportunity to let off steam and to give the first impression of their performances; second that he emphasizes their successes. Even if results have been meagre, it is advisable to start by praising the positive points before correcting the less successful ones. In the discussion of weaknesses the therapist has to check whether patients recognize their failures in feedback, before giving concrete suggestions as much as possible. Finally, it must be stressed that several solutions are possible. We continue with the treatment of Alex.

First session

After the line of treatment has been explained, the therapist and Alex make an inventory of the situations and skills that cause special trouble. Alex emphasizes the problems of having to begin and continue a conversation. He never knows what to say and is terrified of pauses. During the first interview it has already transpired that, when in company, he is particularly tense. This is apparently connected with his fear of saying or doing peculiar things, so that as a result everybody will immediately turn their eyes on him. The therapist has already noticed that Alex usually speaks softly, quickly and monotonously. He has difficulty in listening, while he often looks downward and as a rule is sitting somewhat hunched up. The therapist intends bringing these points up at the general skills ("attention-giving behaviour") training. Alex agrees that six sessions will be spent on the following skills: first of all the practising of attentive behaviour or active listening, extending this later on with asking questions himself and trying to keep conversations going. Next come the first steps in the direction of responding to criticism, followed by giving and receiving compliments, as well as making requests to others (for example, requests for help or for doing things together). Alex himself feels that being able to keep a conversation going and to respond to criticisms are major skills for him to master. The remaining time of the session is spent on attention-giving behaviour and active listening. At first Alex protests weakly against "just listening", as he thinks that listening is the type of skill he can master best of all; he now wants to learn how to tell a story. The therapist, sympathizing with him on this point, suggests carrying out an experiment first. It will be a demonstration of Alex's listening capacities. Alex agrees and the therapist tells him about one of his hobbies. After a while the therapist asks Alex to repeat what he has said. This appears to be very difficult for him. Although Alex has said almost nothing in the meantime he can recall hardly anything of the therapist's story. The therapist then wants to know if Alex can still remember the things he was thinking of while listening. It turns out that Alex was mainly busy pursuing his own thoughts, such as: "I don't know what to say once more", "What an utter bore I am", "My hobbies aren't much fun" and the like. The therapist praises Alex for his honesty and self-knowledge and takes an opportunity to explain the difference between active and passive listening. He defines active listening as listening in such a way that one can repeat what the other has said and be able to put questions about it. After this the listening technique is practised a few times more, Alex being taught to repeat steadily growing pieces of the therapist's stories. It is agreed that Alex will continue practising active listening among his family to start with whenever an opportunity presents itself. In addition, he is given hand-outs describing not only the active listening skill, but also the issue of "how to ask open-ended questions".

Second session

Alex reports that he has practised very hard during the past week, mainly in the family circle; active listening had been quite a revelation to him. Yet he is worrying about the pauses that might crop up. The second session is spent on the development of active listening skills. Such matters as eye-contact, attitude and giving verbal comment (putting in little words or questions such as "then what?", "hm, hm", etc.) are practised. To make this kind of interruption gives Alex some trouble as he feels that, in doing so, he is going a bit over the top. The therapist can persuade him with the argument that every newly adopted skill makes most people feel ill at ease at first. Of course, Alex may decide for himself whether this is his style or not; on the other hand, it is essential for him that he should have a thorough command of it. After having practised four times he is doing better. It is followed by the next part of the active listening training, namely "asking open-ended questions" (questions that cannot be answered by a simple "yes" or "no", as contrasted with closed-ended questions). As Alex finds it hard to think up this sort of question, the therapist introduces an additional exercise. He formulates various closed-ended questions at a time, which Alex must try to turn into open ones. For example, the therapist's question: "Did you watch TV last night?" has to be turned into "What did you do last night?" This exercise soon makes clear the difference between the two kinds of questions. At the end of the second session Alex can maintain a good eye-contact, follow the therapist's talks more actively, recap them concisely and ask a few open-ended questions. The training of these skills is set again as homework.

Third session

During this session the subject "how to tell a story" is practised. Alex is first asked to show how this usually works out on him. This demonstration makes it clear that he is inclined to speak very quickly and in a rather rambling way. It makes him start floundering and then lapse into silence. Obviously there are several negative cognitions underlying this behaviour ("He isn't actually interested in what I'm saying" and "Look here, I know I'm a drag"). The therapist, in turn, decides not to take this subject up for the moment. The next activity is role-playing. Alex is asked to tell a story for 5 minutes, while in between the therapist will ask him encouraging questions. Alex, after having practised twice, is doing fairly well. By mutual agreement the assignment is made more demanding. Now Alex has to tell a story for 5 minutes while the therapist is observing him, but does not encourage him at all. This proves to be very difficult. At first Alex falls silent every now and then, just as the therapist had predicted at the preparatory discussion. The therapist keeps silent too (as agreed), so after a while Alex can pick up the thread again. This situation is run over four times, during which it is remarkable that Alex starts to make spontaneous comments about this rather awkward piece of training. It already anticipates the skill of "communicating about discussions on meta-level". At the end of the session the therapist points out that there may be a link with Alex's fear of using telephones. Is it possible that Alex gets into trouble as it is again a situation that causes minimal response from the other side? These situations obviously call for a rather stiff adherence to a self-reliant talking. Alex had never really thought about that, but he can imagine that lack of response is undoubtedly a major problem for him.

Fourth session

Alex enters the room rather depressed. To his mind everything has gone wrong this week. He has got the impression that he has not made any progress. He has practised telling things himself but that gave him a lot of trouble. He got the idea that others did not find his stories interesting at all and had noticed at once that he had been busy "practising", as he usually hardly ever talks spontaneously. The therapist is very understanding but at the same time he gives the events a positive twist: Alex has obviously done his utmost, and the information is important enough to be used in the current session. After all, Alex's story shows clearly that it is essential to continue practising frightening situations, such as people asking him for instance: "What's the matter with you? I never heard you talk that much". This and similar reactions are role-played several times, teaching Alex to respond in different ways. During the rest of the session attention is paid to learning to respond to criticism, a topic on which he had been given hand-outs the week before. It had just occurred that he had gone through a "crash situation" that week. As he had had no time to do his homework for school, the teacher had made a remark about his negligence. It had left him completely clammed up and unable to speak a word afterwards. Looking back he is thoroughly displeased about his reaction but also has his doubts about how he could have best reacted. After having exhaustively discussed the situation with the therapist Alex comes to the conclusion that in this case it had not been necessary to react very differently from how he actually did. He wished he had said in plain language: "I had no time to study the subject indeed, but I promise to catch up before next time". This situation is practised a few times; after that Alex does not find it difficult to respond adequately. Another point of discussion has also been made clear to Alex; any response to criticism depends greatly on the way that criticism is expressed, the question of whether it is reciprocal and, above all, whether it is considered appropriate. Several instances of these aspects are discussed and practised.

Fifth session

During the fifth session responding to criticism is practised again, this time in combination with expressing criticisms personally. On going through this subject it transpires that Alex hardly ever makes comments. He does not lose his temper quickly, he says, and if it happens, he seldom comes out with it. If, however, he feels pressed to react he is so worked up that he cannot speak normally any more and either begins to shout or gets blocked. Usually the latter will happen. Apart from training in relevant skills the therapist advises Alex to express his irritations at an earlier stage. On the other hand, however, it is clear that this can be difficult when one does not know exactly how to achieve it. The therapist then highlights a few points that should be observed when expressing criticism. Briefly: first, try to focus on the points you want to criticize, preferably in a most concrete way. After that you can move on to telling the other what exactly you want to criticize. This may for instance be introduced by the sentence: "I'd like to have a word with you". Once you have started speaking try to give examples and talk about your feelings towards the other person's behaviour. In addition, it will be all right to be straightforward in saying how you would like the other to behave; sometimes you can indicate in which way you can behave to make that easier. And finally, do not forget to obtain some response from the other. It needed several runs of role-playing to gain control of this kind of situation, which also made a strong appeal to Alex's imagination as the therapist was constantly changing roles.

Sixth session

For the time being this session is the last in which skills will be taught. In consultation with Alex it is decided which skills will be put into practice. Alex opts for taking initiatives in the sphere of making contacts with other people (for example proposals to collaborate on something) and learning to refuse requests made of him. This includes trying on clothes in a shop and walking out without buying anything. The therapist suggests killing two birds with one stone while practising taking initiatives: Alex, who is asked to ring the therapist from another room, will start a social chat about how he is getting on (the therapist role-playing an old schoolmate from secondary school). Alex will eventually propose spending the evening out together. This situation is practised twice, the therapist playing different persons. It shows that Alex has meanwhile learned a lot. Although conversations tend to pass off somewhat chaotically at times, Alex has evidently become a better listener and, what is more, also dares to ask questions. Pauses are less frightening; at least, they do not block him up any more. To propose doing things together is no problem either. The session is closed with an evaluation of the treatment given so far. Alex declares that it has been useful for him to learn skills. He feels that he has learned to respond more adequately, especially in his role-playing with the therapist. However, turning the acquired knowledge into daily routine is still very difficult for him. He knows exactly how to do the right thing, but when it really comes to a head, he soon feels quite lost. The therapist stresses that feelings of the kind are very common. In his opinion it will still take rather a lot of time and practice before the training will have produced lasting results. He concludes with the remark that Alex cannot expect to be freed of a problem in six sessions; a problem that has been so important to him in the past.

This concludes the description of six sessions of social skills training. Although Alex has practised a lot over a short period (generally speaking the pace is usually slower), it is obvious that more practice is desirable. The general principle remains the same. First, the skills that patients do not (sufficiently) master are inventoried, by means of diaries and demonstrations in role-play. Subsequently, it is discussed how their behaviour can be improved; the therapist demonstrating several possibilities. He can show some faulty examples as well, which gives the patient the opportunity of experiencing the effects of socially inadequate behaviour. Next, the desired behaviour is practised several times. In conclusion to this review we present some examples of exercises. Some creativity is often required to adjust them to the patient's personal circumstances. It is frequently found that eye-contact and volume of voice need attention, sometimes the posture of the patient is involved. Preceding practising eye-contact, the therapist can demonstrate several kinds of eye-contact (no contact at all, very short glances, or a fixed staring as the other extreme), after which the patient tries to imitate the right example. Volume of voice can be practised by reading texts aloud with a soft, medium loud and very loud voice, recorded on audiotape and listened back to by the patient. Once speaking loud and clear has been practised, attention can be given to the right intonation, taking into consideration the content of the sentences. Listening and summarizing can best be practised by asking the patient to repeat short extracts, such as sentences, followed by gradually longer extracts. An exercise in teaching the patient to ask open-ended questions was described earlier in session two. Those exercises in which the patient learns to respond to criticism are important. Most social phobics respond either with silence or by defending themselves. In the fifth session the skills important for responding to criticism are described. Some patients show such a persistent tendency to defend themselves that it makes sense to go into this matter first. Various techniques, some described by Smith (1973), are suitable for diminishing strong defensive reactions. Some of these techniques are not social skills in the first place, but seem to be helpful because they bring about changes on a cognitive level (by associating them with the irrational cognition: "It is disastrous to make mistakes"). The therapist has to emphasize that these techniques are not applicable in every situation.

Problems that may occur during social skills training

The discussion about skills sometimes reveals that the patient disagrees with the therapist about what is meant by socially adequate behaviour. To establish a sound therapeutic relationship it is important that the therapist should approve of the patient's divergent opinion, for example by telling him at an early stage that it is hardly ever a matter of one type of social behaviour being superior. There should always be a check of which reaction suits the patient most, and of which one has his approval. However, it does not imply that the therapist has to bow to patients' opinions all along. Patients' aversions to a certain type of response often weaken considerably if the therapist explains that the first aim is to supply them with more alternatives, and that practising in the session does not automatically imply that the skill must be applied in daily life. Besides, the patient's objections may point to irrational cognitions. This is another reason for the therapist to keep stimulating the patient to raise his objections, so that they can serve as a point of departure for discussion of the relevant cognitions. In the same way the therapist needs to encourage the patient to speak up if he cannot manage to use the skills in daily life situations. The first thing to check is whether the situation was essentially different from what was anticipated during the session, and further whether irrational cognitions had had adverse effects. Especially in social skills training, and to a lesser degree in cognitive therapy as well, the social phobia can impede the therapeutic relationship. Being engaged in role-play is experienced by the patient as a performance situation, with the therapist in the role of assessor (which indeed is only partly an irrational cognition). The fear of negative evaluation often reveals itself by frequent fits of laughter during the role-play, acting out of character, or repeatedly postponing the start of the role-play by continuing "talking about". A thorough explanation by the therapist, emphasizing practice instead of performance and admitting the artificial character of the role-play, is of paramount importance. Apart from that, the therapist has to serve as a proper model by starting to practise over and again, assuming that things will pass off easier after a few sessions. If patients have persistent trouble in role-playing, time has to be spent on an investigation into the origins of this.

Cognitive therapy

Cognitive therapy is based on the assumption that feelings in general, and problematic feelings in particular, are not evoked by reality or certain events, but by the person's cognitions about them. The aim of the therapy is to trace these cognitions, compare them with what really happened and, if necessary, replace them by more realistic or rational thoughts. In Chapter 4 a description was given of several variants that can be distinguished, although essentially they all roughly converge on the same point. We will not go further into this matter, but will give an illustration of the application to social phobics, Alex's treatment being a starting point. In this therapy mainly Rational Emotive Therapy was used, thoughts being challenged by means of ABCDE-schemata. The meaning of the letters, as described in Chapter 4, is:

1. *Activating event*: an objective description of the event.
2. *Beliefs*: the irrational, anxiety-provoking thoughts.
3. *Consequence*: the emotional results of the thoughts.
4. *Discussion*: questions that are posed to test the thoughts against reality.
5. *Evaluation*: the replacement (more rational) thoughts resulting from the discussion.

First session

Alex is given detailed information, the essentials of which are summarized here. "So far we've been mainly occupying ourselves with the way you behave and have been learning social skills. Although these aspects are important, they don't stand alone. Feeling distressed in social situations does not always imply that you don't know how to behave; it may also be connected with the way you're used to assessing certain situations. I'll give an example: Suppose you've become a member of a club and it's the first time you go there. Everybody is sociable, but you're sitting by yourself in a corner. You're definitely ill at ease and think that everybody is watching you. When at last you decide to start talking to somebody, it's hard to find the right words and the person you're talking to breaks off the conversation in no time. Anyhow, when you return home, it's only unpleasant feelings that prevail. When you go to the club next time, your previous experience will surface, which makes you feel out of balance in advance. As soon as you start to talk to somebody you feel your face reddening slowly. You feel worse than the time before and you return home early. Next time you decide to stay away because there isn't the least bit of fun in going there. The point is that people who have to cope with this sort of problem generally think too much of what can go wrong. Anxious people are often too concerned and frequently worry about things they're afraid of. The negative sides of a situation can be grossly exaggerated. Take that club: right from the start you think: 'If only I haven't to fumble for words', 'Suppose I've to sit aside the whole evening again' and so on. Thoughts like that make you feel more nervous and distressed than ever, so that exactly those things will happen that tend to scare you stiff. It's the vicious circle of blushing, being tongue-tied and building up excessive distress. It's basically your own negative and unreasonable thoughts about a specific situation that are troubling you so much, not the situation itself. What I want to get across to you in the coming sessions is that you can change your outlook on things that happen. Events that make you anxious and tense are mostly not the real cause of your failures, it is the way you judge them; in other words a question of attending thoughts. Can you imagine your feelings being stirred up by your own vision and thoughts? Over the years these things tend to become an automatic process. Of course, it isn't in your line to check your thoughts when something happens. Seemingly, certain events automatically evoke certain feelings. But if you really want to get rid of or do something about feelings of anxiety, distress, disappointment or upset, it is all important for you to become conscious of these feelings so that you can trace them back to their source. This can be done by realizing what you think every time you feel uncomfortable and also if what you're telling yourself is rational or not. This procedure will probably not be an instant success but if you try again and again you will find out soon that in the long run things straighten out according to your wishes." Alex can accept the therapist's views and explanation. However, he has difficulty in imagining how this will work out for him personally. He is inclined to think that in social situations he cannot think of anything, that his mind goes completely blank. The remaining part of the session is spent on discussing the ABCDE scheme by giving attention to a situation that frequently harasses Alex: asking questions in class. Winding up the session, the therapist asks Alex to write down (at home) not more than one situation daily. The situation must have displeased him and, what is more, Alex must try to recall the thoughts he had when he was in that particular situation. The therapist emphasizes that cognitive strategies are hard to master, adding that he would be very pleased if Alex could manage to fill in the ABC part of the form only. It would offer an opportunity to spend the next session together provoking the thoughts he had when he was going through those situations.

Second session

Alex has written down various situations at home. It had given him a lot of trouble, however, to arrange them according to the scheme. To give a description of the situations (A) had been quite easy, as had the feelings going with them (C). Enumerating his thoughts, however, had been a complete failure. He had been able to figure out only one thought, so he wondered whether the situation itself had been well-chosen. The scheme runs as follows:

A. The telephone is ringing (at home); I have to answer it.
B. Who is on the phone?
C. Distress, shuddering.

The therapist thinks it is an excellent situation for Alex to start with and stresses again that in principle every situation that evokes certain feelings can serve the purpose. The remaining time of the session is spent on working out the following analysis. First a closer look is taken at Alex's description of the situation (A). Alex agrees with the therapist that the description of A has not been very objective (done as a camera could have done it). The point is that the second part anticipates a thought that would better have been described under B. Thus the correct sequence is: A: the telephone rings (at home) and C: feelings of distress and trembling. Alex must admit that generally people do not get stressed in similar situations, obviously because they consider them from a different point of view. Discussing these thoughts, the therapist wonders why Alex gets stressed at the question "who's on the line?" He does not think that there is anything exciting about that question. Anyhow, it seems not to correspond with the sense of distress mentioned under C. He asks Alex to replace the question by a more definite statement. However, the only thought Alex can produce is: "I know I'll be lost for words again". To check if perhaps additional factors have to be taken into account, the therapist proposes role-playing an imaginary exercise together. This is a kind of exercise that stimulates Alex, with his eyes closed, to relive the situation of the ringing telephone with the assistance of the therapist. The latter helps him by giving at the same time a realistic review of the situation. At first Alex shows signs of distress, thinking that the therapist is scrutinizing him. As time goes by it comes more naturally to him, enabling him to produce new thoughts after only a few minutes activation of his imagination. These cognitions are a basis for further treatment. At the end of the sessions the analysis runs as follows:

A. The telephone is ringing (at home).
B. I have to answer it. I'd rather not do it. My brother Theo may come in a few minutes and then I'll be at a loss what to say. What an awful duffer I am, I bet I've to say "no" in a few moments and I'm sure I can't manage. I'm trembling badly; I'm sure people can tell from my shaky voice that I'm stressed.
C. Distressed, shaky.
D. Who is telling you to answer the phone? How do you know Theo will come in soon and why would you become tongue-tied that very moment? Do you really think it will serve your purpose (that is, being more relaxed and able to answer the telephone) when you keep telling yourself you're an awful duffer? Who says that somebody will ask you something you cannot but refuse? How do you know your voice will tremble and if it does, who cares? Why be upset when other people notice you're distressed?
E. Of course, there isn't anything that compels me to take action. Why bother about ringing telephones? However, if I do not answer it, I'm sure I'd hate myself all the more for it, so I'd better answer it right away. I don't know if Theo will come in and if he does, I can speak a few words all the same; maybe it'll sound a bit tense. I could kick myself but that wouldn't do any good. I know it's an uphill task right from the start, so I would be greatly relieved if only I could take up the receiver and listen.

Third to sixth sessions

These sessions pass off in the same way. However, they gradually shift from "superficial" cognitions such as: "I'll surely be at a loss what to say" or "I can't allow myself to feel stressed" to more profound thoughts. In Alex's case the basic assumptions in particular are important, for example: "I expect people to like me" and "I shall be perfect in everything". Repeated discussions of these points teach Alex that he can recognize them in all kinds of situations, giving him an opportunity to make less excessive demands of himself. In Chapter 6 a fragment of a therapeutic interaction is given. It illustrates how such thoughts can be challenged.

In Chapter 4 several general aspects important for the implementation of cognitive therapy were mentioned. The essential point probably is that the therapist has to make sure he does not become a severe judge, who holds patients responsible for their unreasonable thoughts. Cognitive therapy is most effective when patients learn, by means of a Socratic-like dialogue with the therapist, to study their own cognitions intensively, and to put question marks against them if necessary. Experience has shown that with social phobics cognitive therapy has raised some specific problems, that will be briefly discussed. The therapist needs to have an eye for the patient's fear of being judged and, what is more, of being at fault. This fear can surface in several ways, to begin with during a session. Comments such as: "My mind is empty" or "I don't know what my thoughts are" can refer to fear of judgement. More intelligent patients in particular often seem to understand very quickly what the therapist is aiming at, and are capable of enumerating various rational thoughts, which can give the therapist the impression that cognitions are no problem. However, this kind of behaviour can be the result of the fear of judgement, a kind of fear that urges patients to hold back essential thoughts they are ashamed of. The incapacity to make analyses at home may be caused by fear of negative evaluation as well. Moreover, the principles of cognitive therapy are quite simple and patients can learn fairly soon to trace their irrational thoughts. The therapist, however, needs to bear in mind that much more time is required before patients are capable of responding on the basis of realistic attitudes to daily life. As regards the contents of the thoughts, it has become obvious that social phobics often report similar irrational expectations and wishes. These phenomena have been described in several publications, for example by Ellis (1962). Smith (1973) put a number of rational variants of these cognitions in ten "assertive fundamental rights", namely:

1. The right to judge one's own behaviour, thoughts and feelings.
2. The right to withhold excuses or explanations of one's own behaviour.
3. The right to decide to search or not to search for a solution for other people's problems.
4. The right to change one's opinion.
5. The right to make mistakes and be held responsible for them.
6. The right to say: "I don't know".
7. The right to be irrational in taking decisions.
8. The right to say: "I don't understand".
9. The right to say: "I don't care".
10. The right not to exert oneself to be liked by others in order to be able to socialize with them.

Apart from dealing with the contents of cognitions, it is important to pay attention to irrational styles of thinking. Examples are applying double standards, black and white thinking, and concentration on negative aspects of events, while neglecting the positive sides.

Exposure *in vivo*

In many phobic complaints gradual exposure *in vivo* has proved to be very effective in reducing anxiety, as was stated earlier. Exposure *in vivo* is based on the principle that individuals tend to avoid situations that provoke feelings of distress, that the avoidance behaviour is reinforced by means of stress reduction, and that this behaviour generalizes to other situations. The basic principles of exposure, set out in Chapter 4, are simple: overcoming the avoidance behaviour (by again entering, in gradually increasing difficulty, into the feared situations); learning to endure the distress, while noticing that it fades away if duration of the confrontation with the feared stimulus is of adequate length. The application of exposure *in vivo* for social phobia, however, creates a number of specific problems that will be briefly discussed below. We refer to Butler (1985) for an extensive overview.

1. Due to the unpredictability of most social situations (since they depend on the reactions of other people) it is not simple to build up a proper hierarchy of gradually more difficult situations. It is even more difficult to practise them consecutively.
2. Many social situations are time-limited, for example introducing oneself to other people and expressing or accepting criticisms. Generally, it is not long enough for the anxiety to ease off.
3. Many social phobics seem to receive exposure relatively often. Life is a concatenation of social situations, and contacts with other people are daily practice. Nevertheless, it does not reduce distress in social situations. One of our patients, for example, complained that he still felt anxious when looking at other people, in spite of the fact that he hardly ever avoided eye-contact, forcing himself not to cast down his eyes.
4. Whereas agoraphobia centres around the fear of becoming physically unwell or even of having a heart attack or dying, the main fear in social phobia is critical judgement by other people, whether or not it is pronounced. Exposure *in vivo* generally proves to agoraphobics that their most feared event, fainting or a heart attack, does not happen. Social phobics, on the other hand, keep stirring up worries about other people's opinions, and are often convinced that others judge them negatively, being too polite to speak their mind.

These aspects are a serious drawback for the "normal" use of exposure *in vivo* for social phobics, that is searching for situations of gradually increasing difficulty and holding on until the anxiety subsides. It implies that for this group the exposure has to be adjusted in several ways. To start with, it can be wise to emphasize the necessity of frequent practice of difficult situations when it is impossible to practise extensively. In addition, it should be explained to patients that a gradual build-up can be desirable, but is not always possible. When a hierarchy is set up it is urgent to check whether themes can be found in situations feared by the patient. If so, separate hierarchies should be constructed, each around one theme, that may also be practised separately. In doing this, it is conceivable that patients make considerable progress in one hierarchy, while another has not yet even started. Thorough examination of avoidance behaviour is of paramount importance. In the first place situations avoided by patients need to be listed, for example attending meetings, inviting guests at home, and so on. In the second place, and often more important, attention will have to be paid to those behaviours that enable patients to prevent certain situations from occurring. For example, some social phobics are very talkative in order to make sure that other people will not get any opportunity to bring up difficult topics. Similarly, frequent apologizing for "mistakes" cannot always be considered a sign of politeness, since it might in fact be meant to prevent others from making critical remarks. In exposure treatment patients are encouraged to show the kind of behaviour that usually provokes the feared situations, giving them the opportunity to get used to them. In clinical practice the hierarchy is constructed as follows. First, it is determined which themes are significant to situations feared by the patient, for example making contacts with strangers, showing one's feelings, admitting to others about not knowing certain things, bringing up difficult subjects, making mistakes, receiving criticism, telling something in a group, being watched, taking initiatives. Although social phobia essentially centres around fear of being critically judged by others, this fear can fluctuate in strength in various situations. Apart from that, a combination of these themes is supposed to play a part. Next, different assignments concerning the themes are written on cards, which are set by the patient in order of gradually increasing difficulty (according to the principle of the fear thermometer explained in Chapter 4). Some assignments cannot be described exactly at this stage, but that is not a great problem. At the time when the assignment is to be practised, however, it is wise to thoroughly discuss the behaviour the patient has to show in that particular situation, the people he has to practise with, and which restaurants, shops must be involved, and so on.

As examples of assignments around the theme "the adoption of an assertive attitude" can be mentioned:

1. Go to a shop selling tools / domestic appliances / cameras or similar items and ask for detailed advice about one particular article. Think up a few questions in advance, for example about prices and guarantees, and the like. Also ask for demonstrations.

2. Go to a shop selling clothes or shoes and ask somebody to help you. Try on at least five different articles, but do not buy anything.
3. Collect one article in a supermarket at a busy moment, take care to have the exact cash, and ask the first person in front of the queue if he minds your being first.
4. Go to a number of restaurants, cheap as well as expensive ones, and ask if it is possible to make a reservation for a dinner party of 15 persons.
5. Go to a department store, to the section selling alarm clocks, and try out different types. If someone tackles you about it, tell him that you are looking for a clock with a loud and clear sound.
6. Go into a shop and ask if you can make use of the toilet.

It has to be kept in mind that, as a matter of fact, exposure assignments do not aim at practising socially adequate behaviour in the first place, although in some assignments this may happen automatically. On the other hand, it may sometimes be wise to have patients practise socially inadequate behaviour. For example, to apologize for a mistake is generally considered socially adequate; asking the patient to drop this behaviour may be more effective for reducing anxiety in the longer run. In the same way it is not considered socially adequate to keep eye-contact with someone for longer than 5 to 8 seconds. In order to get used to eye-contact, however, it can be very useful to practise for longer periods.

We conclude with a short summary of Alex's exposure treatment.

First session

In the meantime Alex has had a 4 weeks break which, to his mind, passed off reasonably well. He has the impression that he has succeeded in keeping up with the progress he had made during the former sessions. This session is spent on explanation of the principles of exposure *in vivo* and setting up a hierarchy. During the explanation it is emphasized that the treatment includes prolonged or frequent practising of difficult situations, and that abandoning the situation before the anxiety has gradually subsided will be strongly discouraged. During the discussion it becomes clear that Alex still avoids many situations. In his own opinion this behaviour is partly a matter of habit. He has noticed that he is less reluctant to enter into several situations than before. On the other hand, he admits that he still tends to withdraw from difficult situations. Summarizing, the exposure hierarchy is as follows (ranging from the simplest to the most difficult assignment):

Relating to the theme "Being watched by other people":

1. Walk through a busy street in the centre of the city, in a self-confident way. Walk straight on, do not step aside for other people, have a good look at everyone you are passing. Ask some people for the time, or the way to a certain street. Make it more difficult by singing while you walk, or by asking after a street you are already in.

2. Walk in front of busy terraces or visit a number of busy cafés. Make several stops to look closely at everybody on the terrace or in the café. Repeat this several times, until you feel less anxious.
3. Ride in a city bus during the rush hour. Take a seat in front of somebody else and look at that person regularly. Once you are able to do so, make it more difficult by opening a conversation.
4. Take a seat in a busy café and order a cup of coffee. Look around you and observe other people closely. At any rate, stay as long as necessary to get the feeling that you have become less tense, but at least 45 minutes. Repeat the same in another café.
5. Make several telephone calls while other people are around. Start with the easiest calls (for example ask for information about train schedules). First do it in the company of the least "difficult" people you know. Work on to more and more difficult situations.
6. Visit a sauna together with somebody else.

Relating to the theme "Assuming assertive attitudes":

1. Visit several clothes shops and try on various articles. Ask a member of staff to help you. Leave the shop without having bought anything.
2. Ask a few questions during the informatics lessons at school. Keep listening carefully and try to summarize the answer in your own words.
3. Ask some "stupid" questions, that is to say questions to which you already know the answer.

Relating to the theme "Taking initiatives":

1. Start shopping again in the supermarket near your home. If you bump into acquaintances start a conversation.
2. Telephone a friend from your former class and invite him to do something together with you, for example going to the cinema.
3. Try for one day to fall into short conversations with people from your class.
4. During the coffee break at school talk about something you have witnessed in the past few days. Take care to keep the discussion going for at least 10 minutes. Try to draw others into the conversation. Practise with increasing numbers of people.
5. Start a conversation during the coffee break with a girl you like and keep the conversation going for at least 10 minutes.
6. Visit a friend without being invited. Ask if you are welcome. If so, stay for at least one and a half hours. Try to keep the conversation going.
7. Invite a girl to spend an evening out with you.
8. Go out with a girl; invite her to dinner in a restaurant, then go with her to the cinema.

Sessions 2–6

In general, exposure assignments pass off very well. Alex is aware that he usually starts by being very tense, but also that his feelings change quickly. He reports that at last the exposure has restored a feeling of freedom, a feeling that he has regained the ability to go anywhere, anyway, that he can look strangers straight in the eyes. Trying on clothes and asking for information in shops is becoming easier and easier after some initial effort. Making telephone calls is less difficult than he had expected. However, assignments compelling him to take initiatives are still giving trouble. Several "assignments-in-between" appear to be necessary, as the assignments formulated in the first session were too difficult. Thinking up new assignments has now mainly become Alex's business. He gradually develops creative ways of finding new opportunities for practice. After six sessions the exposure block is closed, and 4 weeks without treatment follow. When Alex comes back, he points out that, to his mind, there is an overall improvement. He needs further support, however, and he feels that he has profited most from cognitive therapy and exposure *in vivo*, which is affirmed by the therapist. Therefore it is decided to proceed with a combination of these strategies for a number of sessions. In the beginning the sessions are held weekly, after the eighth session the frequency is gradually reduced. After 15 sessions (33 in total) the treatment can be closed. During the last session Alex says that his life has radically changed. This is partly caused by the fact that he has got a girlfriend. He got to know her by way of an advertisement that he placed on his own initiative. This is one of the reasons for his greatly increased self-confidence. Looking back he feels that he has profited most from cognitive therapy. He has got the impression that he can cope more successfully with possible relapses, now that he has learnt to analyse his own thoughts.

Group treatment versus individual treatment

In discussing the results of treatment studies it was reported that direct comparison of group and individual treatment has not been carried out with social phobics, and further that no differences were found with socially inadequate patients and non-assertive women. Both modalities have their own advantages and disadvantages, which will be discussed briefly. The main advantage of group treatment is the continuous exposure to the situation that many social phobics fear most. In addition, many social phobics are convinced that their fears are uncommon and exclusively theirs. The mere recognition that others share the same problem can put things in the right perspective. Comparison with others can teach a number of patients that their problems are not as serious as they thought them to be. Finally, a definite advantage of group treatment is the possibility of calling on the active assistance of other group members, by acting as a model or opponent in social skills training, and by providing different cognitions that can be used for mutual comparison. Similarly, some exposure assignments, such as making eye-contact, or making a telephone call while being watched by others, can be conducted more easily in a group. The most prominent disadvantage of a group treatment, resulting from time restrictions, is the impossibility of doing sufficient justice to individual problems. In addition, for some patients a group is so threatening that they feel too inhibited to participate sufficiently, which can ruin the effectiveness of the treatment. Finally, comparison with other patients can also have adverse effects: some patients may come to the conclusion that, even among people with similar problems, they are the least skilled and have the strongest fears.

Treatment of fear of trembling or blushing

In Chapter 1 we presented Rob, who was referred to us because of his fear of blushing and sweating when in company. Such complaints are usually considered an expression of a (potentially more generalized) social phobia, and have therefore consequently been treated similarly, for example by means of social skills training or cognitive therapy. However, the results of these treatments have often been disappointing. It seems that this is partly caused by the fact that a treatment for social phobia in general does not pay enough attention to the specific nature of these complaints. Characteristic of the fear of blushing and trembling is a vicious circle: fear of the specific symptoms leads to catastrophizing cognitions and enhanced distress which, in return, make the symptoms even worse. Besides, problems seem to be maintained through an extensive, although sophisticated, avoidance behaviour, which has to be thoroughly inventoried during treatment. Avoidance of blushing can include wearing high-necked sweaters, large, dark-coloured glasses, excessive growth of beards, or thick layers of make-up. Frequently occurring phenomena are also avoiding rooms with bright artificial light, sitting back in a group, stooping quickly to pick something up, and avoiding difficult topics. Avoidance of trembling is generally more connected to specific situations, and can be limited to situations such as drinking or eating with other people, signing cheques or administering injections. This avoidance can take serious forms, which may be illustrated by the case of a 30-year-old woman who became aware, while singing at a party, that her hands were trembling so strongly that she could not hold her music. She disappeared to the toilet and waited until the singing was over. Later in the evening she noticed that her hands started to tremble whenever she had a drink. After that evening she hardly ever took drinks in the company of other people, and only if she had taken a tranquillizer. Avoidance of sweating is often connected with situations which give the person a feeling of being trapped and not being able to leave unnoticed. In this context, having lunch or dinner with others in a restaurant, or participating in certain games should be mentioned. In extreme cases, even situations in which sweating is very normal, such as sports or saunas, are increasingly avoided. Many patients with similar complaints are convinced that they would not have any problems in social situations if only they could be sure never to blush, tremble or sweat again. In fact it seems plausible that the vicious circle makes up the central problem. De Jong (1987) presented a number of strategies to break through this circle. Predominant are the paradoxical intention (asking the patient to blush or tremble as often as possible), and the displaying of the symptoms to other people. The third strategy, to be particularly considered when the former two are too complicated, is called "giving acceptable explanations" for the symptoms. Patients with fear of trembling are often afraid that they will be taken for neurotics or alcoholics, and the mere availability of alternative explanations is sometimes sufficient to break through the vicious circle. In our view such an approach has one serious drawback. That is that it does not have the intended effect on the irrational fear-provoking cognitions; patients do not learn how to deal with the situation that other people indeed perceive them as neurotics. Anyhow, the use of alternative explanations may be a first step in the right direction. At our department a study has been conducted in which the effectiveness of exposure *in vivo* and cognitive restructuring, whether or not combined, have been evaluated in larger groups of patients ($n = 30$) with fear of bodily symptoms. An essential part of this treatment was the establishment of realistic goals for treatment, in consultation with the patient. Blushing or trembling were labelled as individual susceptibilities, or even as handicaps patients would have to learn to deal with. The treatment was aimed not at dispelling blushing or trembling as such, but rather the fear of those symptoms. Nevertheless, it was expected that the symptoms in question would actually become less frequent. Preliminary results indicate that both treatments brought about substantial improvement, with no clear differences among the various treatment conditions as far as the groups are concerned.

Treatment of dysmorphophobia

Dysmorphophobia is described in Chapter 1 as a preoccupation with certain parts of one's own body, although from a purely objective point of view there is no reason for it. This disorder is relatively uncommon. Although it is not considered a variant of social phobia according to DSM-III-R, there are some common grounds, especially with respect to the avoidance of social situations and the fear of social judgement. As yet, researchers have paid little attention to this disorder, with the exception of some case studies. A treatment covering only exposure *in vivo* gave positive results with five patients suffering from this complaint (Marks & Mishan, 1988). Not only did the avoidance behaviour diminish significantly, the delusional conviction weakened as well. In the treatment it is important for the therapist to take the complaint seriously, rather than taking the part of well-meaning relatives and friends, who over and again assure the patient (in vain) that they "don't see anything strange".

Evers (1988) described a strategy that may be effective for a number of dysmorphophobics. In essence, the treatment is based on the proposition that dysmorphophobia is a strong belief that some part of the body looks awful, plus the conviction that other people will undoubtedly notice. The therapist's aim is to succeed in creating a situation proving unequivocally that impartial observers think the patient does not show any abnormality. Then it will be impossible for the patient to hold to the second conviction, which must lead to cognitive dissonance. One method of reducing the dissonance is to change the perception of one's own body.

This ends the discussion about various aspects of treatment of social phobia. However, one point of common knowledge should be stressed here. As stated before, it is hard to discriminate between "normal" and "deviant" social anxiety. Rather, a large number of social phobics have problems in social situations only because they think that they are abnormal. They cannot prevent themselves from feeling some tension in certain situations, and are convinced that other people will notice their distress. Consequently, they shun being exposed to any tension. It is important to spend considerable time on these unreasonable demands during treatment, which may straighten out the problems considerably.

8 Treatment of Obsessive-Compulsive Disorders

Systematic desensitization was the first form of behavioural therapy applied to patients with obsessive-compulsive disorders (Wolpe, 1958). The results, however, were not very encouraging. Beech and Vaughan (1978) and Emmelkamp (1982) presented an overview of the research in this area and came to the conclusion that the success ratio for systematic desensitization was below 50%. The actual success ratio for systematic desensitization may be even lower if one realizes that only case studies were reported, that authors tend to report successful cases only, and that editors of journals usually publish successful treatments. Other treatment procedures that have been reported in the literature are implosive therapy, exposure *in vivo*, imaginary and *in vivo* flooding, aversion therapy, and covert sensitization. Generally, these also related to case studies. Although the theoretical rationales for these procedures differ, all these treatments share a common element, that is exposure to anxiety-inducing stimuli. This exposure can be performed imaginarily as well as *in vivo*. In aversion therapy and covert sensitization the patient is asked to imagine obsessive scenes. When the patient envisions these scenes vividly enough, the therapist introduces a strong aversive stimulus. This may be a mild electric shock or, in the case of covert sensitization, the imagination of aversive consequences. One may wonder, however, whether the use of these aversive stimuli is necessary, considering the fact that recent literature shows that exposure procedures *per se* and exposure *in vivo* procedures in particular are effective as treatment in obsessive-compulsive patients.

Exposure and response prevention

Meyer and his colleagues (Meyer, Levy & Schnurer, 1974) developed a treatment for obsessive-compulsive inpatients consisting of response prevention, modelling and exposure *in vivo*. After a functional analysis of the obsessive-compulsive behaviour had been made, nurses were instructed to prevent the patients from performing their obsessive-compulsive rituals. As soon as this response prevention had led to the elimination of compulsive rituals, the patients were gradually exposed to more stressful situations in which the compulsive rituals were usually provoked (i.e. exposure *in vivo*). During this treatment phase modelling was applied. First, the therapist performed the action of which the patient was afraid, for example touching "contaminated" objects, such as underwear, and next he encouraged the patient to copy this behaviour. Meyer and his colleagues described the results of this programme in 15 patients. In most of them treatment appeared to be successful. Next, a number of researchers studied the various components of this package on their merits. The results are discussed briefly.

1. *Gradual exposure* in vivo *is as effective as flooding* in vivo (Boersma, den Hengst, Dekker & Emmelkamp, 1976; Marks, Hodgson & Rachman, 1975). This implies that it is not necessary to invoke maximal anxiety during exposure *in vivo*. Therefore this method is preferred to flooding, because little exposure invokes less tension and is easier for the patient to carry out.

2. *Generally modelling by the therapist does not lead to greater treatment effect*. Although empirical research in a limited number ($n = 5$) of patients (Hodgson, Rachman & Marks, 1972) suggests that modelling enhances the effect of exposure *in vivo*, later studies suggest this is not the case (Boersma et al., 1976; Rachman, Marks & Hodgson, 1973).

3. *Treatment can be carried out by the patient in his or her natural environment without the therapist being present*. Emmelkamp and Kraanen (1977) compared therapist-controlled exposure and self-controlled exposure. In the latter method, the patient carried out the exposure programme on his own by means of homework assignments, without the therapist being present. Although no significant differences in effects were found between the two treatments, at the follow-up, a month after completion of the treatment, self-controlled exposure *in vivo* proved more effective than therapist-controlled exposure. In a study by Emmelkamp, van Linden van den Heuvell, Riiphan and Sanderman (1989) self-controlled exposure appeared to be as effective as exposure when the therapist was present. Combining the results of both studies, it can be concluded that treatment of obsessive-compulsive patients in their own homes without the therapist being present is equally effective and obviously more cost-effective.

4. *Engaging the partner in the treatment is no more effective than treating the patient alone*. From studies by Emmelkamp and De Lange (1983) and Emmelkamp, de Haan and Hoogduin (1990) it appeared that engaging the partner in exposure *in vivo* did not enhance the treatment effect. In the study by Emmelkamp and De Lange the partner-condition appeared to be more effective at the end of treatment, but at the follow-up a month later this effect had disappeared.

5. *Exposure sessions of long duration are more effective than those of short duration*. Rabavilas, Boulougouris, Stefanis and Vaidakis (1977) investigated the optimal duration of exposure sessions in obsessive-

compulsive patients. Exposure *in vivo* of long duration (2 hours) appeared to be significantly more effective than a short duration exposure. The latter consisted of 10 minutes exposure followed by 5 minutes of neutral material, followed by 10 minutes exposure and so on, for a period of 2 hours. These repeated series of short exposures proved to produce a negative effect on the patients' mood. Therefore it can be concluded that exposure sessions should be of long duration in order to be effective.

6. *Exposure to the anxiety-provoking stimuli as well as response prevention of the compulsive action are both essential components.* In several studies the respective effects of exposure alone and response prevention alone were compared in obsessive-compulsive patients. Exposure generally led to more anxiety reduction than response prevention, whereas response prevention generally led to a greater decrease of compulsive rituals than exposure did. The combination of both procedures proved to yield the most favourable effect (Foa, Steketee & Milby, 1980a; Foa, Steketee, Graspar, Turner & Latimer, 1984). A remarkable number of patients appeared to relapse when treatment consisted of only one of the components. In summary, both exposure *in vivo* and response prevention are essential elements in the treatment of obsessive-compulsive disorders.

7. *Exposure* in vivo *versus exposure in imagination.* Although exposure *in vivo* has proved to be more effective in simple phobia and agoraphobia than exposure in imagination, the differential effect of both forms of exposure in obsessive-compulsive patients is less clear. There is only little research reported thus far and this renders no unequivocal results (Rabavilas et al., 1977; Foa, Steketee & Milby, 1980a; Foa et al., 1980c; Foa, Steketee & Grayson, 1985). In general, however, exposure *in vivo* seems to be more effective than exposure in imagination. However, in patients with checking compulsions imaginary exposure appears to be as effective as exposure *in vivo*. This could be explained by the fact that it is more difficult to expose patients with checking compulsions to situations they fear. For example, in patients who have to carry out all kinds of checking actions for fear of a disaster (for example, a war or something dreadful happening to their family), it is easier to have these scenes imagined than to apply exposure *in vivo*.

8. *Frequent exposure is no more effective than spaced exposure.* Emmelkamp et al. (1989) studied the influence of frequency of exposure *in vivo* sessions on the treatment results. They compared ten massed practice sessions with ten spaced practice sessions. In the massed practice condition four sessions were given each week, whereas in the spaced practice condition there were only two sessions each week. The results indicated that massed practice was equally as effective as spaced practice. Although patients in the latter condition had the possibility of

avoiding fear-arousing situations between sessions this did not hinder their improvement. Theoretically, one could have expected anxiety to increase in the spaced condition, but this was not found empirically. The anxiety between sessions could possibly have increased in the spaced exposure condition if the duration between each session had been shorter or when treatment had been restricted to one session a week. In this study each exposure session lasted 2 hours to make sure that there would be habituation. The results of this study have direct practical consequences. The fact that there was no difference between frequent and less frequent exposure sessions indicates that it is not necessary to carry out exposure every day. The results imply that it is possible to carry out exposure treatment with a limited frequency of two sessions a week.

9. *Outpatient treatment is often equally as effective as clinical treatment.* For most obsessive-compulsive patients hospital admission is no longer necessary because treatment in their own environment yields similar results. In a study by Van den Hout, Emmelkamp, Kraaÿkamp and Griez (1988) no difference was found between a gradual exposure programme carried out by patients in their own homes and a behavioural treatment of long duration in a psychiatric hospital.

10. *Treatment effects are lasting.* Several follow-up studies indicate that the effects of exposure *in vivo* and response prevention are still present 2 years after treatment (Kasvikis & Marks, 1988). In the study by Visser, Hoekstra and Emmelkamp (1990) it appeared that after 4 years patients showed no more compulsive behaviours than at the beginning of treatment, and also that their mood was considerably less depressed. At the follow-up 28 patients (64%) appeared to have improved considerably, 9 patients (20%) improved and only 7 patients (16%) did not improve.

11. *The amount of improvement varies among patients.* The following factors appeared to relate to a less favourable treatment result: severity and duration of complaints (Basoglu, Lax, Kasvikis & Marks, 1988; Hoogduin, 1985), nature of the obsessive-compulsive behaviours (checking compulsions have a less favourable prognosis than washing compulsions, Basoglu et al., 1988; Rabavilas & Boulougouris, 1979); delusion obsessions (Basoglu et al., 1988; Foa, Steketee, Grayson & Doppelt, 1983); and negative rearing experiences (Visser, Hoekstra & Emmelkamp, 1990).

12. *Cognitive therapy is equally as effective as exposure* in vivo. In two studies (Emmelkamp, Visser & Hoekstra, 1988; Emmelkamp & Beens, 1991) the effectiveness of self-controlled exposure *in vivo* was compared with cognitive therapy (RET) in obsessive-compulsive patients. The results showed cognitive therapy to be equally effective as exposure *in vivo*. In addition, a combination of exposure *in vivo* and cognitive therapy proved to be no more effective than exposure *in vivo* alone.

13. *In some cases the obsessive-compulsive disorder appears to serve another function than anxiety reduction.* According to our experience many obsessive patients are socially anxious and non-assertive. In some of them the obsessive-compulsive behaviours have the additional function of helping the patient to avoid other people. In such cases exposure *in vivo* and response prevention are only of limited use, and should be aided by other interventions. Emmelkamp (1982) described the successful treatment of some obsessive-compulsive patients by means of assertion training.

In some patients obsessive-compulsive behaviours serve to conceal painful emotions. Occasionally, we meet obsessive-compulsive patients trying to conquer loneliness and boredom by compulsive actions. It seems that in these patients anxiety reduction begins to play a role later in the onset of the obsessive-compulsive disorder. An example may illustrate this.

Carol is a young woman who enjoyed working at the office until she got married. After her marriage, she left her job and tried to pass the time by tidying her house. She did not have any other contacts in the place where she lived, and as long as she kept herself busy with housekeeping, boredom and feelings of loneliness remained in the background. Within a year the initially innocent habit of tidiness had developed into a cleaning compulsion. She now becomes anxious when her house is not clean enough according to her standards, and she continues cleaning even until late at night. The compulsion really became a problem when the couple decided to have a child. They hoped that having a baby would prevent Carol from spending so much time tidying the house. Caring for her little daughter, however, took so much time that she could not find any opportunity for her household requirements. At present her husband is also engaged in cleaning the house in the evenings and at weekends. By now her daughter has started to walk and touches everything with her little fingers so that the situation has become unbearable. Carol has started hitting her little daughter when she touches something or when she gets in the way when Carol is cleaning. She feels very guilty about her own behaviour and this is the direct reason for referral.

It is evident that in such cases treatment is not very effective when it is aimed only at getting rid of the compulsions, without tackling the source of tension (e.g. boredom and loneliness). In other cases compulsions are fed by unresolved emotions from the past. In these cases patients try to suppress painful memories, feelings, thoughts or images by occupying themselves all day long with obsessive-compulsive rituals.

One of our patients had been successfully treated with exposure *in vivo* and response prevention for an elaborate checking compulsion. A year after treatment he relapsed, but after a limited number of exposure *in vivo* sessions the compulsive complaints virtually disappeared. Eighteen months later he was admitted again, because his compulsions had returned in a severe way. In the sessions that followed the patient was able to talk for the first time about his being sexually abused as a child by his grandfather, who slept in his room. Although he had been asked about such experiences in his previous treatment, the patient dared not answer these questions because his grandfather was still alive at that time. However, he often wondered whether these traumatic experiences were connected with his compulsions. Other traumatic experiences that he kept to himself in previous treatment referred to occasional physical abuse by his father in his childhood. In addition to treating his compulsions by means of exposure *in vivo* and response prevention, treatment now consisted of working through these traumatic experiences. In a number of sessions the therapist asked the patient to imagine these traumatic situations. As was to be expected, this was accompanied by intense emotions that, however, subsided by the end of the session. In order to guarantee a sufficient decrease of emotions it was sometimes necessary to make the sessions last about 90 minutes. At the follow-up, one and a half years after termination of treatment, the compulsive complaints had not returned.

CONDUCTING TREATMENT OF OBSESSIVE-COMPULSIVE BEHAVIOURS

Exposure *in vivo* and response prevention

Before being able to carry out an exposure programme, it is essential for the therapist to have all relevant information concerning the maintenance of the obsessive-compulsive behaviours. In order to obtain a complete picture of the problems, the therapist should interview the patient in great detail. A number of patients tend to avoid mentioning situations in which they are afraid or tense, and in which they have to carry out their compulsions. There may be various reasons for this avoidance, and very often a strong sense of shame plays an important role. It might not be easy for a patient to have to admit to an unknown person (i.e. the therapist) that they are occupied all day long with completely useless things (even in the eye of the patient). With regard to particular matters, such as going to the toilet, washing, having a period, having sexual intercourse, it is important that the therapist finds out empathically to what extent there may be problems in these areas. The patients themselves do not usually take the initiative in discussing such situations. Apart from interviews, questionnaires and diaries (see Chapter 3) a house call may yield much information.

Ms Williams is an unmarried woman aged 45, who was referred to us for treatment of her compulsions. During the initial interview she complains about cleaning and checking compulsions. After some hesitation she allows a house call by the therapist. When he arrives at her house, the reason for this hesitation becomes evident. The entire house is crowded with objects she dares not touch, such as dirty underwear, used sanitary towels, used coffee filters, and so on. Her living room is filled predominantly with piles of books. The patient also appears to have a buying compulsion. She has to buy all kinds of books that are "cheap". These books, however, she never reads, because once they are at home she dare not touch them. Cupboards are loaded with boxes of coffee and tinned food, which the patient keeps in the event of war. On the top floor there are cupboards with more than a hundred pairs of shoes and countless items of underwear. Everywhere there are boxes with bills and tickets, some over 20 years old. Upstairs there appears to be a room which the patient has not entered for many years and which after some coercion by the therapist is opened up. In the middle of the room there is a large pile of objects which have become "contaminated" and which she dares not approach. The patient moves very cautiously about the house, her arms (sleeves up) in the air, hoping she will not touch anything. Doors are opened with her elbows and kicked shut with her feet. It is clear that during the interviews the therapist's impression of the nature and the severity of the compulsion has been far from complete.

After the therapist has gathered all the information about the compulsion, a hierarchy is constructed. To do this he writes down all kinds of exposure assignments of increasing difficulty. It should be noted that the assignments are formulated as actively as possible, in order to enable the patient to carry them out during the treatment session. The assignments should be formulated in such a way that exposure elements as well as elements of response prevention are present. After a number of assignments have been formulated, the patient is asked to score them on an "anxiety thermometer" which ranges from 0 (no anxiety) to 100 (panic). Especially if the patient is to carry out the exposure programme on his or her own this is a very important phase. Before the treatment commences properly, it is essential that the patient grasps the treatment rationale. The patient should understand that the problems are maintained by both passive and active avoidance (i.e. the compulsions). Below is the verbatim explanation of treatment to a patient with cleaning compulsions.

Because you are afraid of being "contaminated" you avoid all kinds of situations such as touching journals, mail, food containers, money, and so on. You've learned that, by avoiding situations, you can prevent yourself becoming very anxious or panicky. If you, for whatever reason, have touched these objects, you start becoming very tense and feel the urge to wash thoroughly. You then submit to these tendencies because you have experienced that the tension decreases when you wash. However, you can't learn that anxiety will subside even when you do not follow this inclination. It means that your anxiety will subside gradually and all by itself, if you contaminate yourself by touching these objects and do not wash afterwards. The treatment consists of exercises in situations which are difficult for you. The distress or tension will often increase at first and this may seem to be unbearable for you, but if you persist tension will decrease after some time (sometimes after a few hours). Of course we do not start with the most difficult assignment. We start with situations that you can accomplish successfully every now and then and that invoke little tension. Only after these assignments have been repeatedly exercised without problems, that is to say, when you can endure the situation without too much tension, without having to wash your hands afterwards, will we move to the next situation which is a bit more dif ficult. You'll notice that during treatment you'll gradually develop more and more self-confidence. So treatment implies that you have to practise in situations you are avoiding now without washing your hands as you usually do.

It may be wise to make the patient write down the rationale in their own words as a homework assignment. It is essential that the patient understands the rationale (believing may be asking too much at this stage) before exposure is started. Otherwise, if the patient begins to practise anxiety-provoking situations, and continues to carry out compulsions, there is a realistic chance that the problems will increase rather than decrease. Such an experience may undermine all confidence in the treatment. It may also be a good idea to make the patient score their anxiety on a "fear thermometer" every 5 minutes during the exposure assignment. When these data are presented graphically, it may convince the patient more than the therapist's verbal explanation. An exposure programme for cleaning rituals usually consists of two elements: in the first place, the patient is exposed to "dirt" or "contaminated material" without being allowed to clean him or herself. Exposure to these stimuli should last until anxiety and tension subside. The second part of the treatment aims at teaching the patient not to wash or clean in a ritualistic manner. Both elements should be practised separately. If a patient is first exposed to dirt and next allowed to perform cleaning rituals, then exposure is of little use, because cleaning will decrease the anxiety and prevent habituation. In patients with checking compulsions it is essential that they should feel responsible for their behaviour during exposure sessions. For this reason therapist-guided exposure is often not real exposure because the patient may easily put the responsibility for his acts on the therapist. Furthermore, it should be noted that in many cases the nature of the exercise precludes repeating that exercise during the same session. For example, checking the gas can be performed only once during an exposure session. If the patient receives the same assignment twice during one session it is not a proper exposure, because if the patient performs the assignment for a second time he is in fact able to check whether he did it right the first time; thus he can be reassured. For patients who are compulsively precise, exposure consists of disarranging the patient's environment and stimulating the patient to drop the habit of doing everything very precisely and in a specific way. If doubt is the main element of the obsession, exposure treatment should consist of confronting the patient with situations in which he or she must take decisions without getting the opportunity to reconsider. Compulsive buying can be treated by putting patients into situations in which they have the opportunity to buy, whereas actual buying will not be allowed. Treatment of compulsive hoarding consists of throwing away all kinds of superfluous objects. Asking for reassurance, a frequently occurring phenomenon in obsessive-compulsive patients, has basically the same function as compulsive rituals. When a patient feels insecure or anxious reassurance may decrease the amount of distress. Reassurance can be sought from members of the family, from experts in a certain area, or by looking up things in newspapers or encyclopaedias. In such cases, response prevention implies that members of the family must be told about the necessity of not providing reassurance.

Furthermore, the patient is instructed to refrain from asking for reassurance. An example may clarify this.

Wilma is a very insecure woman, who continuously asks her husband for reassurance. This may pertain to all kinds of subjects, related not only to housekeeping but also to all kinds of trivial things such as: "What's the name of the woman on the camping site next to us?", or "Which car did Corinne and John have before they bought a new one?", or "How old was Aunt Annie when she first met her husband?" All these kinds of queries she puts to her husband, her children, and also to relatives and acquaintances in order to get an answer to her pressing questions. As part of the treatment the therapist explains to her husband that continuous reassurance has little effect. Moreover, the husband has to admit that asking for reassurance has in fact increased over the years, despite his efforts to reassure his wife. It is agreed that he will no longer provide answers to her questions, and that together they will tell the children to comply with the same instruction. As well as this, the patient gets the explicit instruction not to consult other people such as family members and relatives. As is to be expected, this initially leads to a severe increase of tension in the patient and also her partner is tempted to yield to her questions in order to stop her nagging. In the next session it is decided after discussion that the only remedy is not to provide any answers whatsoever. Although both partners are reluctant to comply, at the next session it appears that the husband has succeeded in not providing answers, and also that his wife has asked fewer questions than before. After a few weeks, the patient herself observes that tension and insecurity have decreased considerably, as well as the inclination to pose questions to everybody.

The next example gives an extensive description of the background, the assessment, and the treatment of an obsessive-compulsive patient. In this treatment attention was paid not only to the decrease of compulsive behaviours, but also to other problems that appeared to be related to the obsessive-compulsive behaviours.

TREATMENT OF SARAH

The presenting patient is a 26-year-old woman named Sarah who has lived with her boyfriend for about 4 years. She works as a librarian. Her main complaint is that she feels compelled to clean things and to be excessively neat. Every day she must clean the doors, mop the floors, vacuum the house, and clean the couch, including underneath. These activities sometimes take place several times a day. The patient is always dressed very neatly; she cannot stand hairs or dust on her clothes. Every day she takes several showers, changes clothes for working, for cleaning, and for eating. She avoids receiving visitors as much as she can. When people do come to visit her, she takes careful notice of where they walk and sit and what they touch. As soon as the visitors leave, she thoroughly cleans the places where they have been and the things they have touched. This is also the reason why she will not take anyone with her in her car. The patient feels compelled to engage in sports every day. Afterwards she must take a good shower. Although this physical training seems to show obsessive-compulsive characteristics (i.e. when she cannot do her exercises because of illness she becomes very tense), she is reluctant to include this aspect in the treatment. The patient is also very precise; things like paintings, chairs, books, and so on all have their fixed place.

History

As a child the patient suffered from asthma and was very sensitive to dust. Because of this her parental home was kept meticulously clean. She no longer suffers from asthma. At that time she was often subject to temper tantrums. These had already started in her kindergarten years. Her mother could not handle her so she often went to an aunt who spoiled her. This aunt was a house-proud housewife and was very precise. When she was about 10 years old, the patient started to dress very neatly. She cannot remember what induced her to do this, but her sensitivity to dust has probably played a part as well as her aunt's excessive neatness. When she was 15 the family moved and she had to attend a different school, where she did not know anyone. She felt very insecure and it was then that the rituals started.

Assessment

Three information sessions are held. In addition, the patient fills out a number of questionnaires: the Maudsley Obsessive-Compulsive Inventory (MOCI), the Social Anxiety Scale (SAS), Zung's Self-Rating Depression Scale (SDS), and the Hostility and Direction of Hostility Questionnaire (HDHQ). Beginning with the first session, the patient is requested to monitor daily on 0–8 scales how much she is troubled by obsessive-compulsive behaviour, depressed moods, and feelings of hostility. Since the first part of Sarah's treatment is conducted within the context of an experimental study on the effects of exposure in *in vivo* therapy, the information sessions are primarily directed at a micro-analysis of her obsessive-compulsive behaviour. The patient apparently tries to avoid the following situations, and if she fails she feels compelled to wash her hands and/or take a shower: reading the newspaper (dirty hands), travelling by train, using public telephones, touching keys and money, touching bottles, putting her bag on the floor, touching shoe-cleaning implements, touching her glasses, walking barefoot, and receiving people. The more visitors she receives, the tenser she gets; indeed, she cannot keep track of all the things they touch. The cleaning of her house must always take place in a specific order. If there is any deviation from this specific order, she starts all over again. Her precision-compulsion is further expressed in the fact that everything has its fixed place, paintings have to hang straight, and so on. She suffers more from her compulsions at home than at work. Although there is quite a lot of dust at the place where she works—

a library archive—it does not worry her very much. She works in a separate room so that contamination through contacting other people seldom occurs. The patient has no concrete thoughts about falling ill or contaminating other people. She experiences great tension and anxiety when she thinks she is contaminated, but she herself does not know the reason for it. Her boyfriend seems to reinforce her obsessive-compulsive complaints. He takes her complaints into account as much as possible; he seldom invites people home and he never leaves his things lying about because she cannot stand this. Furthermore, he helps her clean up the house.

Treatment

Session three

In the third session the treatment rationale of self-controlled exposure *in vivo* is explained to Sarah. It is explained that by giving in to the urges to clean and to wash her hands and to be very precise, she actually maintains her obsessive-compulsive behaviour, but by exposing herself to situations that provoke anxiety and tension without ritualizing, in the long run her anxiety and discomfort will decrease and with it the urge to ritualize. It is further explained that exposure will be gradual, starting with relatively easy situations. To see just how much she has understood the rationale, Sarah is requested to write it down in her own words when at home and to give this to her therapist in the next session. Subsequently, a detailed inventory is drawn up of situations that provoke anxiety and lead to rituals. All listed situations are written down on notecards and scored by her by means of an anxiety bar (0–100). Then a hierarchy is constructed, ranging from easy to difficult assignments. It is agreed that she will practise the hierarchy items for at least 90 minutes, twice a week. At the end of the last session, the following homework assignments are given to her to practise in the first two homework sessions.

1. Walk barefoot through the house. Do not wash your feet.
2. Do not wear your special eating sweater when eating. Eat in your ordinary working clothes.
3. Visit people without first taking a shower or changing.
4. Hang your paintings crooked. Leave them like this for a week.
5. After you have been to the masseur, soap yourself only once when taking a shower.
6. Do not dust more than once a week.

Session four

Sarah has carried out all of these assignments and is quite pleased about it. Walking barefoot through the house had at first been difficult, but nevertheless she had gone to bed without washing her feet. It is agreed that she will repeat the previous assignments. If these go well once again, the following assignments will be added.

1. Put away your clothes within a minute.
2. Sit behind your desk in your special eating clothes, but do not clean the desk afterwards.
3. Prepare a hot meal. Do not take a shower afterwards. Do not change. Wear the same clothes in the evening and wear them again to work.
4. Do not polish your shoes more than once a week.

Session five

Sarah says that things did not go all that well this week; she still felt compelled to clean her glasses and her watch thoroughly (assignments which had not yet been given to her) and feels very guilty about this. She gives the impression of being very tense. She has succeeded in doing nearly all of the assignments which had been given to her, the new ones included, but she has failed to dust only once a week. She has, however, noticed that tension decreased when she did not give in to the urge to ritualize. The therapist emphasizes that there is no reason at all to feel guilty about failing to do any assignment and that it is not wise to do more assignments than have been agreed. In addition to repeating the old assignments, she is to carry out the following assignments (for the next session).

1. Put on your glasses, go out for five minutes. Do not clean your glasses.
2. Do not wash your hands before dinner.
3. Put the chairs in a different position. Leave them like this for a week.
4. Shake leaves off a plant. Let them lie about.
5. Go to the bank, make a withdrawal, and do not wash your hands afterwards.
6. Eat in your house clothes, without putting on your special eating clothes.
7. Take a shower at home. Do not take your keys with you under the shower.

Session six

Again Sarah is very tense, although she has succeeded in doing nearly all of the assignments. Only the assignment with the keys has failed. This, however, made her so angry that she lashed out at Bob, her live-in boyfriend. Her relationship with Bob is going through a bad period: Sarah feels misunderstood and this is probably also a reason why she has been so tense lately. Before dealing with her relationship problems, however, Sarah wants to finish the exposure assignments. She is given the following assignments for the next session.

1. Do not wash your hands after meals.
2. Take several coins and banknotes from your purse and hold them in your hands for at least two minutes. Do not wash your hands.
3. Use a public telephone. Do not wash your hands or face.
4. Go through the house. In every room touch at least 20 objects. Do not clean anything afterwards.
5. Take your mail to your desk. Go through it, parcels included. Do not clean your desk, do not clean your hands, do not clean the mail.
6. Make a stain on your door. Do not clean it.
7. Mop the kitchen only once a week. Do not take longer than usual.
8. Mop the bathroom once a week. Do not take longer than usual.
9. Mop the shower once a week. Do not take longer than usual.

Session seven

Again she has done the assignments reasonably well. Using a public telephone and touching money were very difficult, but she did not give in to the urge to wash her hands. However, she had not put the receiver against her ear so as not to be contaminated. It is agreed that she will try this assignment again, but this time she has to touch herself with the receiver. The assignments not to mop more than once a week have failed: she has mopped the floors twice because she had visitors. Sarah now sees a clear connection between external events (a quarrel with Bob, problems with her boss at work, insecurity in social situations) and her obsessive-compulsive behaviour. When such events upset her, she is much more troubled by her obsessive-compulsive complaints. She is reasonably satisfied about her progress. Because of her gradually increasing ability to do things without ritualizing, she begins to feel that she can solve her obsessive-compulsive problems.

Session eight to session eleven

Carrying out the assignments (see Table 8.1) has given her little difficulty, but it becomes more and more clear that her obsessive-compulsive behaviour is influenced by insecurity in social situations and her problems with Bob. At the end of this period, Sarah is able to do most of the assignments without tension, but the hierarchy has not yet been completed. She would rather stop treatment for a while, because she needs time to study for an important examination after the summer holidays, but she does want to keep on doing the exposure assignments that have not been practised yet, at her own pace.

Broad-spectrum therapy

About 6 months after exposure treatment there is a follow-up interview with Sarah. She is very tense and depressed and has suicidal thoughts, but her

Table 8.1. Hierarchy items used in sessions eight to eleven

1. Read a book from the library at your desk. Do not clean your desk and do not wash your hands.
2. Go out in your house clothes. Keep them on for the whole evening.
3. Do not sweep the floor of the shed more than once a month.
4. Do not sweep the hall near the front door more than once every two weeks.
5. Wear your special eating clothes the whole evening. Do not clean anything in the house.
6. Vacuum only once a week.
7. Read a newspaper at your desk. Fold it out on your desk. Do not clean your desk and do not wash your hands.
8. Go to a gas station. Go back home and do not wash your hands.
9. Put five books in the bookcase and leave them there for a week.
10. Go out and do some shopping. Put away the goods without cleaning them. Do not wash your hands.
11. Do not clean the doors more than once a week and do not take longer than usual.
12. Do not wash your car more than once a month.
13. Throw your clothes on a chair. Do not cover them with a sweater. Leave your boyfriend's clothes lying about too.
14. Read the newspaper. Immediately after that touch at least 10 objects in the house and clutch them tightly. Do not clean anything and do not wash your hands.
15. Wear the same clothes "day and night" for four days. Do not avoid touching or using things, especially not the couch.
16. After taking a shower put on the same clothes you have worn all day.
17. Put the shoes you want to polish not in the shed but in the kitchen.
18. After dinner do not clean the table with a cloth.
19. Do not take a shower for a day.
20. Buy a book without plastic wrapped around it. Put it in the bookcase among the other books without having a further look at it or cleaning it. Do not wash your hands.
21. Pet a dog thoroughly. Do not wash your hands.
22. Put at least 10 books in a place where they do not belong.
23. Use your glasses when you have to drive your car. Do not clean your glasses more than once a day. This must never take longer than 20 seconds. Clean only the lenses, not the frame. Do not wash your hands and face more often than usual.
24. Leave your glasses anywhere in the house without putting them in their case.
25. Sit behind the desk in the clothes you have worn all day. Do not clean your desk. Do not wash your hands.
26. Do not clean the washstand every morning, but only once a week.
27. Drive your car across a muddy track. Do not wash it.

obsessive-compulsive problems show further improvement. Apart from the obsessive-compulsive problems, the questionnaires show a deterioration in all other respects: Sarah proves to be more depressed, more socially anxious, and more hostile than before the treatment. The situation at home with her boyfriend has proved untenable and this is the immediate cause of her depression. Sarah herself wants to continue the treatment. In view of the crisis atmosphere at home, it seems advisable to invite Sarah's boyfriend (Bob) to attend the next interview, and Sarah agrees.

Communication training

The purpose of the interview is to evaluate their relationship problems. During the initial interview it becomes clear that both partners are distressed and dissatisfied with the relationship. Both have seriously entertained the idea of separation but they have not discussed the issue with each other. Bob is increasingly troubled by Sarah's aggressive moods and her remaining obsessive-compulsive problems. He still cannot receive friends because of Sarah's problems, although he too thinks that the ritual problems have improved. Sarah feels that Bob does not understand her and therefore she feels lonely. When she is very tense, she either smashes her crockery or telephones Bob, who then has to come home immediately to comfort her. He reinforces Sarah's behaviour by immediately giving in to her wishes and taking her on his lap. It is explained to the couple that Sarah's aggressive moods have been learned in her childhood and have first been reinforced by her mother and aunt. Now they are reinforced by Bob. Both readily accept this explanation of Sarah's behaviour, and a contractual agreement is reached in which it is specified that Bob shall not give in to Sarah when she is in an aggressive mood. Since the partners are unable to express their emotions directly toward each other, communication training is proposed to the couple, which they both accept. At this stage, the therapist makes it explicit that the goal of the communication training is not necessarily to improve their relationship, but to teach them skills in expressing their feelings more directly, which eventually can result in a mutually agreed-upon separation. During the communication training, conflict situations which have occurred in the previous week are rehearsed in role-playing. Both have good listening skills, but their main problem is that they are unable to express their wishes in a clear way, which prevents conflict resolution. In communication training emphasis is directed to spontaneous expression of feelings, assertiveness, and empathy training. Behaviour rehearsal is used as the primary therapeutic vehicle, which involves the partners acting out relationship problems with each other in role-plays. The therapist's office provides the couple with a safe place in which to change their behaviour and to practise new ways of communication. Specifically, the therapist begins by asking the couple to explain as much about a particular situation as is needed to enable him to play the role of both partners. Next, the therapist asks Bob and Sarah their goals in the situation (i.e. what they want to say). Then, in a series of role-plays, the partners attempt to change their behaviour. The therapist models appropriate behaviour where necessary by alternately playing the role of either partner. At the end of these sessions the partners are encouraged to use their newly learned skills in their daily interaction. The contractual agreement which has been agreed to in the initial interview with the couple is effective in that Sarah's aggressive moods disappear. The progress that both partners make with respect to their communication skills is remarkable. In the fifth session Sarah and Bob tell the therapist that they have decided to separate for some time in order to find out what they feel for each other and to see whether they can live without each other. In the past week they have been able to discuss this openly with each other for the first time, and both are satisfied with this solution. It is agreed that they will live apart for a month and that they will have no contact at all with each other. Therapy is interrupted during this period. After this month Bob and Sarah see each other again in the therapist's office. Bob is very happy about living alone, a heavy load has fallen off his shoulders and he wants to make the separation definite. Sarah too is satisfied about the separation, but she indicates that she would like to maintain a friendly relationship with Bob. Bob makes it clear, however, that he does not want that, and so Sarah accepts a definite separation. Bob feels relieved that the die has been cast, and both are happy that they have been able to convey their wishes to each other. In addition, there is consensus that the treatment should be continued on an individual basis with Sarah.

Re-evaluation and treatment planning

The next two sessions are devoted to a re-evaluation of Sarah's problems. Sarah is still socially anxious and depressed, although no longer suicidal. Although the obsessive-compulsive rituals have improved, she still keeps avoiding a number of situations, in particular those which involve having contact with other people, such as receiving visitors. Inspection of the daily records of obsessive-compulsive complaints, depressed moods, and hostility reveal that these problems seem to (co)vary from one time to another. From re-examination of the notes that have been made from interviews, it appears that there is some relationship between obsessive-compulsive problems and social situations. Her obsessive-compulsive complaints (and to some extent her hostility and depression) appear to increase because of stressful interpersonal events. It now seems plausible that the obsessive-compulsive behaviour might also provide reinforcement in the form of tension reduction and temporary relief from the worries caused by Sarah's social difficulties. It is further hypothesized that Sarah's depressed mood is partly the result of a lack of social reinforcers, and partly the result of irrational cognitions. On the basis of this analysis, the following treatment plan is formulated. To deal with the social anxiety that was presumed to underlie the remaining obsessive-compulsive problems, assertion training is proposed. Further, cognitive restructuring seems appropriate to deal with the irrational cognitions. Finally, to overcome the remaining compulsive problems, Sarah is instructed to continue to practise difficult *in vivo* exposure tasks on her own. There is a consensus on the problems and goals of therapy, and it is decided to commence with assertion training on a once-a-week basis. The reason for giving priority to assertion training over dealing with the irrational cognitions is twofold. First, part of her current depressed feelings is presumably related to grief due to the loss of her partner. As grief is a normal reaction to the loss of a love object, there seems to be no need for a therapeutic intervention to deal with this. Since it is anticipated that the mourning process might interfere with the cognitive restructuring approach, it is decided to postpone cognitive therapy for some time. The other reason for beginning with assertion training is that it probably will be easier to change irrational cognitions when Sarah already has the necessary social skills and is engaged in social interactions, rather than to treat irrational cognitions in a vacuum of social relationships. Generally, assertion training using role-playing to change behaviours can be used without worrying about cognitions unless there are clear indications that these cognitions will interfere with the practice of assertion skills in daily life.

Assertion training

The next ten sessions are devoted mainly to assertion training. The first two sessions are devoted to a more detailed analysis of Sarah's assertion problems. Inspection of her responses on the Social Anxiety Scale has already provided a number of social situations in which Sarah finds it difficult to express herself. In these sessions a number of social situations are role-played to observe Sarah's behaviour in such situations. Difficult situations for Sarah are refusing a request, and giving and receiving negative expressions; receiving and giving positive expressions (such as a compliment) are less of a problem. Further, Sarah's non-verbal behaviour, such as eye-contact, distance and posture, and voice quality, is generally good. Therefore it is decided to focus on the training of (1) refusal skills, (2) the expression of negative emotions, and (3) receiving criticism. Since one situation is not clearly more difficult than another, there is no need for using a hierarchy ranging from less anxiety-arousing situations to situations that provoked high anxiety. To increase Sarah's motivation, it is decided to use only situations that she encounters in real life. Therefore Sarah is instructed to record difficult situations on pre-coded sheets and to bring these with her to the therapy session. Each session starts with a brief discussion of the assertive problems that she has encountered. Then a few of these problems are rehearsed in role-playing, the therapist modelling more appropriate behaviour when necessary. When sufficient progress has been made in role-playing, Sarah is instructed to practise this particular behaviour as a homework assignment. Examples of situations that are rehearsed in this way are:

1. Inviting people to visit her.
2. Being invited herself to visit people.
3. Telling a lesbian acquaintance who wants her to stay the night that she is not interested.

4. Making it clear to her neighbour, who really wants a relationship with her, that she is interested only in drinking a cup of coffee with him occasionally.
5. Making it clear that she likes a man and inviting him for dinner.
6. Criticizing acquaintances and her boss.

Cognitive therapy

After eight of these sessions, progress is evaluated. Sarah now has a number of social contacts; she regularly goes to a bar after work with some colleagues, and both Sarah and the therapist find that the assertion skills have improved remarkably. Her obsessive-compulsive complaints have also continued to improve. Sarah has regularly received visitors without having been overly concerned about what they touched. Neither does she feel compelled to clean the entire house after the visitors left. She seems to have dealt with her separation from Bob reasonably well. Therefore a cognitive therapy is begun to change the irrational cognitions that remained unchanged. Cognitive therapy is based on Ellis (1962, see Chapter 4). After having had the rationale of this therapy explained, Sarah is instructed to read a booklet describing the basic principles of rational emotive therapy. The first stage of cognitive therapy is directed to teaching Sarah to observe and record her cognitions. By using pre-coded A-B-C homework sheets (see Chapter 4), Sarah learns to discriminate between the actual event and her own thoughts. She readily understands the relationship between irrational cognitions and negative feelings, and she is able to offer a number of irrational cognitions associated with her negative feelings after the first week of monitoring these thoughts. The next stage of therapy involves rationally disputing the irrational cognitions. First the therapist challenges the irrational beliefs in a Socratic-like fashion and later on Sarah is instructed to do this on her own as a homework assignment. At least four major themes run through the cognitive therapy:

1. She needs to have a relationship in order to be happy, but is unfit for such a relationship since her previous relationship have failed because of her faults.
2. She has to engage in sports every day and is not allowed to eat "fat food"; otherwise she will not have a good figure and hence will be unable to find a lover.
3. If she is not precise and neat, she will feel insecure and "loss of control" would be intolerable.
4. Tension is intolerable and must immediately be given in to by means of rituals or aggressive moods (e.g. smashing crockery).

It is important to note that the irrational beliefs depicted above operate on a pre-conscious level in a more or less automatic fashion. That is, they only become part of Sarah's conscious awareness after her training in discriminating these beliefs through her homework assignments and through the therapist's intervention during therapy sessions. After rationally disputing these ideas, Sarah receives behavioural assignments. For example, when it has become clear to her on a cognitive level that it is an irrational idea that she can find a partner only if she participates in sports every day and eats as little as possible, she is given the homework assignment not to do sports for a week and to eat well without paying attention to calories and without checking whether she has gained weight. After this week, Sarah is able to skip sports when she does not feel like it and her eating habits have changed without her becoming fat. After ten sessions of cognitive therapy, the situation is re-evaluated. Sarah is markedly less depressed and has a number of satisfying social relationships, while the obsessive rituals are less of a problem. Because there are still a number of exposure assignments left, which Sarah cannot bring herself to do on her own, it is decided to do one *in vivo* exposure session at her home, to tackle the remaining bits of her obsessive-compulsive problem. During this session the therapist contaminates all kinds of objects in the house and Sarah has to touch the ground, her clothes and bedclothes, without washing her hands or cleaning anything. Although Sarah dreads doing this, her tension does not increase very much (a maximum of 6 on a 0–10 anxiety scale). After half an hour, tension has decreased, and after an hour it has completely disappeared. At the next session it appears that Sarah has succeeded in not cleaning anything and that she has repeated a number of these assignments. Because Sarah does reasonably well, it is decided to terminate regular therapy on a weekly basis. There are seven follow-up visits over a period of 9 months, during which period progress appears to continue. Sarah is reassessed at the last follow-up visit 9 months after the end of formal treatment. This time Sarah does extremely well; the obsessive-compulsive problems have markedly improved and she is no longer depressed. She now enjoys social relationships and has had an affair that lasted for 5 months. In addition, she has recently started a new relationship.

Overall evaluation

The focus of this case was a change in the obsessive-compulsive problems of the patient. During the course of therapy a number of other treatment targets emerged that seemed partly related to the obsessive-compulsive behaviour and had to be dealt with separately. Although treatment was broad-spectrum, it was behavioural in that strategies applied were procedures specifically directed at dealing with the various target problems in succession. In this case it was felt necessary to deal with the "underlying" problems (e.g. social anxiety) to eliminate the obsessive-compulsive problems. Exposure therapy alone was not very effective until assertion training and cognitive therapy were implemented to deal with social anxiety and irrational cognitions. It is unlikely, however, that assertion training and cognitive therapy on their own would have resulted in a definite improvement of the obsessive-compulsive problems. It should be noted that when starting therapy, Sarah was so much distressed by her obsessive-compulsive problems that these problems had to be dealt with first. Moreover, at the start of the therapy Sarah was unaware of her uncertainty in social situations, as shown in her low score on the Social Anxiety Scale at the pre-test. Only during the course of exposure therapy dealing with her compulsive behaviour did the problems in social situations become evident to her.

CONDUCTING TREATMENT OF OBSESSIONS

In studies reported in the literature there is less emphasis on the behavioural treatment of obsessions than on the treatment of compulsions. This may be explained by the fact that pure obsessions without compulsions are relatively rare phenomena, which precludes studies with larger groups. Nevertheless, over the past decade a number of researchers have tried to systematically evaluate the effect of several behavioural procedures in patients with pure obsessions. These treatments can be divided into three categories:

1. Treatments aimed at stopping the obsession (for example, thought-stopping and aversion therapy).
2. Treatments aimed at habituation (prolonged exposure and satiation training).
3. Treatments directly aimed not at obsessions, but at some underlying problem.

Thought-stopping procedures

Wolpe (1958) introduced the thought-stopping procedure and described its successful application in a number of patients with obsessions. Other authors also reported successful treatments by means of thought-stopping procedures. (For an overview see Emmelkamp, 1987.) The procedure is illustrated with the next case.

Mr Jones (aged 50) is a teacher who for a number of years has been suffering from harming obsessions, implying that he might run over a person with his car, insult or attack someone. Recently, his obsessions have increased to such an extent that he dare not be in the classroom with his pupils. After explaining the procedure the therapist asks him to sit comfortably, to close his eyes and to visualize one of his obsessions. He chooses the obsession of running over a person with his car. As soon as he imagines this clearly enough, he indicates the fact by raising his hand. The therapist immediately produces a very loud sound with a hooter. This makes the thought disappear instantly, upon which the therapist asks him to imagine his obsession again. Again Mr Jones indicates that he sees the picture clearly. The therapist now calls out "STOP". This is repeated over and over again, with the role of the therapist gradually decreasing. At first the therapist says "STOP" in a low voice, and then Mr Jones has to perform this himself. First he has to call out loudly "STOP" as soon as he imagines his obsessions, and then saying this more and more softly. Finally, he is instructed to do this only mentally. In six sessions several obsessions are taken care of. After a few sessions Mr Jones is instructed to carry out the procedure at home as soon as he is troubled by one of the obsessions. Treatment evidently has a favourable effect. Although obsessions occur regularly, their frequency has decreased considerably. Furthermore, the patient has ceased to be anxious when he gets these thoughts.

In controlled studies the effect of thought-stopping varies considerably (for an overview see Emmelkamp, 1987.) In the four studies published up to now thought-stopping was no more effective than controlled procedures. Also the effect of aversion therapy on obsessions has been insufficiently studied. Kenny, Mowbray and Lalani (1978) investigated the effectiveness of electrical aversion therapy. As soon as their patients reported obsessive thoughts, an electrical shock was applied, which proved to be more effective than no treatment. A problem, however, is the general lack of discrimination between obsessive thoughts that provoke anxiety, and thoughts that serve to reduce anxiety. Anxiety-provoking obsessions can be followed by either compulsions or obsessive thoughts with the function of reducing tension. Obsessive patients often show neutralizing thoughts to undo the allegedly hazardous effects of their obsessions. One of our patients, for example, had an obsessive thought implying "God who fucked" (an anxiety-inducing obsession). This thought was always followed by neutralizing thoughts such as "Neither God nor the Holy Spirit". Thinking this neutralizing thought led to a reduction in anxiety which was provoked by the blasphemous thought.

Exposure to obsessions

Rachman (1976) stated that obsessions can be considered as aversive stimuli to which it is difficult to habituate. He suggested satiation training as a method for treating obsessions. In this treatment patients are asked to produce their obsessions during increasingly longer periods ranging up to 15 minutes. Rachman uses a hierarchical presentation (Rachman & Hodgson, 1980, p. 282). Instructions for response prevention are provided if patients appear to possess neutralizing thoughts or neutralizing compulsions. The effectiveness of this treatment has not been investigated in obsessive patients. Emmelkamp and Kwee (1977) developed a method which is also based on the idea of habituation. In this procedure patients are continually exposed to their obsessions. The duration of an exposure session lasts minimally 60 minutes, during which patients are instructed to sit comfortably and close their eyes. Next, the patient is asked to imagine as vividly as possible an obsession described by the therapist. Imagining this scene may not be avoided in any way at all. Here the therapist emphasizes the prevention of neutralizing tension caused by the obsessive thoughts. Consecutively, those obsessions are described that evoke the most anxiety. Only when a certain obsessive scene does not provoke anxiety any more, does its presentation cease. The therapist describes the scene in a matter of fact way, to avoid inducing additional anxiety. Emmelkamp and Kwee's method differs in some respects from Rachman's satiation training. In the first place, the therapist leads the active imagining of the obsessions in order to prevent the patient from avoiding and neutralizing them. In the second place, the presentation of the scenes is of long duration and is continuous, in order to facilitate habituation. Another difference from Rachman's method is the use of the most difficult obsessions from the very beginning, which implies that there is no hierarchical presentation. Furthermore, it is important that there should be no opportunity to recuperate from the exposure session, apart from a few seconds after every presentation in which the patient is asked to rate his anxiety. Habituation appears to take place in these exposure treatments. In a number of patients Emmelkamp (1982) had the patients rate their subjective anxiety on a scale from 0 to 10. It was apparent that anxiety, after an initial peak at the beginning of the session, gradually subsided at the end of the session. It is not always clear which patients will benefit most from thought-stopping as opposed to imaginal exposure. In a study into the effect of both methods, Emmelkamp and Kwee (1977) found them to be equally effective. The results of this study suggest that a common mechanism in both treatments may be responsible for the effects attained. In another study (Emmelkamp & Giesselbach, 1981) it appeared to be important to expose patients to their own obsessions instead of other anxiety-inducing scenes. When a patient imagined being torn apart by a tiger, having a plane-crash, being burned or strangled, this appeared to have less effect on the obsessions, in comparison to the situation in which the patients had to imagine their own obsessions. It may be concluded that it is not so much habituation to anxiety in general, but the habituation to obsessions that is the active treatment ingredient. Results of both studies show that prolonged imagery exposure can be an important treatment for obsessions. The next example illustrates the application of this procedure in an obsession with the theme of dying.

Susan

Susan is a 27-year-old female suffering from fear of dying. She is subject to obsessions in which she sees herself dying. This happens several times a day. Cue selection also plays an essential part here before the actual exposure is begun. Part of the cue selection is given below.

THERAPIST: Can you describe what is going on with you at that moment?
PATIENT: Well, I begin to get hot in my head and so I think I have a tumour.
T: What happens next?
P: Well, I become anxious and say 'Oh, God, I feel odd' and then I see that it has all ended.
T: What do you see exactly?
P: Well, for example, that I'm running to my neighbour—she's a nurse—to call a doctor and then all of a sudden....I'm gone.
T: And then?
P: Well, I'm dead and the neighbour phones David [her husband] and he tells my parents and then they say: 'So sudden, she was so young'.
T: You see all that before you?
P: Yes, it is just like in a film.
T: And then what happens?
P: I don't know.
T: Try to concentrate; go ahead and close your eyes. Imagine you're dying . . .
P: (She closes her eyes)
T: Tell me what you see.
P: Well . . . I'm dying, and . . . the funeral . . . and then they see my house isn't tidy.
T: Who sees this?
P: Martha and Iris [sisters-in-law].
T: Keep your eyes closed. How does it continue?
P: Well, later on they tell the family, they say: 'That Susan sure had a mess in her cupboards'.

Further questioning yields the following information: the patient is afraid of illnesses that lead to a sudden death (e.g. cerebral haemorrhage, tumour, heart attack). Because of this she also has body sensations (e.g. hot head, stifling, shortness of breath, a burning pain in chest and arms). Death is always sudden (no long illnesses), and she is terrified of her housekeeping being criticized after her death. She visualizes the funeral vividly. It is important to include all these cues in the scenes to be used during prolonged exposure in imagination. Following is a scene used during the treatment:

Imagine you're at home, the weather is fine, but you don't feel well. You have a headache and you think: "I'd better take an aspirin to make it go away." You lie down in bed but it doesn't pass. It is a very strange feeling, a different kind of headache. You get up . . . you feel dizzy, warm in your head and then you think—if this only turns out all right—you feel even stranger, can no longer tell where you are . . . you have to go to the neighbour . . . you think you're having a seizure . . . she has to phone the doctor . . . you ring the neighbour's bell—she opens the door: "What's the matter with you?" she asks. But you can no longer say anything—you fall down, just like that . . . and then you feel that you are going to die . . . then it is over . . . you're dead . . . on the neighbour's step. David dashes home . . . your parents as well. They do not understand: "How is this possible, she is only 27?" Your mother is crying, your father is trying to console her—you can never speak to them again, never go out with them—you are dead. Then there's the funeral—you are lying in your coffin . . . at the front of the church . . . Everybody is there ... the whole family ... your friends ... and then the Reverend says that it is so incomprehensible that such a young woman should be snatched away in the prime of her life, and the people cry—then they go to the graveyard ... you are lying in your coffin in the grave ... slowly the coffin is lowered—your mother is crying—David is crying—and then for the last time they wish you goodbye—then they leave ... they leave you behind in the graveyard. After the funeral Iris and Martha go to your house to prepare dinner for the family. Iris opens the kitchen cupboards and says to Martha: "What a mess, just look at that, she had little to do and still the place is a mess." They tell the family what a mess the place is in ... Iris wipes her fingers across the windowsill, sees all the dog's hairs on the floor, and shows the others ... that you could be so untidy.

It is important to correspond to patients' factual thought in these scenes and not to exaggerate. The best way to present the scenes is in a matter-of-fact tone. Dramatization usually leads to ridicule and offers an opportunity for cognitive avoidance: "This is not real—this is not how it happens in real life." The recording of these scenes is not advised, because such a method of presenting a situation generally has little effect.

The therapist is constantly on the look out for outward signs of anxiety to discover whether certain items especially evoke anxiety. Such an item can then be offered repeatedly until habituation has occurred. With exposure in imagination, too, it is useful to score patients' subjective anxiety levels after each scene. Care must be taken, however, that no breaks are introduced in the actual exposure since such breaks obstruct habituation. For the same reason, it is not sensible to ask for further information during an exposure session; this should be done before or after the exposure session. Duration of exposure sessions depends on whether anxiety has diminished; therefore, there are no general rules to be given. After one and a half hours, however, it becomes impossible for most people to continue concentrating on scenes. It is advisable not to introduce new material or variations at the end of an exposure session as the chances are that little time will remain for reducing the anxiety. Such a mistake was made with Susan during the second exposure session. The anxiety had decreased on the presentation of scenes so much that the patient was made to describe the scenes herself. As a result of this variation, the anxiety level increased again. This caused the patient to suffer some days of anxiety and led to justified feelings of guilt in the therapist.

Variation of scenes is necessary to prevent patients from habituating to the text instead of to the situation. When patients have difficulty in identifying themselves with their roles, it helps to have the patient describe the scenes aloud. The therapist should pay attention to subtle avoidance behaviour. In the example mentioned above (Susan) the patient kept referring to *it* when in fact she was referring to herself or the coffin. The therapist must correct this, for example by asking "Who is lying in the coffin?" After some time—if exposure sessions have been successful—the patient may be given exposure for homework. The patient must make the time, once a day for at least an hour, to go through the scenes until anxiety has decreased. If the patient cannot do this (too threatening) alone at home, it may help to use successive approximation to achieve this.

Other treatments

Harming obsessions constitute an important category within the realm of obsessive-compulsive disorders. These patients suffer from obsessions of killing themselves or other people. We hypothesized that these patients have problems in handling their aggression, since often substantial levels of non-assertive behaviours are observed in them. More precisely, our hypothesis was that these harming obsessions could be generated by a failure to express aggressive feelings adequately, and by related guilt feelings. We wondered whether a more adequate way of coping with aggression (for example by assertion training), would result in a decrease of harming obsessions. In order to investigate this issue we used a cross-over design with six patients to compare the application of thought-stopping and assertion training (Emmelkamp & Van der Heyden, 1980). Each patient received both treatments, but the sequence was varied among patients. The results showed assertion training to be equally as effective as thought stopping. In four out of six cases there was a considerable reduction in obsession frequency after teaching of assertive skills. The results with thought-stopping were less favourable; a decrease of obsession frequency appeared to be present in only two cases.

CONCLUSIONS

The studies on obsessions discussed thus far cannot lead to firm conclusions, because only a limited number of patients were involved. Nevertheless, imaginary exposure seems to be a relevant treatment for obsessions, whereas the effects of thought-stopping are less stable. In harming obsessions, assertion training may be important, but at present it is not clear whether other obsessive patients may profit from this type of training as well.

9 The Treatment of Other Anxiety Disorders

POST-TRAUMATIC STRESS DISORDER AND GENERALIZED ANXIETY DISORDER

In the previous chapters a number of anxiety disorders have been discussed, each having a long history. The attention received by the disorders mentioned in this chapter, that is post-traumatic stress disorder and generalized anxiety disorder, is of more recent date. Epidemiological data and treatment research regarding these disorders are very sparse.

POST-TRAUMATIC STRESS DISORDER

Empirical results

The learning theoretical model explains the development of post-traumatic stress disorder in terms of classical and operant conditioning. The traumatic event serves as an aversive unconditioned stimulus, leading to extreme tension. The process of conditioning transforms the neutral stimuli associated with the traumatic event to conditioned stimuli which in turn provoke anxiety reactions. This leads to the avoidance of these conditioned stimuli. The behavioural treatment of post-traumatic stress disorder generally consists of some form of exposure. This exposure can be in imagination, in which the patient imagines all kinds of aversive images until habituation takes place, or *in vivo*. In the latter form of treatment the patient is confronted with all kinds of real situations related to the trauma until habituation occurs and anxiety diminishes. The treatments may be conducted gradually, in which case increasingly difficult situations are presented, but in many cases it seems necessary to confront the patient with the worst possible scenario from the beginning (flooding). This applies particularly to patients who are afraid of being overwhelmed with painful sensations, and who avoid thinking of aspects of the traumatic situation. Most studies have involved rape victims and people suffering from war traumata.

War trauma

Until now the effect of flooding on persons with war trauma has primarily been studied in case histories. Imaginal flooding proved to be effective in a treatment of war traumata (see Emmelkamp, 1990a, for a review). Kipper (1977) reported a successful treatment of people with war traumata by means of exposure *in vivo* to stimuli related to the traumatic events (such as injured persons, films about war, the sound of aeroplanes, helicopters and shooting). Only one controlled study has been published on the behavioural treatment of war trauma (Keane, Fairbank, Caddell, & Zimmering, 1989). Treatment consisting of relaxation and imaginal exposure resulted in significant reduction of symptoms associated with post-traumatic stress disorder.

Rape trauma

Two behavioural and cognitive-behavioural treatments are now widely applied in the treatment of rape victims: stress-management/stress inoculation training and exposure. Stress-management was found to be effective in studies by Veronen and Kilpatrick (1983), Frank, Anderson, Stewart, Dancu et al. (1988), Resick, Jordan, Girelli, Kotsis-Hutter and Marhoefer-Dvorak (1988) and Foa, Rothbaum, Riggs and Murdock (1991). In the latter study exposure, stress inoculation training and supportive counselling were compared. Exposure consisted of imaginal exposure in order to relive the rape scene in imagination. Homework involved *in vivo* exposure to 'safe' feared and avoided situations. At the end of treatment stress inoculation was more effective than the other conditions on measures of PTSD symptoms. However, at follow-up 3.5 months later exposure was found to be the most effective treatment. The application of flooding in rape victims has been criticized by Kilpatrick (Kilpatrick & Best, 1984). Her main objection implies that flooding could result in a habituation of patients to similar rape situations, which would make them less cautious in future if faced with a new threat. Steketee and Foa (1987) state that there is no evidence that flooding would lead to a disregard for one's own safety. Kilpatrick's second point of criticism relates to the fact that a treatment by means of flooding does not pay any attention to the learning of coping strategies. In our opinion, this does not mean that flooding cannot be beneficial. It does imply however, that in some patients treatment should be directed at acquiring coping skills in addition to fear reduction.

Conducting treatment

In the treatment of post-traumatic stress disorder there is greater emphasis on the quality of the therapeutic relationship than in the treatment of other anxiety disorders. The therapist should manoeuvre carefully in order not to upset the patient's confidence, because for the latter it might have been a great step to seek help in the first place. This is probably caused by the fact that many patients try to avoid reactivating the traumata by all means. The diagnostic criteria of PTSD include several forms of avoidance, such as active avoidance behaviour and psychogenic amnesia. It seems to be a good start to have the patient first utter his fears, worries, and experiences of the event. This serves the purpose of building an understanding contact and helps in estimating the influence of the experiences. Furthermore, it is very important to assess the resilience of the patient and to gain insight into the risks of decompensation and suicidal behaviour. The exposure paradigm mentioned above seems to be an important element of the treatment of these kind of complaints as illustrated by the following case.

Mr Johnson suffered forced labour in Germany during the Second World War and in that situation he had been exposed to various traumatic situations. He saw many of his comrades die, but he himself miraculously escaped this fate. After the war he, like many others, helped to re-establish the economy by working hard and not looking back. When he retired several years ago, he experienced bad times. Since that time he has worried a lot, is irritable, smokes and drinks rather too much, and sleeps badly. Although his wife tries to support him, he is not able to talk with her about his war memories and the emerging feelings. All he can do is stare out of the window. In the course of the admission interview the carefully hidden memories are gradually disclosed. Since the war he has never been abroad and refuses to go to places where many German tourists gather. During all these years, he has not talked with anyone about his war experiences. The treatment we offered Mr Johnson consists of several forms of exposure. During the sessions Mr Johnson speaks about his experiences in detail. Furthermore, he writes them down and is encouraged by the therapist to talk about them with his wife. Their talking about the war is stimulated by watching war documentaries together. In the course of treatment Mr Johnson indicates that he feels more free to express himself and that he shows less tendency to hide his emotions of anger, sadness and frustration.

In post-traumatic stress patients, the therapist should be alert not to move too fast in therapy. Sometimes the therapist may get the false impression that the problems are only minor, which may be caused by the persistent avoidance of the trauma-associated emotions and conversational issues. It often happens that patients dare to relate their trauma only in the course of treatment or after contacts with several professionals. Often post-traumatic stress disorder does not occur in isolatation but emerges in addition to other complaints, such as depression and anxiety disorders. The next example shows this can be the case (Elsenga & Emmelkamp, 1989).

During the treatment of an agoraphobic woman, it becomes clear that she fell victim to sexual violence and abuse prior to the onset of agoraphobia. Initially this information is not known to the therapist and the patient is treated for her agoraphobia with exposure *in vivo*. Although treatment proves reasonably successful in the town where the treatment takes place, the patient remains fearful while practising in her own area. She also indicates that she is suffering from headaches, nightmares and sleepwalking, and from growing irritability. The problems during the exercises seem to be related to the fact that she has met her father while practising in her home town. In the next session the patient very reluctantly admits that she has been involved in an incestuous relationship with an elder brother, that she was assaulted by an acquaintance, that she was nearly raped and also that she had been sexually abused by her father. This new information leads to the hypothesis that the agoraphobia is very much controlled by the avoidance of anxiety related to her father. The second hypothesis is that many stimuli associated with the traumatic incestuous experience are conditioned to emotional and avoidance reactions. Stimuli are both tangible (such as pictures and gifts) and cognitive (memories) in nature. It is assumed that prolonged imaginal exposure to these fear-provoking thoughts, images, memories and concrete objects will result in habituation. In addition, an important source for the maintenance of agoraphobia may be reduced. In the following phase of treatment the patient is confronted with prolonged exposure to the various rape and incest experiences. During these sessions she becomes more and more able to mention these experiences and to work through the associated feelings. The resistance to being confronted with the incestuous experiences with her father appears to be very great, which prompts the therapist to postpone further confrontations for some time. Although imaginal exposure leads to her working through events in which her father was not involved, the effect on the agoraphobia appears to be very negative. The patient has relapsed completely. She does not seem to be able to work through the emotional experiences related to her father. Therefore, it seems most practicable to increase her self-esteem first by repeating the exposure exercises to the agoraphobic situations, and then proceeding with improving her social skills. As a result of the repeated exposure *in vivo* exercises, the patient is able to go out into the street and do her shopping. This result is maintained during the assertiveness training which in turn reduces the amount of tension in social situations. At this point the patient feels that she has reached her goal, that is as far as the agoraphobia is concerned. She is still experiencing all kinds of complaints related to the incestuous experiences with her father, such as irritability and nightmares. The patient herself indicates that she wants to handle the problems related to her father. Therefore, the next 20 sessions are devoted to imaginal exposure to the traumatic situations. As may be expected, this phase in treatment evokes even more emotions than the previous imaginary exposure. The treatment has a clear effect on the working through of the traumatic events. However, its effect on the agoraphobia is again negative. Therefore, a brief repetition of the exposure *in vivo* exercises for the agoraphobia is necessary and successfully accomplished. The most remarkable result is that the patient now for the first time is able to walk in her home town without feeling tense.

This case illustrates the complex relationship between agoraphobic complaints and a history of traumatic events. It seems that the agoraphobia has the function of reducing or hiding the painful memories of the traumatic experiences. The post-traumatic stress disorder emerged when the avoidance of traumatic situations no longer succeeded. By being exposed to the agoraphobic situations, the patient ran the risk of being confronted with situations reactivating the hidden traumatic memories. Both phases of imaginary exposure in turn led to anxiety and avoidance of agoraphobic situations, although they were successful with respect to working through the traumatic events.

GENERALIZED ANXIETY DISORDER

Empirical results

The development of psychological treatments for generalized anxiety disorder has been greatly stimulated by the fact that many people suffering from this anxiety disorder are strongly dependent on (or addicted to) anxiolytic drugs and alcohol. Over the past few years several treatments have been proposed and have been evaluated in research. In particular, relaxation training and the modification of anxiety-inducing cognitions have received much attention. The most important findings will be briefly discussed.

Relaxation techniques

It is central to relaxation exercises that the patient learns to relax, that he learns to recognize somatic phenomena of tension and subsequently to apply relaxation when the first signals are actually perceived. This implies an active way of treating anxiety complaints. A great deal of research has been conducted into the effectiveness of relaxation training in generalized anxiety disorder in non-clinical groups of volunteers, such as students. Although the results give a positive impression of the effects of relaxation the findings are not immediately relevant to clinical groups. Anxiety management training (AMT), applied relaxation (AR) and cue-controlled relaxation (which will be discussed later on in this chapter) are frequently-used techniques. Anxiety management training consists of a combination of relaxation, comforting self-talk, and eliciting of anxiety-inducing and comforting images (which is called image-switching). Jannoun, Oppenheimer and Gelder (1982) investigated the effects of anxiety management training in apprehensive outpatients. This approach was found to produce a reduction both in fear and in the use of anxiolytic drugs in comparison with the findings in a no-treatment group. The patients, however, found image-switching difficult to carry out. Therefore, Butler, Gelder, Hibbert, Cullington and Klimes (1987b) replaced image-switching by exposure *in vivo* in situations which were occasionally avoided. In the latter study patients in the anxiety management group appeared to improve significantly more on measures of anxiety, depression and general problems than a waiting list group. Two studies were conducted on the effectiveness of group treatment, by Eayrs, Rowan and Harvey (1984) and (an uncontrolled study) by Powell (1987). Eayrs, Rowan and Harvey (1984) compared anxiety management training with relaxation exercises, both performed in group, and found the two approaches to be equally effective. Blowers, Cobb and Mathews (1987) compared anxiety management training (consisting of cue-controlled relaxation and cognitive therapy according to Beck) with both a non-directive counselling and a waiting list control group. The former package appeared to be more effective than no treatment, although patients in the non-directive therapy condition improved equally. Furthermore, in this study the effects of anxiety management training were less pronounced than in the study by Butler et al. (1987b) who, as mentioned above, included exposure *in vivo* in their package. We may therefore conclude that anxiety management training does lead to clinically significant results, but that relaxation training *per se* or non-directive therapy are equally effective. Furthermore, a study by Butler et al. shows that additional exposure *in vivo* appears to be an important ingredient of the treatment. Finally, a number of studies focus on the role of biofeedback in the reduction of fear. Two reviews (Emmelkamp, 1982, and Rice & Blanchard, 1982) show that biofeedback training has no additional value in the treatment of generalized anxiety; relaxation training accomplishes a comparable result.

Cognitive therapy

The cognitive paradigm holds that anxiety is prompted by specific cognitions and assumptions by the patient. Treatments are therefore directed at modifying these anxiety-related cognitions linked to irrational estimations of danger. In one of the studies into cognitive restructuring (Woodward & Jones, 1980) the patients were asked to imagine anxiety-provoking situations and then to replace the negative self-statements by positive self-statements. A second group received an adapted form of systematic desensitization (of which relaxation training is a part), whereas a third group was treated with a combination of both methods. The results showed that the combined treatment group improved most, whereas the cognitive restructuring group did not improve at all. Studies encompassing an elaborate package of cognitive interventions (according to Beck & Emery, 1985) on the whole show a considerably more favourable result than the study mentioned above. A more intensive cognitive therapy, therefore, appears to be equally as effective as other behavioural therapies. Because of a number of methodological flaws in these studies, no further conclusions can be drawn.

Conducting treatment

Relaxation training appears to be an important element in the treatment of these anxiety complaints. Applied relaxation has been introduced by Öst (1986) as a technique in which the patient learns to recognize the first signs of anxiety and subsequently learns to cope with anxiety instead of being overwhelmed by it. The explanation of the treatment rationale focuses on the fact that anxiety is accompanied by bodily sensations. Furthermore, the patient is told that he will learn some skills which can be easily and quickly applied, and which need a lot of practice. The first homework assignment consists of the patient's self-observation in daily life, the monitoring of the first signs of anxiety and the monitoring of situations in which anxiety emerges. A number of consecutive phases can be discerned in the training of applied relaxation. In the first phase, the patient is trained in progressive relaxation, as described in detail by Bernstein and Borkovec (1973). According to this technique two main groups of muscles are discerned which are treated in one session each. One group consists of the muscles of the hands, arms, face, neck and shoulders; the muscles of the back, chest, belly, hips, legs and feet form the other group. Every muscle of such a group is tensed for about 5 seconds, and then relaxed for the next 10 to 15 seconds. The patient practises this exercise twice daily as a homework assignment, taking about 15 to 20 minutes for each. In the second phase, muscle tension is omitted and then the patient practises the immediate relaxation of each of the muscles. The total practice time is reduced to 5 or 7 minutes. This relaxation is related to breathing, for which the therapist gives the following instruction:

> Breathe with calm, regular breaths and feel how you relax more and more for every breath... Just let go... Relax your forehead... eyebrows... eyelids... jaws... tongue and throat... lips... your entire face... Relax your neck... shoulders... arms... hands... and all the way out to your fingertips... Breathe calmly and regularly with your stomach all the time... Let the relaxation spread to your stomach... waist and back... Relax the lower part of your body, your behind... thighs... knees... calves... feet... and all the way down to the tips of your toes... Breathe calmly and regularly and feel how you relax more and more by each breath... Take a deep breath and hold your breath for a couple of seconds... and let the air out slowly... slowly... Notice how you relax more and more. (Öst, 1986, p.409)

Öst advises one or two weeks practising. The third stage of treatment consists of so-called cue-controlled relaxation. In this phase the patient learns to condition relaxation to the word "RELAX". Initially the therapist cooperates actively by giving instructions on the rhythm of the breathing pattern. On inhalation he says "INHALE" and just prior to exhaling he says "RELAX". After one or two weeks practice at home the patient will be able to relax in about 3 minutes. Differential relaxation, the fourth phase of applied relaxation, aims at generalizing relaxation to various circumstances, for example, when the patient is writing, making a telephone call, or talking to somebody else. Also the patient needs to practise relaxation while walking. In the fifth phase of the treatment, fast relaxation is taught by relaxing 15 to 20 times a day (which takes place in about 30 seconds), for example when the patient is watching a clock or making a telephone call. After about eight or ten sessions, the patient is able to apply the skills in daily life to reduce anxiety. In the next three sessions, the therapist presents fear-provoking stimuli for about 10 minutes during which the patient is instructed to regard these as a signal for relaxation skills. Lastly, by way of a maintenance programme, the patient is advised to check every day at a fixed time, whether it will be necessary to relax. In the previously mentioned study by Blowers, Cobb and Mathews (1987) a condensed form of relaxation is used, beginning with relaxation by means of calm breathing. Butler et al. (1987b) in their anxiety management training added several cognitive interventions to the relaxation, in which they encouraged the patient to check out the maintaining factors of fear and to eliminate them. Such factors may be anticipation anxiety, fear of fear, avoidance of difficult situations, and loss of self-esteem. These comforting thoughts are investigated and the patient is encouraged to check whether they can be replaced by more realistic and helpful thoughts. Furthermore, the therapist will encourage the positive sides of the patient's functioning in order to increase his self-esteem. The authors mentioned above record only briefly how they handled the patients' use of anxiety-reducing drugs. Butler et al. (1987a) in a pilot study showed that 15% of people suffering from generalized anxiety disorder used medication or alcohol as a means of reducing anxiety. In their treatment outcome study Butler et al. (1987b) succeeded only in encouraging their patient to refrain from anxiolytic drugs, while Blowers, Cobb and Mathews (1987, p. 495) left this completely to the patients and told them "that they could consult their general practitioner at any time should they wish to stop taking medication". It seems, however, to be highly desirable that a psychological approach in treating anxiety complaints should be added by using a structured approach to reduce the use of anxiolytic drugs and/or alcohol. Many patients consider giving these up as a big step and are predominantly concerned with the withdrawal symptoms.

CONCLUSIONS

Little is known about the two disorders we have discussed in this chapter. Diagnostic criteria have only recently been formulated, which in the case of generalized anxiety disorder are anything but clear. As a consequence, the research groups differ considerably, which hinders the interpretation of the results. Some of Butler et al.'s patients for example, are diagnosed as 'generalized anxiety disorder', but report panic attacks as well. In the case of post-traumatic stress disorder, the patients are treated with caution, which may explain the relatively small number of studies applying random assignment to treatment conditions. Consequently, it is difficult to compare the various treatment approaches in this group. Future studies with more homogeneous groups and clear treatment protocols should produce more specific results. Thus, we realize that the present conclusions will have to be reformulated in the near future in the light of new research findings.

10 Psychopharmacological Treatment

Several neuro-transmitter systems appear to be involved in the regulation of anxiety:

1. the benzodiazepine-GABA system;
2. the noradrenergic system; and
3. the serotonergic system (Hoehn-Saric & McLeod, 1988).

The neuro-transmitter GABA appears to play a role in the decrease of arousal. It is presumed that the overactivity of the noradrenergic system plays a role in the onset of panic attacks. It is hypothesized that both the noradrenergic system and the serotonergic system have a function in the tendency to worry and that both play an important role in obsessive-compulsive disorders. More recently it has been suggested that disorders in the serotonergic system correlate with the occurrence of panic attacks (Den Boer, 1988). For an overview of research into pharmacological models the reader is referred to Wamboldt and Insel (1988).

GENERALIZED ANXIETY DISORDER

There is only a limited number of studies in which the effect of psychopharmacology has been investigated in patients with a generalized anxiety disorder. The majority of these studies have been directed to the effect of benzodiazepines. In three controlled studies the effect appeared to be greater than that of the placebo (Buchbaum, Hazlett, Sicotte, Stein et al., 1985; Ceulemans, Hoppenbrouwers, Gelders & Reyntjens, 1985; Fontaine, Annable, Chouinard & Ogilvie, 1983); in three others, however, benzodiazepine was no more effective than the placebo (for a review see Perry, Garvey & Noyes, 1990). In general no difference in effect has been found between several kinds of benzodiazepines. Benzodiazepines possess relatively few side-effects and are also virtually non-toxic. An important objection against the use of benzodiazepines is the danger of habituation and addiction. Withdrawal symptoms often occur after sudden termination of medication (Noyes, Garvey, Cook & Perry, 1988), the symptoms being worst if the drugs have been taken for longer periods and in higher dosages. In addition, some benzodiazepines, particularly those with a short or middle–long half-life (such as lorazepam, oxazepam, temazepam and alprazolam), tend to cause serious symptoms such as trembling, nausea, vomiting, loss of concentration, restlessness, sleeplessness, perspiration, fatigue and irritability. Other known effects are the so-called rebound phenomena, occurring after a sudden termination of the medication, which are in many cases worse than the original complaints (Zitman, 1982). In view of those effects, benzodiazepines should be prescribed only for a limited period of time (Van Praag, 1988). Although it is generally suggested that tricyclic anti-depressants have little use in the treatment of generalized anxiety, two recent studies have been published from which it appears that imipramine had as much effect as chlordiazepoxide (Kahn, McNair, Lipman et al., 1986) and alprazolam (Hoehn-Saric, McLeod & Zimmerli, 1988). In the latter study imipramine in particular led to an elevation of mood and reduction of worrying, whereas alprazolam had an effect on the somatic symptoms and on tension.

PANIC AND AGORAPHOBIA

Benzodiazepines

Although benzodiazepines are often prescribed for patients with panic attacks and agoraphobia, there is no clear evidence that the commercial medications lead to reduction of panic attacks. Recently it has been suggested that a relatively new drug, alprazolam, could be of use for patients with a panic disorder. In a multi-centred study by Ballenger, Burrows, Dupont et al. (1988) alprazolam appeared to be more effective than a placebo: after 4 weeks 50% of the patients using alprazolam were no longer bothered by panic attacks, whereas the same results were found in only 28% of the patients in the placebo group. However, after 8 weeks, both treatments appeared to be equally effective. After the withdrawal of the medication many patients relapsed and appeared to be worse than the patients in the placebo condition (Pecknold, Swinson, Kuch & Lewis, 1988). Despite the fact that the medication was tapered off it led in 27% of the patients to rebound phenomena and in 35% to withdrawal phenomena. There are also other studies suggesting severe withdrawal phenomena and rebound panic attacks after termination of treatment with this drug (Fyer, Liebowitz, Gorman, Campeas, 1987; Juergens & Morse, 1988). One-third of a group of patients treated with alprazolam for panic disorder appeared to show major depression. Klosko, Barlow, Tassinari and Cerny (1988) compared the effectiveness of alprazolam with that of a cognitive behavioural intervention. The cognitive behaviour therapy had considerably better results than the alprazolam condition. At the end of treatment only 13% of the patients in the condition with cognitive therapy had panic attacks, whereas these occurred with 50% of the patients treated with alprazolam; with regard to the frequency of panic attacks the latter group could not be discriminated from the placebo condition. Marks and Swinson (1990) reported the results of an international multi-site study in which alprazolam was compared with exposure *in vivo*. Exposure had an effect twice as great as did alprazolam by the end of treatment, and an even greater effect during tapering off and treatment-free follow-up. The effect of alprazolam was actually worse than that of the placebo after treatment ended. Panics improved just as much with the placebo as with each of the two treatments. In summary, the effectiveness of benzodiazepines in panic disorder has not been convincingly demonstrated. Because of the possibility of addiction, withdrawal phenomena and rebound panic attacks that has been predominantly (but not exclusively) reported for alprazolam, use of this drug is not advised in the treatment of panic disorder.

Mono-amine-oxidase-inhibitors

Results from only a limited number of studies suggest that mono-amine-oxidase-inhibitors (MAO-inhibitors), and in particular phenelzine, may produce favourable results in patients with panic disorder and agoraphobia (Lipsedge, Hajioff, Huggins, Napier et al., 1973; Solyom, Heseltine, McClure, Solyom et al., 1973; Sheehan, Ballenger & Jacobson, 1981; Tyrer, Candy & Kelly, 1973). Solyom, Solyom, La Pierre, Pecknold and Morton (1981), however, found no difference between the effectiveness of phenelzine and a placebo. In most of the studies the patients were instructed to go out and practise in phobic situations (exposure *in vivo*) which hampered the interpretation of the results. The effect of MAO-inhibitors without exposure *in vivo* has not been determined. In the only study in which it has been tried to separate the effects of exposure *in vivo* and phenelzine (Solyom et al., 1981), phenelzine did not appear to be more effective than a placebo. Furthermore, it appeared that many patients relapsed as soon as the drugs were withdrawn (Lipsedge et al., 1973; Solyom et al., 1973; Tyrer, Candy & Kelly, 1973). In view of the limited number of positive results of MAO-inhibitors and the vast number of disadvantages connected with their use (Van Praag, 1988), extreme caution should be observed in prescribing this drug.

Tricyclic anti-depressants

The effects of these drugs have been best documented for panic attacks. Up until now a great number of studies have been published on the effect of imipramine in comparison with that of a placebo in patients with panic disorder and agoraphobia. Most studies show that imipramine is more effective than a placebo (Marks, 1987). However, in two studies this did not appear to be the case (Marks, Gray, Cohen et al., 1983; Evans, Kenardy, Schneider & Hoey, 1986). Up until now only one controlled study into the effect of clomipramine in panic disorders has been published, in which it appeared that clomipramine was more effective than a placebo (Johnston, Troyer & Whitsett, 1988). It should be noted, however, that in most studies the patients received exposure *in vivo* assignments, which hampers the interpretation of the results (Emmelkamp, 1982). A number of studies showed that imipramine with exposure *in vivo* was more effective than imipramine alone (Mavissakalian & Michelson, 1983; 1986a; 1986b; Telch, Agras, Taylor et al., 1985). In the latter study imipramine appeared to have no effect on agoraphobia and panic attacks if the patients were given instructions not to practise in phobic situations. In panic patients, no relationship was found between the dosage of imipramine in the blood level and the amelioration of panic disorder (Marks et al., 1983; Mavissakalian & Michelson, 1986a). These results show that claims made by Klein (1964) that imipramine has a specific "anti-panic" effect are as yet unfounded. It seems more plausible that the medication leads to an amelioration of mood, which motivates the patient to become involved in situations in which he previously has either had or was afraid to get, panic attacks. The final improvement of the agoraphobia can be seen as a result of the habituation that occurs during exposure *in vivo*. If imipramine does have a specific anti-panic effect one would expect this effect also to occur when the patient has no exposure assignment, which was not the case in the study by Telch et al. (1985). A serious danger in the treatment of panic patients with tricyclic anti-depressants is the risk of an increase of anxiety at the beginning of treatment. Furthermore, side-effects often occur and the therapeutic effect can be expected only after a number of weeks. This leads to a large number of drop-outs (about 30% during treatment). In patients who have completed treatment relapse appears to occur after the medication has been withdrawn. Telch, Tearnan and Taylor (1983) summarized the literature and found relapse percentages from between 27% and 50%.

Selective 5HT-uptake inhibitors

In the past few years chemical compounds have been developed that have a selective influence on the serotonergic system rather than acting via the GABA-system. Recent studies show that fluvoxamine reduces anxiety and panic in patients with a panic disorder (Den Boer, 1988). Fluvoxamine, however, has less effect on agoraphobic avoidance behaviour. At the end of the study, the mean score on the Agoraphobia subscale of the Fear Questionnaire was 24, indicating that after 2 months patients were still considerably agoraphobic. After 3 weeks of behaviour therapy, consisting of prolonged exposure *in vivo*, the mean score on this scale in a comparable group of agoraphobics decreased to 15 (Arrindell, Emmelkamp, & Sanderman, 1986).

Beta-adrenergic inhibitors

A number of studies have evaluated the effect of beta-adrenergic blockers in patients with panic disorder and agoraphobia. Beta-blockers influence the nervous system by blocking the transmission of certain stimulators. As a result all kinds of autonomic somatic reactions such as palpitations, trembling and perspiring, are reduced. For this reason it has been suggested that the use of beta-blockers may be useful in disorders in which somatic phenomena of anxiety, and as a result of this, fear of the somatic phenomena, play a prominent role. It has been presumed that these drugs should be useful as assistance to exposure *in vivo* in treating agoraphobia because they could suppress the somatic phenomena of anxiety which often occur in exposure *in vivo*. Results of studies conducted up to now show, however, that the use of beta-blockers has no influence on the effect of exposure *in vivo*. Neither alprenolol (Ullrich, Crombach & Peikert, 1972), propanolol (Hafner & Milton, 1977) nor bupranolol (Butollo, Burkhardt, Himmler & Müller, 1978) appeared to increase the effect of exposure *in vivo*. In a study by Griez and Van den Hout (1986) repeated CO_2 inhalation appeared to be more effective than treatment with propanolol. Beta-adrenergic inhibitors therefore do not seem to be indicated in the treatment of patients with panic disorder.

SOCIAL PHOBIA

Studies have also been conducted into the effects of benzodiazepines, MAO-inhibitors and beta-blockers on patients with social phobia. Only three studies were conducted in social phobics, the other studies related to volunteers with stage fright. Table 10.1 summarizes the results of studies over the past 15 years.

Benzodiazepines

Although benzodiazepines are frequently prescribed for tenseness in social situations, up until now there has been no study in which their effectiveness has been evaluated in clinical social phobics. In a study of volunteers with anxiety about musical performances (James & Savage, 1984), it appeared that diazepam was considerably less effective than the beta-blocker nadolol, and even led to a slight deterioration compared to the performances that were given without use of the drug. The use of alprazolam has been described in a case study (Lydiard, Laraia, Howell & Ballenger, 1988) and in an uncontrolled study (Reich & Yates, 1988). In the latter investigation alprazolam was combined with exposure *in vivo* assignments. After 8 weeks, treatment appeared to be effective, but as soon as the medication was terminated, the patients became as anxious as they were at the beginning of the treatment. In view of the fact that the administration of alprazolam in other anxiety disorders causes a number of undesirable side-effects (strong dependence, panic attacks, and depression after termination) care should be taken in prescribing these drugs.

Beta-adrenergic blockers

Since social anxiety is often combined with all kinds of somatic phenomena, such as palpitations, perspiration, trembling and blushing, it has been suggested

Table 10.1. Results of controlled studies on effectiveness of pharmacological treatments for social anxiety

Study	Complaint	Group	N	Drug	Design	Results
Brantigan et al. (1982)	Stage fright	V	29	(1) Propanolol* (40 mg) (2) Placebo	Double-blind Cross-over	1 > 2
Falloon, Lloyd & Harpin (1981)	Social phobia	P	12	(1) Propanolol (160–320 mg) (2) Placebo	Double-blind Between-group	1 = 2
James et al. (1977)	Stage fright	V	24	(1) Oxprenolol* (40 mg) (2) Placebo	Double-blind Cross-over	1 > 2
James et al. (1983)	Stage fright	V	30	(1) Pindolol* (5 mg) (2) Placebo	Double-blind Cross-over	1 > 2 on anxiety 1 = 2 on performance
James & Savage (1984)	Stage fright	V	33	(1) Nadolol* (40 mg) (2) Diazepam* (2 mg) (3) Placebo	Double-blind Cross-over	1 > 2 and 3
Liden & Gottfries (1974)	Stage fright	V	15	(1) Alprenolol* (50 & 100 mg) (2) Placebo	Double-blind Between-group	1 > 2
Liebowitz et al. (1986)	Social phobia	P	21	(1) Atenolol (50–100 mg) (2) Phenelzine (60–90 mg)	Open study Between-group	1 = 2 No random assignment
Liebowitz et al. (1988)	Social phobia	P	41	(1) Atenolol (50–100 mg) (2) Phenelzine (60–90 mg) (3) Placebo	Double-blind Between-group	2 > 1 = 3
Neftel et al. (1982)	Stage fright	V	22	(1) Atenolol* (100 mg) (2) Placebo	Double-blind Between-group	1 > 2 on anxiety 1 = 2 on performance

1 > 2 : Treatment 1 better than treatment 2. 1 = 2 : Treatment 1 equals treatment 2. N = Number of subjects; V = Volunteers; P = Patients.
* Single dose before performance

that beta-adrenergic inhibitors could reduce anxiety in these patients. The use of beta-blockers would supposedly break the vicious circle because these phenomena should have been blocked by the drug. Therefore, it is not surprising that the bulk of publication on pharmacological treatment of social anxiety relates to the effects of beta-blockers. Most of the studies have been conducted on volunteers with a form of stage fright (e.g. musicians with performance anxiety). Unfortunately, these results cannot be generalized to social phobics. In the latter group three investigations have been conducted. In a study by Falloon, Lloyd and Harpin (1981) no difference was found between the effectiveness of propanolol and that of a placebo. Liebowitz et al. (1986) found no differences between the beta-adrenergic blocker atenolol and the MAO-inhibitor phenelzine, but because of a number of methodological flaws (no placebo control group and no random assignment) results are hard to interpret. In a better designed study (Liebowitz, Gorman, Fyer et al., 1988) phenelzine appeared to be more effective after an 8 week period than atenolol and placebo. Atenolol appeared to be equally ineffective as a placebo. The indication area of beta-adrenergic blockers in social anxiety therefore seems to be restricted to stage fright, for which the drug should be taken one hour before the performance. It is important to note that beta-adrenergic blockers have many side-effects, such as nausea and vomiting, predominantly in short-term or incidental use. The use of beta-adrenergic blockers is not without danger. In CARA-patients they may lead to a deterioration of asthmatic conditions. Furthermore, withdrawal after long-standing use may lead to dangerous rhythm disorders of the heart, and even to cardiac arrest.

Mono-amine-oxidase-inhibitors

Social phobics took part in a number of previously discussed studies in which the effect of phenelzine was evaluated in agoraphobics, but the results have not been analysed for the social phobic group separately. Recent research by Liebowitz et al. (1986, 1988) into the effect of phenelzine gave inconclusive results. In the Liebowitz et al. (1986) study phenelzine did not appear to be more effective than placebo, whereas the reverse seemed to be the case in the study by Liebowitz et al. (1988). Given the limited number of studies, the conflicting results and the complications in the use of MAO-inhibitors, great caution in prescribing this drug is recommended.

OBSESSIVE-COMPULSIVE DISORDERS

In a number of studies the effects of tricyclic anti-depressants in compulsive patients have been evaluated. Most studies were carried out with clomipramine, because it was supposed that, particularly in compulsive patients, the serotonergic system would be disturbed and because clomipramine is partially a 5HT-uptake inhibitor. Clomipramine appeared to be more effective than placebo, but no more effective than other tricyclic anti-depressants (Marks, 1987). The latter findings do not support the hypothesis that the serotonergic system in compulsive patients is necessarily disturbed, since tricyclic anti-depressants which have less effect on this system lead to comparable results. In the long run the effects of tricyclic anti-depressants disappear (Mawson, Marks & Ramm, 1982; Kasviskis & Marks, 1988). In two studies it has been investigated whether clomipramine enhances the effect of exposure *in vivo* and response prevention. This appeared to happen in the study by Marks et al. (1980) only in the case of compulsive patients who were depressed at the same time. In a more recent study (Marks, Lelliott, Basuglu et al., 1988) clomipramine plus exposure instructions appeared to be more effective than a placebo plus exposure instructions; this difference, however, disappeared after 8 weeks. Clomipramine showed hardly any effect on patients with anti-exposure instructions. Treatment with tricyclic anti-depressants therefore seems particularly relevant in compulsive patients who are also depressed (Marks et al., 1980; Thoren, Asberg, Cronholm, Jörnestedt & Träskman, 1980) in supporting a programme of exposure *in vivo* and response prevention. When the depressed mood has been ameliorated these patients are more prepared to carry out exposure assignments. Similarly to panic patients, however, relapses often occur when medication has been withdrawn. A few studies have now been reported in which the newer 5-selective uptake-inhibitors fluvoxamine and fluoxetine have been studied with obsessive-compulsive patients. Both newer compounds were found to have some effects on obsessive-compulsive symptoms, but more placebo-controlled studies are needed before recommendations can be made.

CONCLUDING REMARKS

A big problem is the diagnostic discrimination between depressions and anxiety disorders. The considerable symptomatological overlap between these phenomena hampers a clear interpretation of the results of the "anti-depressants" in anxiety disorders. The favourable effects of these anti-depressant drugs on anxiety can in a number of cases also be explained by a reduction in depression.

References

Abe, K. & Masui, T. (1981) Age–sex trends of phobic and anxiety symptoms in adolescents. *British Journal of Psychiatry*, **138**, 297–302.

Abraham, K. (1927) *Selected Papers*. London: Hogarth Press.

Agras, W.S., Chapin, H.N. & Oliveau, D.C. (1972) The natural history of phobia: Course and prognosis. *Archives of General Psychiatry*, **26**, 315–317.

Agras, W.S., Sylvester, D. & Oliveau, D. (1969) The epidemiology of common fears and phobias. *Comprehensive Psychiatry*, **10**, 151–156.

Ainsworth, M.D.S. (1984) Attachment. In N.S. Endler & J. McV. Hunt (Eds), *Personality and the behavioral disorders. Vol I*. New York: Wiley.

Aitken, R.C.B., Lister, J.A. & Main, C.J. (1981) Identification of features associated with flying phobia in aircrew. *British Journal of Psychiatry*, **139**, 38–42.

Alström, J.E., Nordlund, C.L., Persson, G., Harding, M. & Ljungqvist, C. (1984) Effects of four methods on social phobic patients not suited for insight- oriented psychotherapy. *Acta Psychiatrica Scandinavica*, **70**, 97–110.

American Psychiatric Association (1980) *Diagnostic and Statistical Manual of Mental Disorders* (3rd edition). Washington, DC: APA.

American Psychiatric Association (1987) *Diagnostic and Statistical Manual of Mental Disorders* (3rd revised edition). Washington, DC: APA.

Ameringen, M. van, Mancini, C., Styan, G. & Donison, D. (1991) Relationship of social phobia with other psychiatric illness. *Journal of Affective Disorders*, **21**, 2, 93–99.

Amies, P.L., Gelder, M.G. & Shaw P.M. (1983) Social phobia: a comparative clinical study. *British Journal of Psychiatry*, **142**, 174–179.

Appleby, I.L., Klein, D.F., Sachar, E.J. & Levitt, M. (1981) Biochemical indices of lactate-induced panic: a preliminary report. In D.F. Klein & J. Rabkin (Eds), *Anxiety: New Research and Changing Concepts*. New York: Raven Press.

Arkowitz, H. (1977) The measurement and modification of minimal dating behavior. In M. Hersen, R.M. Eisler & P.M. Miller (Eds), *Progress in behavior modification, Vol. 5*. New York: Academic Press.

Arkowitz, H., Lichtenstein, E., McGovern, K. & Hines, P. (1975) The behavioral assessment of social competence in males. *Behavior Therapy*, **6**, 3–13.

Arrindell, W.A. (1987) Marital Conflict and Agoraphobia: Fact or Fantasy? PhD thesis, University of Groningen, The Netherlands.

Arrindell, W.A. & Emmelkamp, P.M.G. (1985) Psychological profile of the spouse of the female agoraphobic patient: Personality and symptoms. *British Journal of Psychiatry*, **146**, 405–414.

Arrindell, W.A. & Emmelkamp, P.M.G. (1986) Marital adjustment, intimacy and needs in female agoraphobics and their partners: A controlled study. *British Journal of Psychiatry*, **149**, 592–602.

Arrindell, W.A., Emmelkamp, P.M.G., Monsma, A. & Brilman, E. (1983) The role of perceived parental rearing practices in the aetiology of phobic disorders: A controlled study. *British Journal of Psychiatry*, **143**, 183–187.

Arrindell, W.A., Emmelkamp, P.M.G. & Sanderman, R. (1986) Marital quality and general life adjustment in relation to treatment outcome in agoraphobia. *Advances in Behaviour Research and Therapy*, **7**, 139–185.

Asso, D. & Beech, H.R. (1975) Susceptibility to the acquisition of a conditioned response in relation to the menstrual cycle. *Journal of Psychosomatic Research*, **19**, 337–344.

Ballenger, J.C., Burrows, G.D., DuPont, R.L., Lesser, I.M., Noyes, R., Pecknold, J.C., Rifkin, A. & Swinson, R.P. (1988) Alprazolam in panic disorder and agoraphobia: Results from a multicenter trial. *Archives of General Psychiatry*, **45**, 413–422.

Bandura, A. (1977) Self-efficacy: Toward a unifying theory of behavioral change. *Psychological Review*, **84**, 191–215.

Bandura, A., Adams, N.E. & Beyer, J. (1977) Cognitive processes mediating behavioral change. *Journal of Personality and Social Psychology*, **35**, 125–139.

Barlow, D.H. & Cerny, J.A. (1988) *Psychological Treatment of Panic*. New York: Guilford Press.

Barlow, D.H. & Hersen, M. (1984) *Single case experimental design*. New York: Pergamon Press.

Barlow, D.H., Leitenberg, H., Agras, W.S. & Wincze, J.P. (1969) The transfer gap in systematic desensitization: An analogue study. *Behaviour Research and Therapy*, **7**, 191–196.

Basoglu, M., Lax, T., Kasvikis, Y & Marks, I.M. (1988) Predictors of improvement in Obsessive-Compulsive Disorder. *Journal of Anxiety Disorders*, **2**, 299–308.

Beck, A.T. & Emery, G. (1985) *Anxiety Disorders and Phobias: A Cognitive Perspective*. New York: Basic Books.

Beech, H.R. (1974) *Obsessional States*. London: Methuen.

Beech, H.R. & Vaughan, M. (1978) *Behavioral Treatment of Obsessional States*. New York: Wiley.

Beidel, D.C., Turner, S.M. & Dancu, C.V. (1985) Psychological, cognitive and behavioral aspects of social anxiety. *Behaviour Research and Therapy*, **23**, 109–117.

Berg, I. (1976) School phobia in children of agoraphobic women. *British Journal of Psychiatry*, **128**, 86–89.

Bergler, E. (1944) A new approach to the therapy of erytrophobia. *Psychoanalytic Review*, **44**, 452–456.

Bernstein, D.A. & Borkovec, T.D. (1973) *Progressive Relaxation Training. A Manual for the Helping professions*. Illinois: Research Press.

Biran, M., Augusto, F., Wilson, G.T. (1981) In vivo exposure versus cognitive restructuring in the treatment of scriptophobia. *Behaviour Research and Therapy*, **19**, 525–532.

Biran, M. & Wilson, G.T. (1981) Treatment of phobic disorders using cognitive and exposure methods. *Journal of Consulting and Clinical Psychology*, **49**, 886.

Black, A. (1974) The natural history of obsessional neurosis. In H.R. Beech (Ed.) *Obsessional States*. London: Methuen.

Bland, R.C., Orn, H. & Newman, S.C. (1988) Lifetime prevalence of psychiatric disorders in Edmonton. *Acta Psychiatria Scandinavica*, (suppl. 338): 24–32.

Blowers, C., Cobb, J. & Mathews, A. (1987) Generalized anxiety: A controlled treatment study. *Behaviour Research and Therapy*, **25**, 493–502.

Boersma, K., Hengst, S. den, Dekker, J. & Emmelkamp, P.M.G. (1976) Exposure and response prevention in the natural environment: A comparison with obsessive-compulsive patients. *Behaviour Research and Therapy*, **14**, 19–24.

Bonn, J.A., Readhead, C.P.A. & Timmons, B.H. (1984) Enhanced adaptive behavioural response in agoraphobic patients pretreated with breathing retraining. *The Lancet*, **2**, 665–669.

Bourque, P. & Ladouceur, R. (1980) An investigation of various performance-based treatments with acrophobics. *Behaviour Research and Therapy*, **18**, 161–170.

Bowlby, J. (1973) *Attachment of loss: Vol. II: Separation, Anxiety and Anger*. New York: Basic Books.

Brantigan, C.O., Brantigan, T.A. & Joseph, N. (1982) Effect of beta blockade and beta stimulation on stage fright. *American Journal of Medicine*, **72**, 88–94.

Bruch, M.A. (1989) Familial and developmental antecedents of social phobia: Issues and findings. *Clinical Psychology Review*, **9**, 1, 37–47.

Bruch, M.A., Heimberg, R.G., Berger, P. & Collins, T.M. (1989) Social phobia and perception of early parental and personal characteristics. *Anxiety Research*, **2**, 57–65.

Buchbaum, M.S., Hazlett, E., Sicotte, N., Stein, M., Wu, J. & Zetin, M. (1985) Topographic EEG changes with benzodiazepine administation in generalized anxiety disorder. *Biological Psychiatry*, **20**, 832–842.

Buss, A.H. (1980) *Self-consciousness and social anxiety*. San Francisco: Freeman.

Butler, G. (1985) Exposure as a treatment for social phobia: Some instructive difficulties. *Behaviour Research and Therapy*, **23**, 651–657.

Butler, G., Cullington, A., Hibbert, G., Klimes, I. & Gelder, M. (1987a) Anxiety management for persistent generalized anxiety. *British Journal of Psychiatry*, **151**, 535–542.

Butler, G., Cullington, A., Munby, M., Amies, P. & Gelder, M. (1984) Exposure and anxiety management in the treatment of social phobia. *Journal of Consulting and Clinical Psychology*, **52**, 642–650.

Butler, G., Gelder, M., Hibbert, G., Cullington, A. & Klimes, I. (1987b) Anxiety management: Developing effective strategies. *Behaviour Research and Therapy*, **25**, 517–522.

Butollo, W., Burkhardt, P., Himmler, C. & Müller, M. (1978) *Mehrdimensionale Verhaltenstherapie und Beta-Blocker bei functionellen Dysrytmien und chronische körperbezogenen Angstreaktionen*. Paper presented at the Konferenz für psychosomatische Medizin, Cologne.

Carr, A.T. (1974) Compulsive neurosis: A review of the literature. *Psychological Bulletin*, **81**, 311–318.

Carruthers, M. & Taggart, P. (1973) Vagotonicity and violence: biochemical and cardiac responses to violent films and TV programs. *British Medical Journal*, **3**, 384–389.

Casat, C.D. (1988) Childhood anxiety disorders: A review of the possible relationship to adult panic disorder and agoraphobia. *Journal of Anxiety Disorders*, **2**, 51–60.

Ceulemans, D.L.S., Hoppenbrouwers, M., Gelders, Y. & Reyntjens, A.J.M. (1985) The influence of Ritanserin, a serotonin antagonist, in anxiety disorders: A double-blind placebo controlled study versus lorazepam. *Pharmacopsychiatry*, **18**, 303–305.

Chambless, D.L. (1982) Characteristics of agoraphobics. In D.L. Chambless & A.J. Goldstein (Eds), *Agoraphobia: Multiple perspectives on theory and treatment*. New York: Wiley.

Charney, D.S., Heninger, G.R. & Jatlow, P.I. (1985) Increased anxiogenic effects of caffeine in panic disorders. *Archives of General Psychiatry*, **42**, 232–243.

Clark, D.M. (1986) A cognitive approach to panic. *Behaviour Research and Therapy*, **24**, 461–470.

Clark, D.M. (1991) Cognitive Therapy for Panic Disorder. Paper presented at the NIH Consensus Development Conference, September 1991, Maryland, US.

Clark, D.M. & Salkovskis, P.M. (1989) *Manual*. Oxford: Warneford Hospital.

Clark, D.M., Salkovskis, P.M. & Chalkley, A.J. (1985) Respiratory control as a treatment for panic attacks. *Journal of Behaviour Therapy and Experimental Psychiatry*, **16**, 23–30.

Cobb, J.P., Mathews, A.A., Childs-Clarke, A. & Blowers, C.M. (1984) The spouse as co-therapist in the treatment of agoraphobia. *British Journal of Psychiatry*, **144**, 282–287.

Cohn, C.F., Kron, R.E. & Brady, J.P. (1976) A case of blood-illness-injury phobia treated behaviourally. *Journal of Nervous and Mental Disorders*, **162**, 65–68.

Connolly, J.C., Hallam, R.S. & Marks, I.M. (1976) Selective association of fainting with blood-injury-illness fear. *Behavior Therapy*, **7**, 8–13.

Costello, C.G. (1982) Fears and phobias in women: A community study. *Journal of Abnormal Psychology*, **91**, 280–286.

Craske, M.G., Sanderson, W.C. & Barlow, D.H. (1987) The relationship among panic, fear, and avoidance. *Journal of Anxiety Disorders*, **1**, 153–160.

Crowe, M.J., Marks, I.M., Agras, W.S. & Leitenberg, H. (1972) Time-limited desensitization, implosion and shaping for phobic patients: A cross-over study. *Behaviour Research and Therapy*, **10**, 319–328.

Cullington, A., Butler, G., Hibbert, G. & Gelder, M. (1984) Problem-solving: Not a treatment for agoraphobia. *Behavior Therapy*, **15**, 280–286.

Den Boer, J.A. (1988) Serotonergic mechanisms in anxiety disorders. PhD thesis, University of Utrecht, The Netherlands.

Derogatis, L.R. (1977) SCL-90 Administration, scoring and procedures manual 1 for the R(evised) version and other instruments of the psychopathology rating scale series. Baltimore, MD.: Clinical Psychometrics Research Unit, Johns Hopkins University School of Medicine.

DiNardo, P.A., Barlow, D.H., Cerny, J.A., Vermilyea, B.B., Vermilyea, J.A., Himadi, W.G. & Waddell, M.T. (1985) Anxiety Disorders Interview Schedule–Revised (ADIS-R). Albany, NY: Center for Stress and Anxiety Disorders.

DiNardo, P.A., Guzy, T., Jenkins, J.A., Bak, R.M., Tomasi, S.F. & Copland, M. (1988) Etiology and maintenance of dog fears. *Behaviour Research and Therapy*, **26**, 3, 241–244.

DiNardo, P.A., O'Brien, G.T., Barlow, D.H., Waddell, M.T. & Blanchard, E.B. (1983) Reliability of DSM-III anxiety disorder categories using a new structured interview. *Archives of General Psychiatry*, **40**, 1070–1075.

Dow, M.G., Biglan, A. & Glaser, S.R. (1985) Multimethod assessment of socially anxious and socially unanxious women. *Behavioral Assessment*, **7**, 273–282.

Dyckman, J.M. & Cowan, P.A. (1978) Imagining vividness and the outcome of in vivo and imagined scene desensitization. *Journal of Consulting and Clinical Psychology*, **48**, 1155–1156.

Eagle, M. & Wolitzky, D.L. (1988) Psychodynamics. In C.G. Last & M. Hersen (Eds), *Handbook of Anxiety Disorders*. New York: Pergamon Press.

Eayrs, C.B., Rowan, D. & Harvey, P.G. (1984) Behavioural group training for anxiety management. *Behavioural Psychotherapy*, **12**, 117–129.

Edelmann, R.J. (1985) Dealing with embarrasing events: socially anxious and non-socially anxious groups compared. *British Journal of Clinical Psychology*, **24**, 281–288.

Ehlers, A. & Margraf, J. (1989) A psychological model of panic. In P.M.G. Emmelkamp, W.T.A.M. Everaerd, F. Kraaimaat, M.J.M. van Son (Eds), *Annual Series of European Research in Behavior Therapy, Vol. IV: Fresh perspectives on anxiety disorders*. Amsterdam: Swets & Zeitlinger.

Ellis, A. (1962) *Reason and emotion in psychotherapy*. New York: Lyle-Stuart.

Elsenga, S. & Emmelkamp, P.M.G. (1989) Agorafobie en incest. *Directieve Therapie*, **9**, 4–17.

Emmelkamp, P.M.G. (1974) Self-observation versus flooding in the treatment of agoraphobia. *Behaviour Research and Therapy*, **12**, 229–237.

Emmelkamp, P.M.G. (1975) Effects of expectancy on systematic desensitization and flooding. *European Journal of Behavioral Analysis and Modification*, **1**, 1–11.

Emmelkamp, P.M.G. (1979) The behavioral treatment of clinical phobias. In: M. Hersen, M. Eisler & P. Miller (Eds.) *Progress in Behavior Modification*. New York: Academic press.

Emmelkamp, P.M.G. (1982) *Phobic and Obsessive-compulsive Disorders: Theory, Research and Practice*. New York: Plenum Press.

Emmelkamp, P.M.G. (1986) Behavior therapy with adults. In S.L. Garfield & A.E. Bergin (Eds), *Handbook of Psychotherapy and Behavior Change*. New York: Wiley.

Emmelkamp, P.M.G. (1987) Obsessive-compulsive disorder. In L. Michelson & M. Ascher (Eds), *Anxiety and Stress*. New York: Guilford Press.

Emmelkamp, P.M.G. (1990a) Anxiety Disorders. In A. Bellack, M. Hersen & A. Kazdin (Eds.), *The International Handbook of Behavior Modification and Therapy*. New York: Plenum Press.

Emmelkamp, P.M.G. (1990b) Obsessive-compulsive disorders in adulthood. In M. Hersen & C.G. Last (Eds), *Handbook of child and adult psychopathology: A longitudinal perspective*. New York: Pergamon Press.

Emmelkamp, P.M.G. en Beens, H. (1991) Cognitive therapy with obsessive-compulsive disorder: A comparative evaluation. *Behaviour Research and Therapy*, **29**, 293–300.

Emmelkamp, P.M.G., Brilman, E., Kuiper, H. & Mersch, P.P. (1986) The treatment of agoraphobia: A comparison of self-instructional training, rational emotive therapy and exposure in vivo. *Behavior Modification*, **10**, 37–53.

Emmelkamp, P.M.G. & Cohen-Kettenis, P. (1975) Relationship of locus of control to phobic anxiety and depression. *Psychological Reports*, **36**, 2, 390.

Emmelkamp, P.M.G., Dyck, R. van, Bitter, M., Heins, R., Onstein, E.J. & Eisen, B. (1992) Spouse-aided therapy with agoraphobics. *British Journal of Psychiatry*, **160**, 51–56.

Emmelkamp, P.M.G. & Emmelkamp-Benner, A. (1975) Effects of historically portrayed modeling and group treatment on self-observation: A comparison with agoraphobics. *Behaviour Research and Therapy*, **13**, 135–139.

Emmelkamp, P.M.G. & Felten, M. (1985) The process of exposure in vivo: Cognitive and physiological changes during treatment of acrophobia. *Behaviour Research and Therapy*, **23**, 219–223.

Emmelkamp, P.M.G. & Giesselbach, P. (1981) Treatment of obsessions: Relevant versus irrelevant exposure. *Behavioural Psychotherapy*, **9**, 322–329.

Emmelkamp, P.M.G., Haan, E. de & Hoogduin, C.A.L. (1990) Marital adjustment and obsessive-compulsive disorder. *British Journal of Psychiatry*, **156**, 55–60.

Emmelkamp, P.M.G. & Heyden, H. van der (1980) Treatment of harming obsessions. *Behavioural Analysis and Modification*, **4**, 28–35.

Emmelkamp, P.M.G. & Hout, A. van den (1983) Failure in treating agoraphobia. In E.B. Foa & P.M.G. Emmelkamp (Eds.), *Failures in Behavior Therapy*. New York: Wiley.

Emmelkamp, P.M.G., Hout, A. van den & De Vries, K. (1983) Assertive training for agoraphobics. *Behaviour Research and Therapy*, **21**, 63–68.

Emmelkamp, P.M.G. & Kraanen, J. (1977) Therapist controlled exposure in vivo versus self-controlled exposure in vivo: A comparison with obsessive-compulsive patients. *Behaviour Research and Therapy*, **15**, 491–495.

Emmelkamp, P.M.G., Kuipers, A. & Eggeraat, J. (1978) Cognitive modification versus prolonged exposure in vivo: A comparison with agoraphobics. *Behaviour Research and Therapy*, **16**, 33–41.

Emmelkamp, P.M.G. & Kwee, G.K. (1977) Obsessional ruminations: A comparison between thought-stopping and prolonged exposure in imagination. *Behaviour Research and Therapy*, **15**, 441–444.

Emmelkamp, P.M.G. & Lange, I. de (1983) Spouse involvement in the treatment of obsessive-compulsive patients. *Behaviour Research and Therapy*, **21**, 341–346.

Emmelkamp, P.M.G., Van Linden van den Heuvell, C., Rüphan, M. & Sanderman, R. (1989) Home-based treatment of obsessive-compulsive patients: Intersession interval and therapist involvement. *Behaviour Research and Therapy*, **21**, 341–346.

Emmelkamp, P.M.G. & Mersch, P.P. (1982) Cognition and exposure in vivo in the treatment of agoraphobia: Short-term and delayed effects. *Cognitive Therapy and Research*, **6**, 77–90.

Emmelkamp, P.M.G., Mersch, P.P., Vissia, E. & Van der Helm, M. (1985) Social phobia: A comparative evaluation of cognitive and behavioral interventions. *Behaviour Research and Therapy*, **23**, 365–369.

Emmelkamp, P.M.G. & Ultee, K.A. (1974) A comparison of successive approximation and self-observation in the treatment of agoraphobia. *Behavior Therapy*, **5**, 605–613.

Emmelkamp, P.M.G., Visser, S. & Hoekstra, R. (1988) Cognitive therapy versus exposure in vivo in the treatment of obsessive-compulsives. *Cognitive Therapy and Research*, **12**, 103–114.

Emmelkamp, P.M.G. & Wessels, H. (1975) Flooding in imagination versus flooding in vivo: A comparison with agoraphobics. *Behaviour Research and Therapy*, **13**, 7–16.

Evans, L., Kenardy, J., Schneider, P. & Hoey, H. (1986) Effect of a selective serotonin uptake inhibitor in agoraphobia with panic attacks: A double-blind comparison of zimeldine, imipramine and placebo. *Acta Psychiatrica Scandinavia*, **73**, 49–53.

Evers, R. (1988) Een behandeling van dysmorfofobie. *Directieve Therapie*, **9**, 326–335.

Falloon, I.R.H., Lindley, P. Mc.Donald, R. & Marks, I.M. (1977) Social skills training of out-patient groups. A controlled study of rehearsal and homework. *British Journal of Psychiatry*, **131**, 599–609.

Falloon, I.R.H., Lloyd, G.G. & Harpin, R.E. (1981) The treatment of social phobia. *Journal of Nervous and Mental Disease*, **169**, 180–184.

Fenichel, O. (1945) *The Psychoanalytic Theory of Neurosis*. New York: Norton.

Foa, E.B., Rothbaum, B.O., Riggs, D.S. & Murdock, T.B. (1991) Treatment of posttraumatic stress disorders in rape victims: A comparison between cognitive behavioral procedures and counseling. *Journal of Consulting and Clinical Psychology*, **59**, 715–723.

Foa, E.B., Steketee, G. & Milby, J.B. (1980a) Differential effects of exposure and response prevention in obsessive-compulsive washers. *Journal of Consulting and Clinical Psychology*, **48**, 71–79.

Foa, E.B., Jameson, J.R., Turner, R.M. & Payne, L.L. (1980b) Massed versus spaced exposure sessions in the treatment of agoraphobia. *Behaviour Research and Therapy*, **18**, 333–338.

Foa, E.B., Steketee, G., Turner, R.M. & Fischer, S.C. (1980c) Effects of imaginal exposure to feared disasters in obsessive-compulsive checkers. *Behaviour Research and Therapy*, **18**, 449–455.

Foa, E.B., Steketee, G., Graspar, J.B., Turner, R.M. & Latimer, R.L. (1984) Deliberate exposure and blocking of obsessive-compulsive rituals: Immediate and long-term effects. *Behavior Therapy*, **15**, 450–472.

Foa, E.B., Steketee, G. & Grayson, J.B. (1985) Imaginal and in vivo exposure: A comparison with obsessive-compulsive checkers. *Behavior Therapy*, **16**, 292–302.

Foa, E.B., Steketee, G., Grayson, J.B. & Doppelt, H.G. (1983) Treatment of obsessive-compulsives: When do we fail? In E.B. Foa & P.M.G. Emmelkamp (Eds.), *Failures in Behavior Therapy*. New York: Wiley.

Fontaine, R., Annable, L., Chouinard, G. & Ogilvie, R.I. (1983) Bromazepam and diazepam in generalized anxiety. *Journal of Clinical Psychopharmacology*, **3**, 80–87.

Frank, E., Anderson, B., Stewart, B.D., Dancu, C., Hughes, C. & West, D. (1988) Efficacy of cognitive behavior therapy and systematic desensitization in the treatment of rape trauma. *Behavior Therapy*, **19**, 403–420.

Fremouw, W., Gross, R., Monroe, J. & Rapp, S. (1982) Empirical subtypes of performance anxiety. *Behavioral Assessment*, **4**, 179–193.

Freud, S. (1909) *Analysis of a phobia in a five-year old boy.* Standard Edition (Vol. X). London: Hogarth Press, 1966.

Freud, S. (1947) Wege der Psychoanalytische Therapie. In *Gesammelte Werke WII Band. Werke aus den Jahren 1917-1920.* London: Imago.

Frisch, M.B., Elliott, C.H., Atsaides, J.P., Salva, D.M. & Denney, D.R. (1982) Social skills and stress management training to enhance patients' interpersonal competencies. *Psychotherapy: Theory, Research and Practice*, **19**, 349–358.

Fry, W.F. (1962) The marital context of anxiety syndrome. *Family Process*, **1**, 245–252.

Fyer, A.J., Liebowitz, M.R., Gorman, J.M., Campeas, R., Levin, A., Davies, O., Goetz, D. & Klein, D.F. (1987) Discontinuation of Alprazolam treatment in panic patients. *American Journal of Psychiatry*, **144**, 303–308.

Garssen, B., Veenendaal, W. van & Bloemink, R. (1983) Agoraphobia and the Hyperventilation Syndrome. *Behaviour Research and Therapy*, **21**, 643–649.

Garvey, M.J. & Tuason, V.B. (1984) The relationship of panic disorders to agoraphobia. *Comprehensive Psychiatry*, **25**, 529–531.

Gelder, M.G., Bancroft, J.H.J., Gath, D.H., Johnston, D.W., Mathews, A.M. & Shaw, P.M. (1973) Specific and non-specific factors in behaviour therapy. *British Journal of Psychiatry*, **123**, 445–462.

Gelder, M.G. & Marks, I.M. (1966) Severe agoraphobia: A controlled prospective trial of behaviour therapy. *British Journal of Psychiatry*, **113**, 53–73.

Gelder, M.G. & Marks, I.M. (1968) Desensitization and phobias: A crossover study. *British Journal of Psychiatry*, **114**, 323–328.

Gelder, M.G., Marks, I.M. & Wolff, H.H. (1967) Desensitization and psychotherapy in the treatment of phobic states: A controlled enquiry. *British Journal of Psychiatry*, **113**, 53–73.

Gerlsma, C., Emmelkamp, P.M.G. & Arrindell, W.A. (1990) Anxiety, depression and perception of early parenting: a meta-analysis. *Clinical Psychology Review*, **10**, 251–277.

Girodo, M. & Roehl, J. (1978) Cognitive preparation and coping self-talk: Anxiety management during the stress of flying. *Journal of Consulting and Clinical Psychology*, **46**, 978–989.

Golden, M. (1981) A measure of cognition within the context of assertion. *Journal of Clinical Psychology*, **37**, 253–262.

Goldfried, M.R. (1971) Systematic desensitization as training in self-control. *Journal of Consulting and Clinical Psychology*, **37**, 228–234.

Goldfried, M.R. & Sobocinski, D. (1975) The effect of irrational beliefs on emotional arousal. *Journal of Consulting and Clinical Psychology*, **43**, 348–355.

Goldstein, A. J. & Chambless, D.L. (1978) A reanalysis of agoraphobia. *Behavior Therapy*, **9**, 47–59.

Goorney, A.B. (1970) Treatment of aviation phobias by behaviour therapy. *British Journal of Psychiatry*, **119**, 159–166.

Goorney, A.B. & O'Connor, P.J. (1971) Anxiety associated with flying. *British Journal of Psychiatry*, **119**, 159–166.

Gormally, J., Sipps, G., Raphael, R. & Varvil-Weld, E.D. (1981) The relationship between maladaptive cognitions and social anxiety. *Journal of Consulting and Clinical Psychology*, **39**, 300–301.

Griez, E. & Hout, M.A. van den (1986) CO $_2$ inhalation in the treatment of panic attacks. *Behaviour Research and Therapy*, **24**, 145–150.

Griez, E. & Hout, M.A. van den (1984) *Carbon dioxide and anxiety. An experimental approach to a clinical claim.* PhD thesis, University of Maastricht, The Netherlands.

Hafner, R.J. (1982) The marital context of the agoraphobic syndrome. In D.L. Chambless and A.J. Goldstein (Eds), *Agoraphobia: Multiple Perspectives on Theory and Treatment.* New York, Wiley.

Hafner, R.J. & Milton, F. (1977) The influence of propranolol on the exposure *in vivo* of agoraphobics. *Psychological Medicine*, **7**, 419–425.

Hafner, R.J. & Marks, I.M. (1976) Exposure in vivo in agoraphobics: Contributions of diazepam, group exposure, and anxiety evocation. *Psychological Medicine*, **6**, 71–88.

Hall, R. & Goldberg, D. (1977) The role of social anxiety in social interaction difficulties. *British Journal of Psychiatry*, **131**, 610–615.

Hardy, G.E. & Cotterill, J.A. (1982) A study of depression and obsessionality in dysmorphophobic and psoriatic patients. *British Journal of Psychiatry*, **140**, 19–22.

Hartman, L.M. (1983) A metacognitive model of social anxiety: Implications for treatment. *Clinical Psychology Review*, **3**, 435–456.

Hatzenbühler, L.C. & Schröder, H.E. (1982) Assertiveness training with outpatients: The effectiveness of skill and cognitive procedures. *Behavioral Psychotherapy*, **10**, 234–252.

Herrnstein, R.J. (1969) Method and theory in the study of avoidance. *Psychological Review*, **76**, 49–69.

Hersen, M. & Bellack, A.S. (1988) *Dictionary of Behavioral Assessment Techniques.* New York: Pergamon Press.

Hibbert, G.A. (1984a) Ideational components of anxiety, their origin and content. *British Journal of Psychiatry*, **144**, 618–624.

Hibbert, G.A. (1984b) Hyperventilation as a cause of panic attacks. *British Medical Journal*, **288**, 263–264.

Hitschmann, E. (1943) Neurotic bashfulness in erytrophobia. *Psychoanalytic Review*, **30**, 438–466.

Hodgson, R. & Rachman, S. (1977) Obsessional-compulsive complaints. *Behaviour Research and Therapy*, **15**, 389–395.

Hodgson, R., Rachman, S. & Marks, I. (1972) The treatment of chronic obsessive-compulsive neurosis: follow up and further findings. *Behaviour Research and Therapy*, **10**, 181–184.

Hoehn-Saric, R. & McLeod, D.R. (1988) Panic and generalized anxiety disorders. In C.G. Last & M. Hersen (Eds.), *Handbook of Anxiety Disorders*, New York, Pergamon Press.

Hoehn-Saric, R., Mc Leod, D.R. & Zimmerli, W.D. (1988) Differential effects of alprazolam and imipramine in generalized anxiety disorder: Somatic versus psychic symptoms. *Journal of Clinical Psychiatry*, **49**, 293–301.

Hoekstra, R.J., Visser, S. & Emmelkamp, P.M.G. (1989) A social learning formulation of the etiology of obsessive-compulsive disorders. In P.M.G. Emmelkamp, W.T.A.M. Everaerd, F. Kraaimaat, M.J.M. van Son (Eds), *Annual Series of European Research in Behavior Therapy, Vol. IV: Fresh Perspectives on Anxiety Disorders.* Amsterdam: Swets & Zeitlinger.

Hoogduin, C.A.L. (1985) *Mislukking en succes bij de ambulante behandeling van dwangneurose.* PhD. thesis, University of Rotterdam, The Netherlands.

Horney, K. (1950) *Neurosis and Human Growth.* New York: Norton.

Hout, M. van den, Emmelkamp, P.M.G., Kraaÿkamp, J. & Griez, E. (1988) Behavioural treatment of obsessive-compulsives: Inpatient versus outpatient. *Behaviour Research and Therapy*, **26**, 331–332.

Hout, M.A. van den & Molen, G.M. van der (1988) De experimentele psychopathologie van paniek. *Directieve Therapie*, **8**, 163–187.

Hugdahl, K., Frederikson, M. & Ohman, A. (1977) "Preparedness" and "arousability" as determinants of electrodermal conditioning. *Behaviour Research and Therapy*, **15**, 345–353.

Hugdahl, K. & Öst, L.-G. (1985) Subjectively rated physiological and cognitive symptoms in six different clinical phobias. *Personality and Individual Differences*, **6**, 2, 175–188.

James, I.M. & Savage, I.T. (1984) Nadolol, diazepam and placebo for anxiety in musicians. *American Heart Journal*, **108**, 1150–1155.

James, I.M., Burgoyne, W. & Savage, L.T. (1983) Effects of pindolol on stress-related disturbances of musical performance: preliminary communication. *Journal of the Royal Society of Medicine*, **76**, 194–196.

James, I.M., Griffith, D.N.W., Pearson, R.M. & Newby, P. (1977) Effects of oxprenolol on stage fright in musicians. *Lancet*, **ii**, 952–954.

Jannoun, L., Oppenheimer, C. & Gelder, M. (1982) A self-help treatment program for anxiety state patients. *Behavior Therapy*, **13**, 103–111.

Jerremalm, A., Jansson, L. & Öst, L.G. (1986) Cognitive and physiological reactivity and the effects of different behavioral methods in the treatment of social phobia. *Behaviour Research and Therapy*, **24**, 171–180.

Johnson, J.H. & Sarason, I.G. (1978) Life stress, depression and anxiety: Internal–external control as a moderator variable. *Journal of Psychosomatic Research*, **22**, 205–208.

Johnston, D.G., Troyer, I.E. & Whitsett, S.F. (1988) Clomipramine treatment of agoraphobic women. *Archives of General Psychiatry*, **45**, 453–459.

Jong, P. de (1987) Angst voor trillende handen; een behandelingsstrategie. *Tijdschrift voor Directieve Therapie*, **7**, 51–62.

Juergens, S.M. & Morse, R.M. (1988) Alprazolam dependence in seven patients. *American Journal of Psychiatry*, **145**, 625–627.

Kahn, R.J., McNair, D.M., Lipman, R.S., Covi, L., Rickels, K., Downing, R., Fisher, S. & Freakenthaler, L.M. (1986) Imipramine and chlordiazepoxide in depressive and anxiety disorders. *Archives of General Psychiatry*, **43**, 79–85.

Kasvikis, Y. & Marks, I.M. (1988) Clomipramine, self-exposure and therapist-accompanied exposure in obsessive-compulsive ritualizers: Two year follow-up. *Journal of Anxiety Disorders*, **2**, 291–298.

Keane, T.M., Fairbank, J.A., Caddell, J.M. & Zimmering, R.T. (1989) Implosive (flooding) therapy reduces symptoms of PTSD in Vietnam combat veterans. *Behavior Therapy*, **20**, 245–260.

Kenny, F.T., Mowbray, R.M. & Lalani, S. (1978) Faradic disruption of obsessive ideation in the treatment of obsessive neurosis: A controlled study. *Behavior Therapy*, **9**, 209–221.

Kilpatrick, D.G. & Best, C. (1984) Some cautionary remarks on treating sexual assault victims with implosion. *Behavior Therapy*, **15**, 421–423.

Kipper, D.A. (1977) Behavior therapy for fears brought on by war experiences. *Journal of Consulting and Clinical Psychology*, **45**, 216–221.

Klein, D.F. (1964) Delineation of two drug-responsive anxiety syndromes. *Psychopharmacologia*, **5**, 397–408.

Kleiner, L. & Marshall, W.L. (1987) Interpersonal problems and agoraphobia. *Journal of Anxiety Disorders*, **1**, 313–323.

Klosko, J.S., Barlow, D.H., Tassinari, R.B. & Cerny, J.A. (1988) Comparison of alprazolam and cognitive behavior therapy in the treatment of panic disorder: A preliminary report. In I. Hand & H.U. Wittchen (Eds), *Panic and Phobias 2: Treatment and Variables Affecting Course and Outcome*, New York: Springer.

Kozak, M.J. & Montgomery, G.K. (1981) Multimodal behavioral treatment of recurrent injury-scene-elicited fainting (vasodepressor syncope). *Behavioral Psychotherapy*, **9**, 316–321.

Kringlen, E. (1965) Obsessional neurotics: A long-term follow-up. *British Journal of Psychiatry*, **111**, 709–722.

Kushner, M.G., Sher, K.J. & Beitman, B.D. (1990) The relation between alcohol problems and the anxiety disorders. *American Journal of Psychiatry*, **147**, 6, 685–695.

Lader, M.H. (1967) Palmar conductance measures in anxiety and phobic states. *Journal of Psychosomatic Research*, **11**, 271–281.

Lader, M.H. & Mathews, A.M. (1968) A physiological model of phobic anxiety and desensitization. *Behaviour Research and Therapy*, **6**, 411–421.

Lader, M.H. & Wing, L. (1966) *Physiological Measures, Sedative Drugs, and Morbid Anxiety*. London: Oxford University Press.

Ladouceur, R. (1983) Participant modeling with or without cognitive treatment for phobias. *Journal of Consulting and Clinical Psychology*, **51**, 942–944.

Lapouse, R. & Monk, M.A. (1959) Fears and worries in representative sample of children. *American Journal of Orthopsychiatry*, **29**, 803–818.

Last, C.G. (1984) Cognitive treatment of phobia. In M. Hersen, R.M. Eisler & P.M. Miller (Eds), *Progress in behavior modification,* Vol 16 (p. 65–82). New York: Academic Press.

Last, C.G., Barlow, D.H. & O'Brien, G.T. (1984) Precipitants of agoraphobia: Role of stressful life events. *Psychological Reports*, **54**, 567–570.

Last, C.G. & Blanchard, E.B. (1982) Classification of phobic versus fearful non-phobics: procedural and theoretical issues. *Behavioral Assessment*, **4**, 195–210.

Lautsch, H. (1971) Dental phobia. *British Journal of Psychiatry*, **119**, 151–158.

Leitenberg, H. & Callahan, E.J. (1973) Reinforced practice and reduction of different kinds of fear in adults and children. *Behaviour Research and Therapy*, **11**, 19–30.

Ley, R. (1985) Blood, breath and fears: A hyperventilation theory of panic attacks and agoraphobia. *Clinical Psychology Review*, **5**, 271–285.

Liden, S. & Gottfries, C.G. (1974) Beta blocking agents in treatment of catecholamine induced symptoms in musicians. *Lancet*, **ii**, 529.

Liebowitz, M.R., Gorman, J., Fyer, A., Campeas, R., Levin, A., Davies, S. & Klein, D.F. (1986) Psychopharmacological treatment of social phobia. *Journal of Clinical Psychopharmacology*, **6**, 93–98.

Liebowitz, M.R., Gorman, J.M., Fyer, A.J., Campeas, R., Levin, A.P., Sandberg, D., Hollander, E., Papp, L. & Goetz, D. (1988) Pharmacotherapy of social phobia: A placebo-controlled comparison of phenelzine and atenolol. *Journal of Clinical Psychiatry*, **49**, 252–257.

Linehan, M.M., Walker, R.O., Bronheim, S., Haynes, K.F. & Yerzeroff, H. (1979) Group versus individual assertion training. *Journal of Consulting and Clinical Psychology*, **47**, 1000–1002.

Lipsedge, M.S., Hajioff, J., Huggins, P., Napier, L., Pearce, J., Pike, D.J. & Rich, M. (1973) The management of severe agoraphobia: A comparison of iproniazid and systematic desensitization. *Psychopharmacologia*, **32**, 67–88.

Lum, L.C. (1976) The syndrome of habitual chronic hyperventilation. In: Hill, O.W. (Ed): *Modern trends in psychosomatic medicine,* vol. 3. London: Butterworths.

Lydiard, R.B., Laraia, M.T., Ballenger, J.C. & Howell, E.F. (1987) Emergence of depressive symptoms in patients receiving alprazolam for panic disorder. *American Journal of Psychiatry*, **144**, 664–665.

Lydiard, R.B., Laraia, M.T., Howell, E.F. & Ballenger, J.C. (1988) Alprazolam in the treatment of social phobia. *Journal of Clinical Psychiatry*, **49**, 17–19.

Mackay, W. & Liddell, A. (1986) An investigation into the matching of specific agoraphobic anxiety response characteristics with specific types of treatment. *Behaviour Research and Therapy*, **24**, 361–364.

Marks, I.M. (1969) *Fears and Phobias*. London: Heinemann.

Marks, I.M. (1987) *Fears, phobias and rituals*. Oxford: Oxford University Press.

Marks, I.M., Boulougouris, J. & Marset, P. (1971) Flooding versus desensitization in the treatment of phobic patients. *British Journal of Psychiatry*, **119**, 353–375.

Marks, I.M. & Gelder, M.G. (1966) Different ages of onset in varieties of phobias. *American Journal of Psychiatry*, **123**, 218–221.

Marks, I.M., Hodgson, R. & Rachman, S. (1975) Treatment of chronic obsessive-compulsive neurosis by in vivo exposure. *British Journal of Psychiatry*, **127**, 349–364.

Marks, I.M., Gray, S., Cohen, D., Hill, R., Mawson, D., Ramm, E. & Stern, R.S. (1983) Imipramine and brief therapist aided exposure in agoraphobics having self-exposure homework. *Archives of General Psychiatry*, **40**, 153–162.

Marks, I.M., Lelliott, P., Basuglu, M., Noshirvani, H., Monteiro, W., Cohen, D. & Kasvikis, Y. (1988) Clomipramine, self exposure and therapist aided exposure in obsessive-compulsive ritualisers. *British Journal of Psychiatry*, **152**, 522–534.

Marks, I.M. & Mathews, A.M. (1979) Brief standard self-rating for phobic patients. *Behaviour Research and Therapy*, **17**, 59–68.

Marks, I.M. & Mishan, J. (1988) Dysmorphophobic avoidance with disturbed bodily perception. A pilot study of exposure therapy. *British Journal of Psychiatry*, **152**, 674–678.

Marks, I.M., Stern, R.S., Mawson, D., Cobb, J. & McDonald, R. (1980) Clomipramine and exposure for obsessive-compulsive rituals: I. *British Journal of Psychiatry*, **136**, 1–25.

Marks, I.M. & Swinson, S. (1990) *Results of the cross-national control study of alprazolam and exposure*. Paper presented at the International Conference on Panic Disorder, September 1990, Geneva.

Marshall, W.L. (1985) Variable exposure in flooding. *Behaviour Research and Therapy*, **16**, 117–135.

Marshall, W.L. (1988) Behavioral indices of habituation and sensitization during exposure to phobic stimuli. *Behaviour Research and Therapy*, **26**, 67–77.

Marzillier, J.S., Lambert, C. & Kellett, J. (1976) A controlled evaluation of systematic desensitization and social skills training for socially inadequate psychiatric patients. *Behaviour Research and Therapy*, **14**, 225–238.

Mathews, A. (1978) Fear reduction research and clinical phobias. *Psychological Bulletin*, **85**, 390–404.

Mathews, A. (1989) Cognitive aspects of the aetiology and phenomenology of anxiety disorders. In P.M.G. Emmelkamp, W.T.A.M. Everaerd, F. Kraaimaat & M.J.M. van Son (Eds), *Annual Series of European Research in Behavior Therapy, Vol. IV: Fresh perspectives on anxiety disorders*. Amsterdam: Swets & Zeitlinger.

Mathews, A.M., Gelder, M.G. & Johnston, D.W. (1981) *Agoraphobia. Nature and treatment*. London: Tavistock Publications.

Mathews, A. & MacLeod, C. (1986) Discrimination of threat cues without awareness in anxiety states. *Journal of Abnormal Psychology*, **95**, 131–138.

Mattick, R.P. & Peters, L. (1988) Treatment of severe social phobia: Effects of guided exposure with and without cognitive restructuring. *Journal of Consulting and Clinical Psychology*, **56**, 251–260.

Mattick, R.P., Peters, L. & Clarke, J.D. (1989) Exposure and cognitive restructuring for social phobia: a controlled study. *Behavior Therapy*, **20**, 3–23.

Mavissakalian, M. & Michelson, L. (1983) Self-directed in vivo exposure practice in behavioral and pharmacological treatment of agoraphobia. *Behavior Therapy*, **14**, 506–519.

Mavissakalian, M. & Michelson, L. (1986a) Agoraphobia: Relative and combined efectiveness of therapist-asssisted in vivo exposure and imipramine. *Journal of Clinical Psychiatry*, **47**, 117–122.

Mavissakalian, M. & Michelson, L. (1986b) Two-year follow-up of exposure and imipramine treatment of agoraphobia. *American Journal of Psychiatry*, **143**, 1106–1112.

Mawson, D., Marks, I.M. & Ramm, E. (1982) Clomipramine and exposure for chronic OCD ritualisers: III. Two-year follow-up. *British Journal of Psychiatry*, **140**, 11–18.

McGuffin, R. & Reich, R. (1984) Psychopathology and genetics. In H.E. Adams & P.B. Suther (Eds) *Comprehensive Handbook of Psychopathology*, New York: Plenum Press.

McKean, J., Roa, B. & Mann, A. (1984) Life events and personality traits in obsessive-compulsive neurosis. *British Journal of Psychiatry*, **144**, 185–189.

McNally, R.J. & Steketee, G.S. (1985) The etiology and maintenance of severe animal phobias. *Behaviour Research and Therapy*, **23**, 4, 431–435.

McReynolds, W.T. & Grizzard, R.H. (1971) A comparison of three fear reduction procedures. *Psychotherapy: Theory, Research and Practice*, **8**, 264–268.

Meichenbaum, D.H. (1975) Self-instructional methods. In F.H. Kanfer & A.P. Goldstein (Eds), *Helping People Change*. New York: Pergamon Press.

Mersch, P.P.A., Emmelkamp, P.M.G., Bögels, S.M. & Van der Sleen, J. (1989) Social phobia: Individual response pattern and the effects of behavioral and cognitive interventions. *Behaviour Research and Therapy*, **27**, 421–434.

Meyer, V., Levy, R. & Schnurer, A. (1974) The behavioural treatment of obsessive-compulsive disorder. In H.R. Beech (Ed.), *Obsessional States*. London: Methuen.

Michelson, L., Mavissakalian, M. & Marchione, K. (1988) Cognitive, behavioral and psychophysiological treatments of agoraphobia: A comparative outcome investigation. *Behavior Therapy*, **19**, 97–120.

Miller, L.C., Barrett, C.L. & Hampe, E. (1974) Phobias of childhood. In A. Davids (Ed.), *Child Personality and Psychopathology: Current topics* (Vol 1). New York: Wiley.

Monti, P.M., Boice, R., Fingeret, A.L. Zwick, W.R., Kolko, D., Munroe, S & Grunberger, A. (1984) Midi-level measurement of social anxiety in psychiatric and non psychiatric samples. *Behaviour Research and Therapy*, **22**, 651–660.

Mowrer, O.H. (1947) On the dual nature of learning—a reinterpretation of "conditioning" and "problemsolving". *Harvard Educational Review*, **17**, 102–148.

Mullaney, J.A. & Trippett, C.J. (1979) Alcohol dependence and phobias: Clinical description and relevance. *British Journal of Psychiatry*, **135**, 563–573.

Myers, K., Weissman, M., Tischler, L., Holzer, E., Leaf, J., Orvaschel, H., Anthony, C., Boyd, H., Burke, D., Kramer, M. & Stolzman, R. (1984) Six-month prevalence of psychiatric disorders in three communities: 1980–1982. *Archives of General Psychiatry*, **41**, 959–967.

Neftel, K.A., Adler, R.H., Kappeli, L., Rossi, M., Dodler, M., Kaser, H.E., Brugesser, H.H. & Vorkauf, H. (1982) Stage fright in musicians: a model illustrating the effect of beta-blockers. *Psychosomatic Medicine*, **44**, 461–469.

Newton, A., Kindness, K. & McFadyen, M. (1983) Patients and social skills groups: do they lack social skills? *Behavioural Psychotherapy*, **11**, 116–126.

Noyes, R., Garvey, M.J., Cook, B.L. & Perry, P.J. (1988) Benzodiazepine withdrawal: A review of the evidence. *Journal of Clinical Psychiatry*, **49**, 382–389.

Ollendick, T.H., Matson, J.L. & Helsel, W.J. (1985) Fears in children and adolescents: Normative data. *Behaviour Research and Therapy*, **23**, 465–467.

Öst, L-G. (1986) Applied relaxation: description of a coping technique and review of controlled studies. *Behaviour Research and Therapy*, **25**, 397–409.

Öst, L-G. (1987) Age of onset in different phobias. *Journal of Abnormal Psychology*, **96**, 3, 223–229.

Öst, L-G. (1989) One-session treatment for specific phobias. *Behaviour Research and Therapy*, 27, **1**, 1–7

Öst, L-G. & Hugdahl, K. (1981) Acquisition of phobias and anxiety response patterns in clinical patients. *Behaviour Research and Therapy*, **19**, 439–447.

Öst, L-G., Jerremalm, A. & Jansson, L. (1984a) Individual response patterns and the effects of different behavioral methods in the treatment of agoraphobia. *Behaviour Research and Therapy*, **22**, 697–707.

Öst, L-G., Jerremalm, A. & Johansson, J. (1981) Individual response patterns and the effects of different behavioral methods in the treatment of social phobia. *Behaviour Research and Therapy*, **19**, 1–16.

Öst, L-G., Johansson, J. & Jerremalm, A. (1982) Individual response patterns and the effects of different behavioral methods in the treatment of claustrophobia. *Behaviour Research and Therapy*, **20**, 445–460.

Öst, L-G., Lindahl, I.-L., Sterner, U. & Jerremalm, A. (1984b) Physiological responses in blood phobics. *Behaviour Research and Therapy*, **22**, 109–177.

Öst, L.-G. & Sterner, U. (1987) Applied Tension: a specific behavioral method for treatment of blood phobia. *Behaviour Research and Therapy*, **25**, 1, 25–29.

Ottaviani, R. & Beck, A.T. (1987) Cognitive aspects of panic disorders. *Journal of Anxiety Disorders*, **1**, 15–28.

Parker, G. (1979) Reported parental characteristics of agoraphobics and social phobics. *British Journal of Psychiatry*, **135**, 555–560.

Pecknold, J.C., Swinson, R.P., Kuch, K. & Lewis, C.P. (1988) Alprazolam in panic disorder and agoraphobia: Results from a multicenter trial. *Archives of General Psychiatry*, **45**, 429–436.

Perry, P.J., Garvey M.J. & Noyes, R. (1990). Benzodiazepine treatment of generalized anxiety disorder. In Noyes, R., Roth, M. & Burrows, G. D. (Eds) *Handbook of Anxiety, Vol. 4: The Treatment of Anxiety*. Amsterdam: Elsevier.

Persson, G. & Nordlund, C.L. (1985) Agoraphobics and social phobics: differences in background factors, syndrome profiles and therapeutic response. *Acta Psychiatrica Scandinavica*, **71**, 148–159.

Powel, T.J. (1987) Anxiety management groups in clinical practice: A preliminary report. *Behavioral Psychotherapy*, **15**.

Praag, H.M. van (1988) *Psychofarmaca*. Assen: Van Gorcum.

Prochaska, J.O. (1971) Symptom and dynamic cues in the implosive treatment of test anxiety. *Journal of Abnormal Psychology*, **77**, 133–142.

Rabavilas, A.D. & Boulougouris, J.C. (1979) Mood changes and flooding outcome in obsessive-compulsive patients: Report of a two-year follow-up. *Journal of Nervous and Mental Disease*, **167**, 495–496.

Rabavilas, A.D., Boulougouris, J.C., Stefanis, C. & Vaidakis, N. (1977) Psycho-physiological accompaniments of threat anticipation in obsessive-compulsive patients. In C.D. Spielberger & I.G. Sarason (Eds), *Stress and Anxiety* (Vol. 4). New York: Wiley.

Rachman, S. (1976) The modification of obsessions: A new formulation. *Behaviour Research and Therapy*, **14**, 269–277.

Rachman, S. & Hodgson, R.J. (1980) *Obsessions and Compulsions*. Englewood Cliffs, N.J.: Prentice Hall.

Rachman, S., Marks, I. & Hodgson, R. (1973) The treatment of obsessive-compulsive neurotics by modelling and flooding in vivo. *Behaviour Research and Therapy*, **11**, 463–471.

Rachman, S. & Wilson, G.T. (1980) *The effects of Psychological Therapy*. Oxford: Pergamon Press.

Rapee, R.M. (1985) Distinction between panic disorder and generalized anxiety disorder. *Australian and New Zealand Journal of Psychiatry*, **19**, 227–232.

Reed, G.F. (1977) Obsessional cognition: performance on two numerical tasks. *British Journal of Psychiatry*, **130**, 184–185.

Reich, J. & Yates, W. (1988) A pilot study of treatment of social phobia with alprazolam. *American Journal of Psychiatry*, **145**, 590–594.

Reiss, S., Peterson, R.A., Gursky, D.M. & McNally, R.J. (1986) Anxiety sensitivity, anxiety frequency and the prediction of fearfulness. *Behaviour Research and Therapy*, **24**, 1–8.

Resick, P.A., Jordan, C.G., Girelli, S.A., Kotsis-Hutter, C. & Marhoefer-Dvorak, S. (1988) A comparative outcome study of behavioral group therapy for sexual assault victims. *Behavior Therapy*, **19**, 385–401.

Rice, K.M. & Blanchard, E.B. (1982) Biofeedback in the treatment of anxiety disorders. *Clinical Psychology Review*, **2**, 557–577.

Robins, L.N., Helzer, J.F., Weissman, M.M., Overaschel, H., Gruenberg, F., Burke, J.D. & Regier, D.A. (1984) Life-time prevalence of specific psychiatric disorders in three sites. *Archives of General Psychiatry*, **41**, 949–958.

Rose, R.J. & Dilto, W.B. (1983) A developmental-genetic analysis of common fears from early adolescence to early adulthood. *Child Development*, **54**, 361–368.

Roth, M. (1959) The phobic anxiety-depersonalization syndrome. *Proceedings of the Royal Society of Medicine*, **52**, 587–595.

Rotter, J.B. (1966) Generalized expectancies for internal versus external control of reinforcement. *Psychological Monographs*, **80**, 1–28.

Rutter, M., Tizard, J. & Whitmore, S. (1970) *Education, Health and Behaviour*. London: Longmans.

Salkovskis, P.M., Jones, D.R.G. & Clark, D.M. (1986a) Respiratory control in the treatment of panic attacks: Replication and extension with concurrent measurement of behaviour and pCO_2. *British Journal of Psychiatry*, **148**, 526–532.

Salkovskis, P.M., Warwick, H.M.C., Clark, D.M. & Wessels, D.J. (1986b) A demonstration of acute hyperventilation during naturally occurring panic attacks. *Behaviour Research and Therapy*, **24**, 91–94.

Sanderman, R., Mersch, P.P., van der Sleen, J., Emmelkamp, P.M.G. & Ormel, J. (1987) The rational behavior inventory (RBI): A psychometric evaluation. *Personality and Individual Differences*, **8**, 561–569.

Schaap, C. & Hoogduin, C.A.L. (1988) The therapeutic relationship in behavior therapy: Enhancing the quality of the bond. In P.M.G. Emmelkamp, W.T.A.M. Everaerd, F. Kraaimaat & M.J.M. van Son (Eds), *Annual Series of European Research in Behavior Therapy, Vol. IV: Fresh Perspectives on Anxiety Disorders*. Amsterdam: Swets & Zeitlinger.

Schindler, L. (1988) Client-therapist interaction and therapeutic change. In P.M.G. Emmelkamp, W.T.A.M. Everaerd, F. Kraaimaat & M.J.M. van Son (Eds), *Annual Series of European Research in Behavior Therapy, Vol. IV: Fresh perspectives on anxiety disorders.* Amsterdam: Swets & Zeitlinger.

Scholing, A. & Emmelkamp, P.M.G. (1989) Individualized treatment for social phobia. In P.M.G. Emmelkamp, W.T.A.M. Everaerd, F. Kraaimaat, M.J.M. van Son (Eds), *Annual Series of European Research in Behavior Therapy, Vol. IV: Fresh Perspectives on Anxiety Disorders.* Amsterdam: Swets & Zeitlinger.

Shafar, S. (1976) Aspects of phobic illness—a study of 90 personal cases. *British Journal of Medical Psychology*, **49**, 221–236.

Shaw, P. (1979) A comparison of three behaviour therapies in the treatment of social phobias. *British Journal of Psychiatry*, **134**, 620–623.

Sheehan, D.V., Ballenger, J. & Jacobson, G. (1981) Relative efficacy of monomamine oxidase inhibitors and tricyclic antidepressants in the treatment of endogenous anxiety. In D.F. Klein & J. Rabkin (Eds), *Anxiety: New research and changing concepts.* New York: Raven Press.

Smith, M. (1973) *When I Say No, I Feel Guilty.* New York: The Dial Press.

Solyom, L., Heseltine, G.F., McClure, D.J., Solyom, C., Ledwidge, B. & Steinberg, S. (1973) Behaviour therapy versus drug therapy in the treatment of phobic neurosis. *Canadian Psychiatric Association Journal*, **18**, 25–31.

Solyom, C., Ledwidge, B. & Solyom, C. (1986) Delineating social phobia. *British Journal of Psychiatry*, **149**, 464–470.

Solyom, C., Solyom, L., La Pierre, Y., Pecknold, J.C. & Morton, L. (1981) Phenelzine and exposure in the treatment of phobias. *Journal of Biological Psychiatry*, **16**, 239–248.

Solyom, L., Beck, P., Solyom, C. & Hugel, R. (1974) Some etiological factors in phobic neurosis. *Canadian Psychiatric Association Journal*, **21**, 109–113.

Son, M.J.M. van (1978) *Sociale vaardigheidstherapie, gedragstherapie en sociaal gedrag.* Amsterdam: Swets & Zeitlinger.

Sperling, M. (1971) Spider phobias and spider fantasies. *Journal of the American Psychoanalytic Association*, **19**, 472–498.

Stampfl, T.G. & Levis, D.J. (1967) Essentials of implosive therapy. *Journal of Abnormal Psychology*, **72**, 496–503.

Stekel, W. (1924) *Nervöse Angstzustände und ihre Bedeutung.* Berlijn/Wenen: Urban & Schwartzenberg.

Steketee, G. & Foa, E.B. (1987) Rape victims: Post-traumatic stress responses and their treatment. *Journal of Anxiety Disorders*, **1**, 69–86.

Stern, R.S. & Marks, I.M. (1973) A comparison of brief and prolonged flooding in agoraphobics. *Archives of General Psychiatry*, **28**, 210–216.

Stravynski, A., Marks, I. & Yule, W. (1982) Social skills problems in neurotic outpatients. *Archives of General Psychiatry*, **39**, 1378–1385.

Sutton-Simon, K. & Goldfried, M.R. (1979) Faulty thinking patterns in two types of anxiety. *Cognitive Therapy and Research*, **3**, 193–203.

Telch, M., Agras, W.S., Taylor, C.B., Roth, W.T. & Gallen, C.C. (1985) Combined pharmacological and behavioural treatment for agoraphobia. *Behaviour Research and Therapy*, **21**, 505– 527.

Telch, M., Tearnan, B.H. & Taylor, C.B. (1983) Anti-depressant medication in the treatment of agoraphobia: A critical review. *Behaviour Research and Therapy*, **21**, 505–527.

Thoren, P., Asberg, M., Cronholm, B., Jörnestedt, L. & Träskman, L. (1980) Clomipramine treatment of obsessive-compulsive disorders. *Archives of General Psychiatry*, **37**, 1281–1285.

Thyer, B.A. & Himle, J. (1985) Temporal relationship between panic attack onset and phobic avoidance in agoraphobia. *Behaviour Research and Therapy*, **23**, 607–608.

Thyer, B.A., Parrish, R.T., Curtis, G.C., Nesse, R.M. & Cameron, G.G. (1985) Age of onset of DSM-III anxiety disorders. *Comprehensive Psychiatry*, 113–122.

Torgersen, S. (1979) The nature and origin of common phobic fears. *British Journal of Psychiatry*, **134**, 343–351.

Torgerson, S. (1988) Genetics. In C.G. Last & M. Hersen (Eds), *Handbook of anxiety disorders*, New York: Pergamon Press.

Trower, P. Casey, A & Dryden, W. (1988) *Cognitive-behavioural Counselling in Action*. London: Sage.

Trower, P. Yardley, K., Bryant, B. & Shaw, P. (1978) The treatment of social failure: A comparison of anxiety reduction and skills-acquisition procedures on two social problems. *Behaviour Modification*, **2**, 41–60.

Turner, S.M. & Beidel, D.C. (1985) Empirically derived subtypes of social anxiety. *Behavior Therapy*, **16**, 384–392.

Turner, S.M., Beidel, D.C., Dancu, C.V. & Keys, D.J. (1986a) Psychopathology of social phobia and comparison to avoidant personality disorder. *Journal of Abnormal Psychology*, **95**, 4, 389–394.

Turner, S.M., Beidel, D.C. & Larkin, K.T. (1986b) Situational determinants of social anxiety in clinic and nonclinic samples: Physiological and cognitive correlates. *Journal of Consulting and Clinical Psychology*, **54**, 523–527.

Turner, S.M., Williams, S.L., Beidel, D.C. & Mezzich, J.E. (1986c) Panic disorder and agoraphobia with panic attacks: Covariation along the dimension of panic and agoraphobic fear. *Journal of Abnormal Psychology*, **95**, 384–388.

Twentyman, C.T. & McFall, R.M. (1975) Behavioral training of social skills in shy males. *Journal of Consulting and Clinical Psychology*, **43**, 384–395.

Tyrer, P., Candy, J. & Kelly, D. (1973) A study of the clinical effects of phenelzine and placebo in the treatment of phobic anxiety. *Psychopharmacology*, **32**, 237–254.

Ullrich, R., Crombach, G. & Peikert, V. (1972) *Three flooding procedures in the treatment of agoraphobics*. Paper at the European Conference of Behaviour Modification. Wexford, Ireland.

Vandereycken, W. & Pollentier, S. (1986) Erytrofobie of de angst om te blozen—een literatuuroverzicht. *Tijdschrift voor Directieve Therapie*, **7**, 1, 36–55.

Verhulst, F.C. (1985) Normale en niet-normale angsten in de kinderontwikkeling. In H. Ras, T. van Rijthoven & R. Beunderman (Eds), *Angsten en fobieën*. Utrecht: Nederlandse Vereniging voor Psychotherapie.

Veronen, L.J. & Kilpatrick, D.G. (1983) Stress management for rape victims. In D. Meichenbaum & M.E. Jaremko (Eds), *Stress Reduction and Prevention*. New York: Plenum Press.

Vila, J. & Beech, H.R. (1977) Vulnerability and conditioning in relation to the human menstrual cycle. *British Journal of Social and Clinical Psychology*, **16**, 69–75.

Vila, J. & Beech, H.R. (1978) Vulnerability and defensive reactions to the human menstrual cycle. *British Journal of Social and Clinical Psychology*, **17**, 93–100.

Visser, S., Hoekstra, R.J. & Emmelkamp, P.M.G. (1990) Follow up Ergebnisse von Verhaltenstherapie bei Zwangspatienten. In: W. Fiegenbaum, J. Margraf, I. Florin & A. Ehlers (Eds) *Zukunftsperspectiven der Klinischen Psychologie*. Berlin: Springer.

Walen, S.R., DiGiuseppe, R. & Wessler, R.L. (1980) *A Practitioner's Guide to Rational Emotive Therapy*. Oxford: Oxford University Press.

Wamboldt, M.Z. & Insel, T.R. (1988) Pharmacologic models. In C.G. Last & M. Hersen (Eds), *Handbook of Anxiety Disorders*, New York: Pergamon.

Watson, J. & Rayner, R. (1920) Conditioned emotional reactions. *Journal of Experimental Psychology*, **3**, 1–22.

Watson, J.P. & Marks, I.M. (1971) Relevant and irrelevant fear in flooding—a crossover study of phobic patients. *Behavior Therapy*, **2**, 275–293.

Weiss, K.J. & Rosenberg, D.J. (1985) Prevalence of anxiety disorders among alcoholics. *Journal of Clinical Psychiatry*, **46**, 3–5.

Williams, S.L. (1985) On the nature and measurement of agoraphobia. In M. Hersen, R.M. Eisler & P.M. Miller (Eds), *Progress in Behavior Modification* (Vol. 19 pp. 109–144). New York: Academic Press.

Williams, S.L., Dooseman, G. & Kleifield, E. (1984) Comparative effectiveness of guided mastery and exposure treatment for intractable phobias. *Journal of Consulting and Clinical Psychology*, **52**, 502–518.

Williams, S.L. & Rappoport, A. (1983) Cognitive treatment in the natural environment for agoraphobics. *Behavior Therapy*, **14**, 299–313.

Williams, S.L. & Watson Newhouse, N. (1985) Perceived danger and perceived self efficacy as cognitive determinants of acrophobic behavior. *Behavior Therapy*, **16**, 2, 136–146.

Wilson, G.T. & Davison, G.C. (1975) Effects of expectancy on systematic desensitization and flooding: A critical analysis. *European Journal of Behavioural Analysis and Modification*, **1**, 12–14.

Windheuser, H.J. (1977) Anxious mothers as models for coping with anxiety. *Behavioural Analysis and Modification*, **1**, 39–58.

Wittchen, H.U. (1988) Natural course and spontaneous remissions of untreated anxiety disorders. In I. Hand & H.U. Wittchen (Eds), *Panic and Phobias, Vol. 2*, New York: Springer.

Wolpe, J. (1958) *Psychotherapy and Reciprocal Inhibition*. Stanford: Stanford University Press.

Wolpe, J. (1963) Quantitative relationships in the systematic desensitation of phobias. *American Journal of Psychiatry*, **119**, 1062–1068.

Wolpe, J. & Lang, P.J. (1964) Fear Survey Schedule for use in behavior therapy. *Behaviour Research and Therapy*, **2**, 27–30.

Woodward, R. & Jones, R.B. (1980) Cognitive restructuring treatment: A controlled trial with anxious patients. *Behaviour Research and Therapy*, **18**, 401–409.

Yuksel, S., Marks, I., Ramm, E. & Ghosh, A. (1984) Slow versus rapid exposure *in vivo* of phobics. *Behavioural Psychotherapy*, **12**, 249–256.

Zitman, F.G. (1982) Bijwerkingen van benzodiazepinen. In H.G.M. Rooymans & F.G. Zitman (Eds) *Benzodiazepinen*. Stafleu, Alphen a/d Rijn.

Index